1951

George Horace Lorimer

and *THE SATURDAY EVENING POST*

by John Tebbel

Garden City, New York

Doubleday & Company, Inc., 1948

To the men and women, writers and editors,
who made *The Saturday Evening Post*,
and to whom George Horace Lorimer will always be—
The Boss.

Foreword

WHEN I WAS A PUBLISHER'S EDITOR, I HAD THE PLEASURE of lunching frequently with the editors of magazines who were on the lookout for novels that might be condensed or serialized. One of these gentlemen was Hugh MacNair Kahler, a veteran writer of fiction for the Saturday Evening Post and other periodicals, now associate editor of the *Ladies' Home Journal*.

My noontide sessions with Hugh Kahler took on a pleasant pattern. We ran through our business in the first ten minutes or so of conversation, after which my friend entertained me with inimitable reminiscences of writers and editors, and their diversions and follies in the less harried earlier years of this century. The Kahler well of memory never ran dry, and I never tired of dipping into it.

One day the storytelling centered particularly on George Horace Lorimer, legendary editor of the Saturday Evening Post, and the constellation of famous writers whom he placed in the American literary sky. Hugh was part of that constellation, knew it and the man who created it intimately, and so my natural question as an editor was: "Why haven't you written the Lorimer story?"

It appeared that Kahler and several other well-known writers had considered doing the biography of Lorimer and his Post, and had all decided against it, ultimately, for the same reason: they had idolized the editor and not one of them believed he could do an objective Lorimer biography. A few had other reasons as well, but the sum of nearly a decade of talk about the project since Lorimer's death in 1937 was that the book remained unwritten. It looked as though the remarkable, significant story of an American publishing era would be allowed to die, as the years closed up one primary source after another. Without undue modesty, I was fully aware that there were at least a dozen people better qualified to tell that story, but nonetheless I asked my friend whether he thought I could do the job, and if so, whether he would help me.

I am profoundly grateful to Hugh Kahler for giving me the confidence to take on the project, for helping me over the initial hurdles, and for standing at my elbow during the progress of what has turned out to be an exciting biographical venture. Had it not been for his inspiration and aid I could not even have begun this book.

I am no less grateful to Graeme Lorimer and his wife Sarah, who made available to me the files of George Horace Lorimer's voluminous private correspondence, on which much of the book is based. And that was only the beginning of their contribution to this volume's creation. They gave me unlimited assistance at every step of the way; I could not have proceeded without it. I am particularly grateful that they made no attempt to censor the material; thus the book is wholly mine, and not in any way "authorized."

Of the others who gave me their time and energy, I want particularly to thank Miss Adelaide Neall and Kenneth Roberts. Miss Neall's firsthand knowledge of a man with whom she worked closely for more than a quarter century was indispensable to this biography, as were the letters and other private papers she permitted me to examine. Kenneth Roberts did me the honor of reading the manuscript, offering me the most valuable criticism, and adding to it from his diary, correspondence and memories of the Boss.

Finally, I want to express my gratitude to Mary Roberts Rinehart, for permitting me to examine her Lorimer correspondence;

Martin

to Wesley Stout, for his help; and to those others who took the time to reminisce about the man they knew: Garet Garrett, Ben Ames Williams, Thomas B. Costain, Joseph Hergesheimer, Martin Sommers, Edwin Balmer, Sophie Kerr Underwood and Alan Jackson.

A special note of thanks, also, to Miss Margaret Davies, for many years Mr. Lorimer's private secretary, who checked my manuscript carefully and added to it from her files.

JOHN TEBBEL

Contents

xi

CONTENTS

George Horace Lorimer

and *THE SATURDAY EVENING POST*

CHAPTER ONE

The Making of an Editor

George Horace Lorimer was the editor of what Will Rogers called "America's greatest nickelodeon," the Saturday Evening Post. When Lorimer went to Philadelphia in 1898 the Post was worth a thousand dollars; it was, as Irvin Cobb put it, "an elderly and indisposed magazine." When he left the editor's chair nearly thirty-nine years later, on the last day of 1936, the Post had been for three decades one of the most successful and significant magazines in the history of American letters.

The man responsible for this achievement left an indelible mark upon his times. He was the articulate voice of millions, the purveyor of entertainment, advice and political sentiment to a considerable body of Americans—yet he was almost unknown to the Post's readers. Of the more than three million people who bought the magazine at the peak of its circulation, only a few knew its editor as more than a name on the masthead. Lorimer remained an anonymous figure until the final issue of the Post under his editorship, when for the first time he signed an editorial. Nevertheless he was a man whom nine Presidents of the United States recognized as the potent spokesman for a sizable bloc of voters, and upon whom thousands of writers, both famous and unknown, looked as a god to whose Olympus every creator of prose aspired.

When Wesley Winans Stout ascended the throne he printed a full-page picture of his predecessor and asked, in the course of an editorial tribute, whether the readers would like to have Lorimer's editorials continued, now that they knew who had been speaking for them these many years. The response was an overwhelming assent, but the thousands of answering letters were more than "yea" votes: they were tributes to George Horace Lorimer. In one way or another all of them said: "When I saw that picture I knew this was the man who wrote those editorials and gave us such a wonderful magazine."

For Lorimer was the Post and the Post was Lorimer. He told people who urged him to write his autobiography that it was being written every week in the Post, and he gave but three interviews in his lifetime. He made speeches only because, as he put it, "it's the thing you're afraid to do that you simply have to do."

From his early youth until he died in 1937, less than a year after his retirement, Lorimer remained a giant among men. Before he was thirty he had achieved business success in the packing industry; and he had been so excellent a reporter for the Boston papers that he would surely have risen to the top in the newspaper business. After he came to the Post, he wrote three best-selling books, two of which are still selling after more than forty years. In fact Lorimer would have been successful at any occupation, but editing the Saturday Evening Post was the job that fitted him best.

As a man destined to inform, entertain, and to a certain extent lead millions of people, Lorimer had more than his natural gifts to prepare him for such a position in the social scheme. There was, first of all, the advantage of a unique background for his editorship. Then there was the profound influence of his father, whose personality, as strong as his son's, was a determining factor in the shaping of Lorimer's life. The psychological truism that behind every man stands a woman, wife or mother, who makes or breaks him was not operative in this case.

George Claude Lorimer, the father, was one of the most powerful evangelical ministers this country has ever known. He stood so far above his brothers in the clergy that the Boston *Transcript*,

when he died, did not hesitate to call him "an important American," a verdict echoed in New York, Chicago, and other cities.

He came to the work of saving souls by a devious but advan-
tageous route. Born in the suburbs of Edinburgh, on June 4, 1838,
he started life as "a wild one," and ran away to sea when he was
only thirteen. One voyage was enough. His parents forgave the
adventure and cast about for something to keep him happy and
useful. His stepfather was W. H. Joseph, manager of Edinburgh's
Theatre Royal and later of Sadler's Wells. His half brother was
John H. Selwyn, a theatrical figure of importance. Thus it was
natural that George Claude should become an actor, and his youth
made him ideal for the female parts in the Shakespearean repertory
troupe controlled by his kinfolk.

This company came to America on tour in 1855 and the youngster came with them. A tall, dramatic-looking boy of seventeen,
he had by this time graduated to hero roles. While they were
playing the Louisville, Kentucky, theater, George and a fellow
actor strolled idly down a tree-shaded street one Sunday morning
and heard sounds of exhortation coming from the open doors of
the Walnut Street Baptist Church. A good member of the congregation accosted them: "Brothers, wouldn't you like to come
to church with me?" George apologized and explained that they
were actors. The accoster seemed undismayed by this intelligence
and persuaded the boys to accompany him.

Passionate evangelism was strange to young George, whose religious sensibilities were accustomed to the dour Presbyterianism
of Edinburgh. Curious, he took a seat at the back with his friend
and listened intently to the service. The drama of the plea for
souls moved him to the heart, and when the call came, the boy
from Scotland joined the repentant Kentuckians who stumbled
down the aisle to be saved.

His conversion was complete. He left the theater, prepared at
once for the Baptist ministry, and in 1860 he was ordained at
Harrodsburg, Kentucky. The church could have found no better-
qualified pleader for its cause. George Claude not only had the
zealous faith of the convert, but he brought to the pulpit all the
elocutionary eloquence he had learned on the stage. The voice

that had declaimed Hamlet so effectively was even more potent in preaching the Gospel. Harrodsburg had never seen such a striking young minister; there were many conversions among the women. One already converted to the faith became as ardent a believer in its expounder. She was Arabella Burford, the black-haired daughter of a deacon. George married Belle soon after he was ordained.

The new preacher discovered that the zeal for war outweighed the desire for grace in Harrodsburg. He saw, too, that he would be an undesirable member of the population, since his sympathies were not with the South, and he welcomed the chance to return to the scene of his conversion and become pastor of the Walnut Street Church in Louisville, in 1861. There he found little difference in political feeling, but the size of the town and the magnitude of the job he had to do made it much safer. The Walnut Street Church was the largest in the state, but it faced extinction, torn by politics and debt-ridden in the bargain.

Lorimer steered a middle course in the sectarian feuding. He devoted his energies to saving souls and clearing the debt. In seven years he united the church membership, wiped out the indebtedness and baptized more than five hundred people. By the last year of his Louisville ministry George Claude had only begun to hit his stride as an evangelist. He was inspired to greater labors that year by the birth of a son to his wife, who had earlier borne him three daughters—Mattie, May and Edith.

George Horace, the son, later gave the year of his birth as 1868. That date appears in Who's Who and in all official biographies. Only a few people knew that he was actually born on October 6, 1867, and those who knew told no one during Lorimer's lifetime because they understood the reason for the innocent deception: he wanted to say that he had become editor of the Post when he was thirty.

It amused him when a Southern newspaper referred to him proudly as a Southerner. His Louisville residence encompassed less than his first year in the world, and the single incident worth recording from it was his cowering with his mother and sisters in the cellar while a race riot turned the streets bloody outside.

George Claude was called to the First Church of Albany, New York, in 1868. There he baptized two hundred and fifty persons in less than two years, a feat which underscored his rapidly growing fame as a minister and brought him the pastorate of Shawmut Avenue Baptist Church, Boston, in 1870, where he stayed for three years before he moved to historic Tremont Temple. It was in the austere Temple that he became famous. From 1873 to 1879, his first period there, he grew to be a celebrity of the Baptist Church and edited its New England paper, the *Watchman*.

During those years in Boston, George Horace got his grammar school education at the Dwight School, where he was the promising pupil of Elizabeth G. Melcher. Miss Melcher remembered him later as "the boy very much interested in Napoleon. You had just read Abbott's Life of Napoleon, and you had very strong opinions of his greatness." She recalled this predilection to him in a letter written in May 1919, and Lorimer replied: "I am still interested in Napoleon, but I have greatly modified my views about him."

His reading in these early years, guided by his parents, was confined to history and religion. He was not permitted to read fiction until he was sixteen, when he began to devour Scott, Dickens and Thackeray in tremendous gulps. Aside from reading, the boy exhibited but one lively interest: he loved the business of planting seeds in the earth. Dr. Lorimer went to England to preach one summer and left his son at home in charge of a nurse. Having exhausted his books, George Horace found a bagful of pumpkin seeds in the kitchen and devoted an earnest afternoon to tearing up the fine lawn, of which the family was so proud, and seeding it with pumpkin. The elder Lorimer disapproved of this labor and did not hesitate to show it. He also ruled against live animals. These prohibitions resulted in the son's keen interest, when he grew up, in all growing things, whether plants or animals. George Horace encouraged his own children in their raising of everything from white mice to alligators in the bathroom, honey bees on the terrace, and pigs in the barn. He drew the line only at permitting his son Graeme to realize a youthful ambition to own a zebra.

Dr. Lorimer was called to the First Baptist Church of Chicago in 1879, and there repeated his Louisville feat by getting it out of heavy debt in two years. He resigned in 1881 to reorganize Immanuel Baptist Church, and for the next decade he worked at a ruinous pace to raise its membership from 170 to 1100. Somehow he also found time to help raise money for the founding of the University of Chicago. His health broke under the strain and European specialists told him he would have to change his occupation; the elder Lorimer felt it was his duty to work even harder.

The growing, lusty Chicago of that time was a happy place for a healthy youngster. George Horace spent his serious hours in Mosely High School, but whatever time he could spare after classes he devoted to hunting prairie chickens. "In those days," he recalled, "I could take my gun after school and within thirty minutes' ride of the Chicago City Hall find jacksnipe, wild duck, prairie chicken and golden plover." To get the money for shells he made a deal with his mother—a dollar for every one of Plutarch's Lives on which he could report in detail.

After high school George Horace entered Yale in the class of 1888, along with such promising students as Irving Fisher, Alonzo Stagg and James Heyworth. He aimed at no particular career; Yale was his father's idea.

Shortly before he was due to return for his sophomore year George met P. D. Armour on the street one day. Armour was one of his father's richest parishioners and the young man greeted the eminent packer respectfully. P.D. recognized him and stopped for a perfunctory chat. He was not in a good mood. The plant was booming, but when he sat with his friends at the Millionaires' Table in the Chicago Club he was seldom in a happy frame of mind. Primarily he worried about the anarchists. In common with George Pullman, Marshall Field and the others, he expected the radicals to take over Chicago momentarily.

When he asked George Horace what he was doing these days and the young man told him he was at Yale, Armour snorted. "Give up that nonsense," the familiar story quotes him, "and come to work for me. I'll make you a millionaire."

That idea appealed to Dr. Lorimer's son, who even then had a good understanding of Armour's philosophy. He asked his father what he should do, and the elder Lorimer remarked sensibly that he would have to decide that for himself. The decision was not difficult. The thought of making some money on his own appealed strongly to him.

Both his parents were saddened when George decided to quit Yale and go to work for Armour. George himself was saddened momentarily when he presented himself at the packing plant.

"I've decided to take your advice," he told Armour.

The great man had forgotten their conversation on the street, and for a moment he had difficulty remembering Lorimer.

"Oh yes," he said finally. "You're the preacher's boy. Give this young man a desk," he ordered a nearby clerk, "and find him something to do."

The job was at the mailing desk, where Armour started his own son. Lorimer got to work at six o'clock in the morning, and he was impressed to find, as often as not, the bulky figure of the chief already at work. His first task of the day was to decode telegraphic dispatches from the far reaches of the Armour empire and place the translations on his employer's desk by seven o'clock. The pay was ten dollars a week for a fourteen-hour day, and twenty-five cents for supper money if there was overtime, which was usually the case.

Lorimer came early and stayed late. He loved business. It never occurred to him for a moment that he was underpaid and overworked, because there was nothing in the world he would rather have been doing at that moment. At first Armour paid no attention to him, addressing him by a system of grunts rather than words, but the old man could not help noticing his employee's unusual industry.

He noticed, too, that young Lorimer learned rapidly the ways of business. When Armour workers rose in one of their sporadic revolts against the appalling conditions then existing in the industry, a supply train ran through the picket lines into a siding in the Armour yards, carrying food to besieged strikebreakers. Lorimer rode the locomotive, a fact he referred to with pride in later years. This and other incidents helped to foster his disillusionment with organized labor.

Phil Armour's young employee, after two years of apprentice-ship, became assistant manager of the canning department. This promotion meant that he had to travel for six months of the year, visiting Armour branches in cities and towns everywhere in the nation.

It was the most valuable kind of training for a potential maga-zine editor. He learned to know the people of America at first hand, and he acquired a knowledge of the places they lived in; he got a sense of the whole living, breathing nation. Sometimes he traveled through the railless South by horse and buggy and thus came to understand that region's economic problems. Again he traveled westward, making his first trip to Colorado over the Kansas Pacific from Kansas City. Two lifelong interests developed from this journey: his love for the Far West and his intense zeal for conservation. The K.P. line ran through unfenced prairie and Lorimer saw herds of antelope running away from the train. The abundant wild life of Colorado was an even greater delight to him, and as he came back home to sprawling Chicago he understood for the first time that America's wild life and natural resources were on the defensive before the rolling tide of urbanization.

As a minor executive of the company, Lorimer had an oppor-tunity to meet and talk with a good many of Armour's friends, the pioneer merchants and railroad men who were creating the American business empire; and he met the empire builders from abroad, such men as Sir Thomas Lipton. Always he asked ques-tions about their careers, and instinctively he performed as an editor would, mentally translating the meaning of their lives into understandable terms.

These meetings were the sources of inspiration for the biog-raphies and autobiographies which so enthralled Post readers. Lorimer well understood from the beginning what there was about the lives of such men that would appeal to the average man. "I have a theory," he once told an English writer who wanted to do Lipton's life for the Post, "that great men are most interesting in the years before their greatness is recognized."

Happy at his work, young Lorimer was soon equally happy at home. Five years after he went to work for Armour he wooed the beautiful Alma V. Ennis, daughter of Judge Alfred Ennis, a prominent Chicago jurist, formerly a tough-minded counsel for the Pullman Palace Car Company. Alma and George were married on June 6, 1892. She was the spoiled youngest daughter of the Ennis family, who called her "Pet." Acknowledged to be the prettiest girl in the city, Alma was a dazzling redhead whose dashing manner made her stand out from all the others.

When the marriage was disclosed to Armour he generously granted the happy bridegroom a honeymoon. "You might call on the trade as long as you're traveling," he added.

Lorimer worked at Armour's for three more years after his marriage. He was made head of the canning department, at a salary of five thousand dollars a year, and it appeared that he was well on the way to becoming one of P.D.'s right-hand men. But ambition moved him to leave the company for a flier in the wholesale grocery business. It was a disastrous venture, and its end was hastened by Lorimer's faith in the merits of the perfect liquid coffee extract, as yet undiscovered. It was a trying period. In the middle of it Alma nearly died of typhoid fever, and subsequently startled her friends by wearing a black wig during her convalescence.

Turning with the resilience of genius to other fields, Lorimer almost instinctively chose the business of writing. He had done nothing in that direction except to continue his omnivorous reading, which now included a half-dozen periodicals as well as books. Magazines excited him and he had some revolutionary ideas about making them, but he knew he was not quite ready. Newspapering, he thought, was the essential springboard.

That he made this choice deliberately is shown from a letter he wrote to an inquisitive Post reader in 1924. "I went into newspaper work," he explained, "with the same spirit that a medical student enters a hospital as an interne—for practical experience and training. I hoped to be both an editor and a writer. . . ."

His first reporting job was on the Boston *Standard*, where he worked until the paper suspended publication, a few months after he had joined the staff. That brief experience was enough to convince him that he needed more preparation if his drastic change in careers was to be successful. At his father's urging, he enrolled as a special student for a year's study at Colby College in Waterville, Maine, where he and Alma lived in the old yellow hotel at the center of town, beside the railroad tracks. At Colby he took courses in English and history under President Roberts, for whom the elder Lorimer had a great admiration, but he spent less time in the classroom than he did in the town library, and in acting as correspondent for the Boston and Maine papers. At night he worked on his first major literary production, a novel called "The Search for Simpkins." He sent it to publisher after publisher. It was a heartbreaking period; every rejection was another discouraging blow to Lorimer.

Eventually "The Search for Simpkins" achieved a piecemeal immortality. Lorimer used its hundred and fifty thousand words as a literary woodpile, both before and after he became editor of the Post. Parts of it appeared in minor magazines; other parts were used in the "Letters from a Self-Made Merchant to His Son"; and still other sections turned up on the editorial page of the Saturday Evening Post. He even cut away from it several sonnets and a rather long serial story. All these dismemberments did not damage "The Search for Simpkins" to any appreciable extent. As Lorimer later told one of his writers: "You see, it was a first novel, so I put everything that I knew in it. Whenever I wanted a story or an article or an editorial, I went to it and sawed out the proper lengths."

At the end of his year at Colby, Lorimer and Alma returned to Boston, where his father got him a job on the Boston *Post*, then the voice of the city's silk-stocking Democrats.

The elder Lorimer was a power in Boston by this time. He had returned to Tremont Temple in 1891 to serve for a decade during which he raised the church's income from twenty thousand to thirty-five thousand dollars annually, and increased its membership by more than eighteen hundred persons. Every Sunday there were congregations of four to five thousand people. The parishioners called him "The Little Giant of Tremont Temple," and the church was never large enough to hold all those who came to hear him. People made virtual pilgrimages to the Temple, arriving by every available means of transport.

In March 1893 the Temple was destroyed by fire for the third time. While the congregation met in the old Music Hall at Hamilton Place, opposite Park Street, Dr. Lorimer successfully conducted an international campaign to raise the more than half a million dollars needed for a new building. When it was completed in 1896 the crowds were so enormous that he had to deliver his dedicatory sermon twice and it was read to a third audience.

Dr. Lorimer declined two calls to London churches, but he preached there summers. His sermons had an almost overwhelming effect, although their manner of delivery was simple enough. At Tremont Temple there were no pulpit trappings when Lorimer preached. He simply rose from his seat among the lay brethren, and with a Bagster Bible in his hands began to talk. In London the setting was a little more ornate, but the effect was the same.

A London reporter, writing of Dr. Lorimer's first sermon at Marylebone Presbyterian Church, described him this way: "His personality is rich. Lean and long, he reminds one of many famous Americans, of Daniel Webster, of Emerson, of Abraham Lincoln —not so much in his features as in his temperament. He is full of a parched solemnity, a crackling melancholy, a dry austerity. Seldom in our pulpits do we see anything so solemn as his solemnity. Solemn presence, solemn face, solemn eyes, solemn mouth, solemn gestures, solemn voice. Not Wordsworth himself wore a longer monotony of countenance. He is built like a skyscraper, tier on tier, of legs and arms and features. His nose is long, his cheeks are long, his chin is long, and all these lengths are poised on a long neck that springs out of a long shaft of black frock-coat, tightly buttoned round a long trunk resting on long legs. Then there is a long perpendicular ridge of wrinkled flesh from the towering cheekbone to the long, lean curve of the jaw. Amid these lengths the dark sunken eyes, set wide apart, glow with that peculiar sad and weary energy which is characteristic of Americans, and over them jut penthouse eyebrows which intensify their mournful fire. His head and his body are strung and strained backward, making an obtuse angle with his legs, and when he folds his long arms one half expects to see the thin white hands clasped behind his back.

"He does not read his sermons. . . . No, he preaches with fresh, not stale, emotions and his words fall molten from his lips. . . . Dr. Lorimer plays with consummate skill on his audience. Indeed, at one point in his sermon, the emotional tension became intolerable. Quickly realizing that the surging tide of emotion was about to break, by a swift transition he swept his theme to a less passionate plane. Like a flash, the whole congregation sighed with relief, handkerchiefs fluttered, and the shy English temperament hastily took refuge in its habitual impassivity. It was strange to see matter-of-fact Englishmen quivering with violent emotion, their breath coming in short gaspings, their eyes moist with tears. And yet the Preacher eschewed claptrap, his appeal being essentially noble and grave and serene."

As Dr. Lorimer developed the theme of his sermon, the London reporter went on, switching to the present tense, "his slow, dragging, syllabic voice hoarsens with rapture, and the live sentences, tearing, grinding, shearing, rasping, hacking, saw their way through our ears. There is a fierce beauty in these raucous huskinesses, these high cacophonous discords, the beauty of escaping energies, of outleaping fires. Giordano Bruno said that God is an interior artist. Well, there is a divine fire working inside this man, and one cannot deny its reality, for the words that break through our indifference are witnesses too passionate for artifice, too fiery for affectation."

Much of the father was in the son. George Horace put George Claude's conviction and sincerity into editing the Post, and he displayed the same dominant will power that was reflected in Henley's "Invictus," his father's favorite poem. The son was the evangelist of business—although he was no apologist for business's sins—and he was the stout defender of faith in the America he knew and loved. In his manner there was always a reminder of his father's austerity, a projection of the preacher's commanding personality.

In the Boston days there was even a physical resemblance. At twenty-nine, Lorimer had not yet filled out into the square-cut block of a man he was to be. He was thin and not so tall as his father, though his thinness made him seem tall and accented his long Lorimer jaw. He had Dr. Lorimer's intense blue eyes and the minister's tremendous vitality. The elder Lorimer was being sapped by a fatal illness, but he gave no sign of it in his indefatigable activity.

There was one resemblance which George Claude found embarrassing. He called himself "George Lorimer" and so did his son. The younger Lorimer began to get an occasional by-line in the Boston *Post* after he joined it—not in the news columns but as the author of bits of folksy verse, much of it flippant and all of it signed "George Lorimer." After some literal Bostonians had inquired of Dr. Lorimer with raised eyebrows whether he had anything to do with these efforts, George Claude took his son aside. "George," he said, "I don't mind if you write these things, but please use all of your name so there won't be any mistake." Thereafter the son signed himself George Horace Lorimer.

In spite of such recognition, George Horace found life on the newspaper a difficult proposition. He worked on the night side for eighteen dollars a week, and the only compensation for hours and salary was the fact that when he came home early in the morning his lovely redheaded Alma would be waiting up for him. To Lorimer it was a vision that remained for long years afterward: the sight of a beautiful woman waiting when he opened the door. It helped him to endure the weary months of apprenticeship.

Life was not all hardship, of course. Lorimer had good friends in the city rooms of the Boston papers, including one, Frederick Bigelow, who was to be his friend for the rest of his life. With these colleagues he had an occasional merry evening, in the traditional manner of newspapermen before the profession became a business. Not infrequently they rendezvoused at the notorious Bell-in-Hand, a reporters' hide-out, where departing customers were aided up the steps from its basement location by means of a ship's line strung along the wall. The technique was hand over hand. Another favorite convening place was a saloon where the literate bartender kept one drawer of his cash register full of copy paper. Reporters coming in from a story would dash off their accounts with one hand while they used the other to propel liquid inspiration.

Lorimer was restless on the Boston *Post*. He asked for a two-dollar raise and it was refused. For years afterward, when the *Post's* managing editor, C. B. Carberry, complained that another of the paper's bright young men was clamoring for a two-dollar-a-week raise and that he wasn't worth it, E. A. Grozier, the publisher, would remark: "Better give it to him, Carberry. We lost Lorimer because of two dollars."

The departure of Lorimer was more than an ordinary loss for the *Post*. It was an aphorism on Newspaper Row that "if Lorimer can't get a story, no one can." The craft talked about such Lorimer exploits as his exposure of a medium by diving at the lady while she was in mid-trance and disclosing her temporal, mechanical connections with the supernatural.

Lorimer got a new job on the Boston *Herald*, where he was more restless than ever. He felt himself exceptionally well qualified for something, but he wasn't sure what it might be. Soon to be thirty-one, in October 1898, he had compiled a backlog of experience that few young Americans his age could match. He had lived in three different sections of his country. He had visited nearly every state in the Union—and not only visited, but done business in most of them; and he had hunted, fished, climbed mountains and talked to people in the others. Thus he saw America both as a nation and as a country made up of sections with different likes and dislikes, interests and resources. Moreover, he had several times accompanied his father on the summer trips to Europe and had come to be familiar with most of western Europe and with England.

In a scant ten years of working life he had been a successful businessman, a top-notch journalist, and a resourceful student. He enjoyed some of the most valuable attributes possessed by his famous father. Above everything else, he was passionately American, without jingoism or sentimentality. At that period in his life —and for more than twenty years afterward—there were few citizens who understood their country so thoroughly. Lorimer knew America's faults and virtues; he understood what it had been; he had a comprehensive knowledge of what it was at that moment in history; and he had a deep faith in what it could be.

He was, in brief, ready for the major turn in his life. It came by way of a short paragraph, tapped out by a telegraph key in the *Herald* office. It was a routine story, an announcement that Cyrus H. K. Curtis, owner of the astonishingly successful *Ladies' Home Journal*, had bought the name and what good will it possessed of the Saturday Evening Post: net paid circulation, 10,473; price, $1000. Mr. Curtis, the story said, hoped to find an outstanding editor who could make the publication successful.

Lorimer wired Curtis within an hour, asking for a job. He did not flatter himself that he was the answer to the new publisher's hope. Curtis wired back that he would be in Boston the following week and would be glad to talk to him. There are numerous stories of that meeting. Lorimer's own version is simple. "I expected to go to Philadelphia," he said. "Mr. Curtis, however, replied that I should meet him at the Hotel Touraine in Boston. There, on a divan in the lobby, we talked one morning for about ten minutes. . . ."

At the end of that time they shook hands and parted. Cyrus Curtis had hired George Horace Lorimer as the first—and last—literary editor of the Saturday Evening Post.

CHAPTER TWO

The Making of the Post

As the first and last literary editor of the Saturday Evening Post, Lorimer found more of a memory than a magazine waiting for him in Philadelphia in 1898. It could boast of a distinguished past but there was no more to be said for it.

After it became rich and successful the Post's detractors were fond of trying to prove that it was an illegitimate offspring of Benjamin Franklin, trading on his illustrious name. While there was room for scholarly hairsplitting in this argument, it was also true that the magazine did not have to apologize for its lineage.

The Post was first published as *The Universal Instructor in All Arts and Sciences and Pennsylvania Gazette*, on the day before Christmas, 1728, Old Style. The first newspaper in the colonies had been published thirty-eight years before; Samuel Johnson was an Oxford freshman; George Washington would not be born for three more years.

The beginning of the Post is a familiar story: how Franklin broached the idea to a printer named Webb, who appropriated it and launched the weekly with the aid of Franklin's ex-employer, Samuel Keimer. The wages of this sin were collected in ten months, when the new publication proved itself unable to get more than ninety subscribers and Franklin bought it for a bargain price.

As the *Pennsylvania Gazette*, issued from Franklin's own press beginning October 2, 1729, it became "a sensible, well-arranged, handsomely printed, straightforward, businesslike sheet," the best-known paper in all the Colonies. Even when the pressure of his active life led Franklin to turn over the actual direction to his partner, Hall, the imprint of his personality remained. As a regular contributor, he submitted articles, essays, and that immortal cartoon depicting a disjointed snake, with the caption "Unite or Die," which appeared in 1754.

The *Gazette* published broadsides instead of regular issues for two weeks in 1765, protesting the Stamp Act, and the subsequent flow of events leading to the Revolution compelled Franklin to turn over his interest in the *Gazette* to David Sellers.

The paper led a stormy life during the Revolution. Twice it was suspended; it was issued from York while the British held Philadelphia. The name was changed again on January 1, 1779, to the *Pennsylvania Gazette and Weekly Advertiser*, which it remained until 1821, when on August 4 it became finally the Saturday Evening Post. Sellers and Hall (later Hall's son and his grandson) had been the publishers; now its owners were Samuel C. Atkinson, the grandson's partner, and a man named Alexander.

The new *Post* had at least four rivals, both daily and weekly, but it flourished and outshone them for the next forty years. Once its name was changed to the *Daily Chronicle and Saturday Evening Post*, but *Daily Chronicle* was removed shortly and there were no more alterations. For years the Post was published in the offices occupied when Franklin was alive; even his type faces were used. The circulation climbed to 90,000, and noteworthy names appeared in its pages. Edgar Allan Poe contributed "The Black Cat" and a spasmodic code-and-cipher department; the Post's editor, Thomas Cottrell Clarke, even sheltered Poe and his wife Virginia at his home and made an effort to stop the author's drinking. Such other contributors as Harriet Beecher Stowe, James Fenimore Cooper, Bayard Taylor, N. P. Willis and G. P. R. James often appeared in the magazine. The Post had several imitators, but it either absorbed them or forced them out of business.

After the Civil War the Post shared the general decline suffered by all American magazines. Much of the blame for that situation rested with *Harper's*, which established in 1855 an English pattern for magazine making and clung to it stubbornly for nearly a half century afterward. Typography improved tremendously in that time, and circulation and advertising grew with the country, but the editorial content and point of view of American magazines remained unaltered.

By the time Lorimer got to Philadelphia the decline had reached its lowest point. Monthly publications led the field. They led it with such articles as these, the lead pieces in three 1899 issues of *Harper's:* "Boston at the Century's End"; "The Ascent of Illimani" (a South American volcano); and "The First American, His Homes and His Households."

Harper's chief rival, *Scribner's*, was no better. Its first twenty pages for the issue of June 1899 included "The Modern Group of Scandinavian Painters," "Between Showers in Dort," "The Portraits of John W. Alexander," "The British Army Manoeuvres" and an essay on William Makepeace Thackeray.

The *Atlantic Monthly*, third of the Big Three, was occupied at the same time with "Australasian Extensions of Democracy" as its leading article. The *Century* led with "A Solar Eclipse in Benares." In succeeding issues it printed Mrs. Schuyler Van Rensselaer's illustrated articles on Niagara Falls and the churches of Auvergne; Benjamin Ide Wheeler's history of Alexander the Great, complete in thirteen issues; "Life among the Nomadic Lapps"; and "Victor Hugo: Draughtsman and Decorator."

The fiction was even more puerile. It followed the worst of the British novels, and Lorimer cannily put his finger on the reason for its failure. "The social scheme in England had no counterpart in America," he once told John B. Kennedy, "so fiction based on their caste system and the theory that a life of leisure is the sole end of man could have no wide appeal in a working democracy that measured human values by achievement, not by inheritance."

As for the Post, it was much worse than its competitors. Its sixteen unillustrated pages rarely carried a column of paid advertising; the fiction was unsigned, or signed with initials; the narrow, small-type columns were filled largely with material clipped from English newspapers and magazines. The paid advertising in its issue of July 2, 1898, totaled two hundred and ninety dollars.

Cyrus Curtis had already made a resounding success of the *Ladies' Home Journal.* Not only did it lead the women's field, but it had the largest magazine circulation in the world. His decision to buy the Post was based on sound reasoning, although on the surface it appeared to be little more than a speculative life belt thrown to a nearly drowned man. Curtis saw that the country needed a vigorous magazine that would do for American males what the *Journal* was doing for women. He was wise enough to see that it should be a weekly. The fine weekly newspapers, like Greeley's New York *Tribune,* which had attracted nationwide followings had been superseded by better dailies and by the rise of magazines like *Frank Leslie's* and *Collier's.* The only other national weeklies of consequence were *Puck* and *Judge,* both humor magazines, and the juvenile *Youth's Companion. Leslie's* and *Collier's* sold for ten cents and were concerned mostly with current events, virtually in competition with the newspapers. Curtis proposed to create a magazine that would sell for five cents, meeting the newspapers on their own financial ground, but he intended to leave the news to them and build a weekly periodical of a quality that a newspaper could not approach. He foresaw that the dailies would quickly occupy a field by themselves, if they had not done so already, and that the magazine market was ripe for something new and non-competitive.

To realize his ambition, Curtis well understood, he had to have an exceptional editor. His genius as a magazine publisher lay in sensing the need, setting up the mechanism to supply it, getting the right man to operate it, and then leaving him strictly alone unless he failed to produce. This formula had proved itself in the case of the *Journal.* Curtis and his wife had seen the magazine through its precarious early days, until the publisher had been able to get Edward Bok as editor. Bok had done the rest.

For some time after he bought the Post, Curtis followed his practice by letting William George Jordan edit the magazine. Jordan did not understand Curtis' idea at all. He did understand the *Journal,* however, and he made the Post as much like it as possible, but without the vigor which Bok instilled. In other respects he relied on the Post's outmoded formula, which Curtis had intended him to change.

Lorimer chafed under Jordan's direction. He was full of ideas for the magazine which the conservative editor would not let him carry out. But the period of watchful, waiting apprenticeship gave him an opportunity to study the Post and perfect his plans for it.

Meanwhile Curtis did some chafing on his own account. The future of his new property was still much in doubt. Outside experts who examined it were unanimous in asserting that it would fail for two reasons: there was no market for a national weekly, and the five-cent price was economic suicide. In fact, said the experts, the weekly as a periodical form was on its way out.

Curtis remained unconvinced. He believed that the market was there and that he had the magazine potentially able to fill it, but not the man to do the job. Early in 1899 his patience with Jordan came to an end at last. He fired his editor and announced that he was leaving for Europe to find a successor. Lorimer saw his chance. He knew that someone had to edit the magazine until Curtis found his man and he felt certain that the publisher had no one else to whom he could turn. The young literary editor asked to be left in charge and Curtis agreed.

While the publisher was in Europe, Lorimer functioned as managing editor. He knew that he had only a short time to show what he could do, and he knew the handicaps he faced. "I had little money to spend and the paper had no reputation," he remarked later. What he did have to offer was something completely new in the magazine field: prompt pay and prompt reading of manuscripts. In this period of his and the Post's trial he inaugurated those two policies which came to figure so markedly in the early success of the magazine. He began, too, the practice of making trips to New York in search of writers, another policy which soon bore fruit.

There are numerous stories, all of them apocryphal, of how Lorimer came to be editor of the Post after Curtis had searched Europe in vain for a man of eminence to take the job. As Lorimer himself explained it: "When Mr. Curtis returned to Philadelphia he liked the way things were going so well that he made me editor in chief of the periodical." That was the simple, accurate truth of the matter. Lorimer ascended to the editor's chair on St. Patrick's Day, 1899.

He had improved the Post, during his few weeks of trial, so noticeably that Curtis had felt justified in giving him the direction of it, but the magazine was still far from successful as a business venture. It lost a staggering amount every week.

Lorimer knew he could not make the publication an instantaneous success. There was a formidable task of reconversion facing him, a task so enormous that the transformation he accomplished in the first six months of 1899 was a monumental achievement. He had to replace such insipid items as "For the Sake of Tom, a Story of Daffodil Time" with vigorous fiction. He had to attune the Post's articles to the national life, particularly politics. He intended to revamp the editorial page and make it the heart of the Post, but meanwhile it was devoted to such solemn considerations as "Newspaper Reading as a Dissipation" and "Putting Children in Hothouses." The latter began: "When your son comes to you with the complaint that he finds Emerson and the Oversoul tiresome, pat the boy on the back and tell him to put the book away for ten years. The day will come when he will cry for the Oversoul and the Platonist Review as the particular morsel for which his intellectual palate holds a craving. . . ."

Editorial changes were made as rapidly as possible, but Lorimer the businessman knew that he could not finance further improvements unless he increased the Post's advertising revenue. The issue for the first week in March 1899 carried the magazine's first full-page advertisement—for a Philadelphia seed house—and that started a flow large enough to turn the financial tide. By the time Lorimer's name appeared for the first time as editor, on June 10, 1899 (Vol. 171, No. 50), he had renovated the Post's insides until they were scarcely recognizable. He had been made editor officially in March, but this was the first issue with his name at the top of the masthead, and consequently he tried to make it as impressive as possible.

The issue led with Mrs. Burton Harrison's romantic serial, "The Circle of a Century, a Story of Old New York and New." There was a short story by Barry Pain; a non-fiction serial, "My Travels and Troubles in the Orient," by Robert Barr; a short story, "A Plantation Diplomat," by Paul Laurence Dunbar; one of Morgan Robertson's sea stories; an article about Cyrus McCormick by Edward G. Westlake; and some nondescript short pieces. The regular column, "Publick Occurrences That Are Making History," usually full of deadly dull clipped material, now told of renewed American interest in the Caroline Islands, of the Baldwin Locomotive Works, and of the Philippines, which were worth "20 million and a fight," the latter an opinion which Lorimer rejected in later years.

There were some echoes of the old days. The regular column, "Men and Women of the Hour," dealt respectfully and respectably with James Whitcomb Riley, William Rainey Harper, Edison and Richard Henry Stoddard. The editorial page's lead piece was a religious meditation by Jordan titled, "The Power of a Purpose in Life," and the magazine still carried its regular sermon, plus such lay exhortations as "The Talent for Work," by William Matthews, LL.D. The book reviews, by Vance Thompson, showed more spirit. Mr. Thompson wrote of Gertrude Atherton's "A Daughter of the Vine" that ". . . her errors of good taste are due largely . . . to her defective sense of humor," but he thought it nevertheless a "powerful novel."

More important for the Post's continued existence was the fact that this issue carried twenty-two advertisements on the last two pages of a sixteen-page edition, lauding the virtues of Hires Root Beer, Eastman Kodaks, Singer Sewing Machines, the products of the National Cloak Company, Swift and Company (health soap), the Mosely Folding Bathtub Company, and Drexel Biddle, Publisher.

In the next issue, June 17, Lorimer ran the first of the pieces which were to tell the story of American business. It was "The Making of a Merchant," by Harlow N. Higinbotham, Marshall Field's credit man, and it bore the Lorimer stamp. That issue also carried Lorimer's first editorial, unsigned as his editorials would always be, and not even on the editorial page but on a revamped "Publick Occurrences" page. Titled "Outlining the Presidential Campaign," the editorial was written unmistakably in Lorimer's style and read much like his later work. The issues of the campaign, he asserted, were "expansion abroad and trusts at home."

The fall fiction number, in September, carried the Post's first cover in color; the first cover of any description had appeared September 2. Fall fiction included "The Sergeant's Private Madhouse," by Stephen Crane, and "Under the Eaves," by Bret Harte. With that issue of September 30, the Post was enlarged to twenty-four pages, with an early prospect of thirty-two, the shape was changed to its present size, and the Quaker Oats Company appeared in the magazine's first full-page color advertisement. There were thirty-two columns of paid advertising and all the fiction and articles were illustrated. A Lorimer editorial declared that in less than a year the magazine had "achieved not only the essence but the substance of success. Hereafter it will be developed on the broad lines which it has marked out in its purpose to present the best and largest weekly magazine in the world." Looking ahead in this editorial, which he titled "A Retrospect and a Prospect," Lorimer promised for the next year a series by Thomas B. Reed, the noted Speaker of the House and "most brilliant of American statesmen"; editorials by Edwin Markham; poetry; correspondence from Washington, Paris and London; and a department on amateur sports and recreation.

"It promises twice as much as any other magazine," he wrote, "and it will try to give twice as much as it promises."

Even before 1899 had ended Lorimer appeared to be fulfilling that promise. He gave the Post's readers two prime examples of Robert W. Chambers, a new Stephen Crane story, and Rudyard Kipling's "Garm—A Hostage." Bliss Carman's poetry introduced a new era of verse in the magazine. But it was the articles that gave readers their first real taste of the Post to come. There were Hamlin Garland's reminiscences of his youth on the prairies and Ian Maclaren's remembrance of his boyhood in a Scottish grammar school. Major J. B. Pond spoke familiarly of the famous writers he had wet-nursed in his lecture agency. Robert C. Ogden told aspiring young capitalists how to get and keep a business position. Edwin Markham explained how and why he had written "The Man with the Hoe," and Joel Chandler Harris held a post-mortem on the failure of the Confederacy. Chicago's stormy mayor, Carter Harrison, anticipated in glowing terms what the twentieth-century city would be like.

No wonder Cyrus Curtis exclaimed later that he "never saw such quick and brilliant action."

It was action accomplished not only by reason of Lorimer's natural genius but through his amazing drive and energy. He worked day and night that first year, and in spite of his compara-tively munificent salary—forty dollars a week—he was so poor that he often had no more dinner than the free lunch that went with a glass of beer in a saloon. He was saving his money so that he could bring Alma and their baby daughter down from Boston. He remarked jokingly that he thought their presence would re-duce the chances of Mr. Curtis' firing him. They arrived in time to share a bleak Christmas with him. Though there was no money to buy a tree, for the baby's sake the young parents hung a few meager ornaments on the lighting fixtures.

At the office, in spite of the growing list of distinguished con-tributors, Lorimer sometimes virtually wrote an issue himself. For a few anxious months, too, his job was at stake and only Cyrus Curtis' faith saved it for him. There was developing within the Curtis Company the long, silent feud between Bok and Lorimer. Edward Bok, a brilliant but self-centered man, watched the struggles of the newcomer in the Curtis family with contempt. He referred to the Post as "the *Journal's* little brother," a term which infuriated Lorimer, who hated that kind of whimsey, particularly when it was applied to his magazine. At the first stockholder's meeting held after Curtis' return from abroad, Bok was for get-ting rid of the Post. He was afraid the magazine's continuing losses would hurt his *Journal* in time, and if it succeeded, Lorimer would be a potentially serious rival in the company.

Bok was supported by the company treasurer, who came to Curtis one day in a cold sweat of anxiety to point out that the Post was seven hundred and fifty thousand dollars in the red.

"Well," said Curtis, unperturbed, "Mr. Lorimer's got two hundred and fifty thousand to go before he touches a million. I like round numbers."

Curtis stood by Lorimer in this crisis as the young editor had supported his publisher in these early days of financial travail by putting his name on some of Curtis' notes, although the only collateral he could offer as a co-signer was his good will.

Such mutual faith was justified eventually. At somewhere near the million mark in debits, Lorimer's magic began to work. The Post made back its losses at an astounding rate as circulation and advertising shot up together. It was never in trouble again.

As the Post began the new century it was in safe waters and Lorimer was solidly at its helm. Curtis made only one attempt to interfere. He protested against one of the short stories that Lorimer had unearthed.

"My wife doesn't think it's a very good piece to be in the Post," he remarked.

"I'm not editing the Saturday Evening Post for your wife," Lorimer told him bluntly.

Curtis turned away and said nothing. He wasn't angry. He knew when he had the man he wanted, and it was his policy to give an editor full control without interference. That policy made millions for him. In Lorimer's case, he raised his editor's salary to two hundred and fifty dollars a week, which was his way of saying, "Go ahead."

Lorimer knew exactly what he wanted to make of the Post. It was to be a magazine without class, clique or sectional editing, but intended for every adult in America's seventy-five million population. He meant to edit it for the whole United States. Wesley Stout wrote later, "He set out to interpret America to itself, always readably, but constructively."

As he settled into the job of interpretation, Lorimer sensed accurately the mood of the country at the beginning of the new century. People were weary of reading about problems, politics, radicalism, war, and even uplift. They wanted to read historical novels and dwell in the past, and Lorimer gave them covers showing Ben Franklin, Washington and Independence Hall in appropriate poses, while inside he displayed the romances of the Rev. Cyrus Townsend Brady and Robert W. Chambers.

The Post had to meet three requirements, as Lorimer saw it: it had to be worth the price, be entertaining, and have a character of its own. The first requirement was well met: the Post was the best bargain in the business at a nickel. Lorimer, however, intended to give the buyer far more for his money than he expected, just as he planned to give the advertiser more circulation than he paid for. As for entertainment, the new editor was sure he had the ability to pick the entertainers in the open market, and do it better than his competitors. The matter of character would take more time—but not much more, for the Post in 1901 was in miniature what it would be at the peak of its success.

Shaping the Post, Lorimer perceived why American magazines were so much alike. The same authors rotated through the better publications. Editors and writers alike copied each other, sometimes quite shamelessly, and since most of the magazines were edited in New York, they had come to have a parochial point of view.

Lorimer eliminated much of this difficulty at one stroke by refusing to look at another magazine. (In later years he skimmed through the current magazines once a year on his vacation, and he perused *Redbook* for pleasure.) He continued to do his own missionary work in the search for new writers. He took the late afternoon train from Philadelphia to New York, where he hunted down authors and showed them his vision of America, hoping they would catch fire. Then he would take the eleven o'clock train back to Philadelphia, so that he would be at his desk when the plant opened next morning. Shades of old Phil Armour!

The result of these labors in the first two years was astonishing. While the fiction had to come mostly from established American and British authors, the Lorimer touch began to be evident in the articles, where he was able to show the public what kind of magazine he intended to make. He persuaded ex-President Grover Cleveland to write a series which brought the Post wide attention. Senator Albert J. Beveridge, who soon became his personal friend, appeared almost weekly. Speaker Tom Reed and Champ Clark followed along in the political parade.

Always the accent was heaviest on business. Charles R. Flint praised the benefits of business combination; the mayors of San Francisco and Baltimore wrote jointly on the need for better business methods in civic administration; Harvard's director of physical culture advised the businessman on home gymnastics; and Harlow Higinbotham contributed his "Tales of the Credit Man."

With these went the interpretations of American life: Bret Harte's colorful depiction of bohemian days in San Francisco; Colonel A. K. McClure's recollections of Lincoln's two campaigns; ex-Senator John J. Ingalls' re-creation of the stormy days of the Hayes-Tilden fight; William Moody's remembrances of his celebrated father, Dwight L.; David Graham Phillips' retelling of famous journalistic feats; and frequent examinations of the Civil War period by Joel Chandler Harris.

Familiar names began to parade through the Post: Rupert Hughes, Marie Corelli, Quiller-Couch, Jerome K. Jerome, Opie Read, Arthur Stringer, Joseph C. Lincoln, Richard Harding Davis, Sewell Ford, Emerson Hough, Owen Wister, Will Payne, William Allen White, Samuel Merwin. With their work appeared the illustrations of such artists as Harrison Fisher, Howard Chandler Christy, George Gibbs and F. R. Gruger.

There was but one dish missing in the basic Post menu that Lorimer planned to serve his readers, and that was business fiction. To him business was a wonderful, romantic adventure. He could chronicle it in articles by and about businessmen, but he was certain that it could also be done in fiction. The first successful attempt to write a business story, Harold Frederic's "The Market Place," had already appeared in the Post, written coincidentally in the month Lorimer was made editor. He bought this serial eagerly and was scarcely surprised to see its instant acceptance by the readers.

Frederic died before the story was published, and none of the other writers Lorimer talked to could be persuaded to enter such strange territory. The Post's new editor persisted. He had a strong feeling that this was the kind of writing which would give Post circulation an even faster upward swing. It had passed the 250,-000 mark by the end of 1900, and no one doubted it would soon reach 500,000. It had still a long way to go before it could over-haul the *Ladies' Home Journal,* whose circulation was already over 800,000 and was destined in 1904 to be the first magazine in America to have 1,000,000 net paid circulation.

Lorimer could not interest any writer in the business story. In vain he pointed out that "the struggle for existence is the loaf, love or sex is the frosting on the cake," and that every business day was full of comedy, tragedy, farce, romance—all the in-gredients of successful fiction. Business was a dominating factor in the lives of Americans, but the nation's writers ignored it.

There was one man specially qualified to write on the subject and that was Lorimer himself. He knew it, and that was why in the summer of 1901 he began writing, nights and week ends, the "Letters from a Self-Made Merchant to His Son," a perennial classic which survives today in a dozen languages. It was, as Benjamin Stolberg pointed out, "a perfect picture of Big Business before it learned to be 'good,' when giants were building it."

The editor turned author showed his work to no one. He labored over the first batch of "Letters" carefully, then sent them, unsigned, to the composing room. Post publication day was Thursday, and Lorimer waited anxiously for the mail the day after the issue carrying his work appeared. There was one letter on that Friday. It came from a young Harvard man, resident in Brookline. He deplored the existence of a writer who doubted the superior intellectual qualifications of a college man. Over the week end, however, a small flood of mail arrived in praise of the "Letters," and as they continued to run serially in 1901 and 1902, Post circulation picked up and passed the 500,000 mark long be-fore it was expected to; in fact, by the spring of 1904 it had reached 700,000. No one doubted that the "Letters" had been the primary impetus of this spurt.

John Graham, the hero of the series, was a direct, cynical, homely, primally simple man who had carved out his Chicago packing business under the hard code of that day. His letters of advice to his son were full of typically American humor. Everyone assumed that John Graham was P. D. Armour, and it was true that Lorimer had based the series on his experiences at the Armour plant. A few of Graham's salty comments probably first issued from the packer's lips at those early morning sessions with his young clerk. But the fictional packer differed in most respects from the Chicago baron. The former was a conglomerate character, a compound of several businessmen whom Lorimer had known well. John Graham's speech was redolent of the Southwest, while Armour always spoke with the accent of the East, where he had been born and raised. Lorimer used some of Armour's stock phrases, like "I simply mention this in passing," and he also utilized one of his former boss's best-known anecdotes in the first letter. The rest was imaginary.

As he went along in the series, Lorimer found material for the letters in his daily life. He lunched one day with a friend who told him about an Indian quack doctor he had met. Scarcely listening to the story, Lorimer's analytical brain picked up the phrase "quack doctor," turned it to "fake doctor," and before the day was over it had become the starting point of a letter. His friends unwittingly contributed many of the "Letters" in the same way, through the casual telling of anecdotes.

Reader response to the series was tremendous. There were five thousand letters before the end of 1901. The young intellectual from Brookline was the only dissenting voice, but there were innumerable suggestions. It was argued by a sizable bloc of readers that the son should be allowed to answer; Lorimer wisely decided against it. Some Post subscribers took the series as fact, and wrote begging letters. One man said he had bet the author wasn't over a certain age; the bet was a box of cigars and the writer urged Lorimer to answer so he could "smoke on the other man."

By far the most unusual letter came from Mississippi. In it was a pass for a Southern railway, and the writer explained that this was an expression of gratitude to the author of the "Merchant Letters," and to Lorimer as editor. He was, he said, the owner of the railroad in question and had tried unsuccessfully for a long time to get a right of way over a stretch of Mississippi pine land.

He had smoked and talked for hours with the man who owned this land, and finally had to admit he was beaten; the farmer was obstinate beyond recall. As the railroad man had departed after his last visit, he left a copy of the Post with the farmer's son, a lazy lout who had shown no inclination to do anything in the world but loaf. A few months later the farmer wrote and said he had decided to sell the land out of sheer gratitude. His son had read John Graham's letters in that and subsequent issues, and had been so inspired that he was doing well in a business of his own.

Lorimer had planned to write only five or six pieces in the series but they were so popular that he was compelled to turn out twenty of them, and six more later on. Their first republication was in pamphlet form, as an inspiration piece for Eastman Kodak workers. Then, in 1902, they were published in book form by Small, Maynard and Company, of Boston, and the author had an instantaneous best seller on his hands.

The publisher asked Lorimer's friend, William Allen White, to write them something that could be used for advertising copy. White wrote back: "The best thing about George Horace Lorimer's 'Letters' . . . is that they tell the truth about Chicago so unconsciously. Lorimer in his 'Letters' has created a paper man as vital as any of the men made by American story writers. John Graham is strong, hard-working, broad-gauged after the Western fashion, mean to his enemies, provincial, country-bred, city-made, an automatic philanthropist and what the country papers call 'a kind father, a loyal husband, a generous friend and a good citizen.' Graham has more philosophy than the Shepherd of Arden, but it is the philosophy of business; cynical as the cold south wind. But the marvel of the whole book, John Graham, Pierrepont, his 'Ma,' Helen Heath, and all of the simple dramatis personae, is the way it reproduces and reflects Chicago. In no other book is the dirt and riches and unformed mass of the town more vividly yet unconsciously set down than in these 'Letters.' The book is Chicago boiled to an essence. The barbaric yawp of protest, and the careless whoop of approval that Chicago voices where she pleases, are in the book. If a statue typical of Chicago were to be made it should represent John Graham writing to his son, 'Repartee makes lively reading but business dull. What the house needs is more orders.' "

White and Lorimer's other friends were loud in their approval, but the author remained self-effacing. His name on the book told readers for the first time that the editor of the Post was the creator of the "Letters." Norman Thompson, his editor at Small, Maynard, had difficulty in persuading him to take advantage of the publicity.

"I understand," Thompson wrote in December 1902, "that your father is going around town informing the trade that he really wrote the Merchant's Letters, but that you are getting the money for it. Now I suspect that your father is a man after my own heart. As a Press Agent I find myself hampered. Haven't you lost any diamonds? And didn't you raise a row because they wouldn't let you take Fido in the hotel? Come, come, give a Press Agent a show.

"Do you play the piano with one finger? I could write a nice literary article around that for a bit of January exploitation. Do you sleep on your left or right side and do you moisten your thumb and forefinger when you deal cards? Of course, I observed a bit at your home. 'This brilliant young author,' says my article, 'sits on his legs like a Chinese Mandarin and blows out huge clouds of smoke and aphorisms.' Another paragraph commences: 'He sings delightfully; he has a deep, rich, natural bass voice and he is kind to his wife.' . . ."

Thompson reported early in 1903 that all the Boston papers were running letters in the Lorimer style: "Letters from a Son to His Self-Made Father," "Letters from a Self-Made Chorus Girl to her Hand-Made Mother," "Letters from a Tailor-Made Daughter to a Home-Made Mother," "Letters from a Custom-Made Son to His Ready-Made Father." One paper made the mistake of using Lorimer's own characters, and brought upon itself an injunction and a damage suit. But as Thompson remarked, "They none of them, however, are dignified and none of them will stand before the public as anything but a temporary, flimsy, catch-penny scheme to sell Sunday papers by cheap, nonsensical literature. . . ."

Nothing stopped the progress of the "Letters." The book was a simultaneous best seller in the United States, England and Germany. Lorimer noted of the German edition: "If they weren't funny before, they are now." Booksellers reported that a large percentage of their sales was to customers who never read novels.

In time the book was translated into more languages and was more generally circulated in all parts of the world than any other book of American authorship since "Uncle Tom's Cabin." Isaac Marcosson, traveling the world for the Post, reported that he saw it on sale in England, France, Germany, Russia, Holland, Switzerland, Austria, Norway, Sweden, Denmark, Spain and Italy. During the first World War, he said, he was traveling between Paris and Rome in a sleeping-car compartment which he shared with a Japanese diplomat, who was reading a Japanese book. Marcosson asked him the book's name and was not surprised to hear that it was "the essays of the American self-made merchant."

There was steady demand for more "Letters," and early in 1903 it was noised around in the trade that Lorimer was doing a second series. This rumor brought a letter from F. N. Doubleday, whose young publishing house was rising rapidly in the business. "We want this new book by Mr. Gorgon Graham," he wrote, "and we think we ought to have it and hope you will agree with us that we ought to have it. We should not trespass upon any other person's preserves were it not for the fact that we were too slow, although our intentions were honorable. I enclose a check for five hundred dollars, which I should like to have you accept to bind the bargain between us. We will give you an advance of a thousand more on publication and twenty per cent on the new book. These are the terms we give Mr. Kipling and we hope under the circumstances you will accept them. . . ."

Always on the lookout for new writers, Mr. Doubleday inquired solicitously as to the current plans of two Post authors, William Allen White and Owen Wister.

Lorimer was evasive with Doubleday, but the publisher was insistent. He wrote on October 30, 1903: "Sunday is the first of November" (the day Lorimer had said he would make up his mind) "and I have been almost tempted to go and camp on your doorstep, to be taken in with your morning paper on the Sabbath morning, and to sign a contract, if you will be so good as to do this, for your new book. But I have feared lest this should be too much importunity, and I enclose you again our check for a thousand dollars to bind the bargain, if you are willing to bind it, which I hope you will be. We just must have this book, and we will hustle to make good all the hot air we have given off about our ability to sell books."

The letter must have been effective, for Lorimer signed the contract. When he received it, Doubleday wrote on January 12, 1904: "This contract seems all right to me, though mighty informal, being written over with various kinds of lead pencil. Still, if it suits you, it suits us; and I have signed it and initialed your lead pencil businesses. . . . I understand that we are to publish the book September 15th. Don't let it be later if you can help it. That is the time we can sell books. By the way, if you see any new books going that will sell a hundred thousand copies, please do not hesitate to give me the straight and narrow tip."

The book was published on schedule, under the title "Old Gorgon Graham," and it was a best seller, although not in the figures established by the original volume. But it marked the beginning of a long friendship between Doubleday and Lorimer. It was more of a business than a personal relationship, in which each acted as an occasional scout for the other. The genesis of this informal arrangement was a letter Doubleday wrote on October 31, 1904:

"After we sell two or three hundred thousand copies of your book, we shall need another book to sell to keep the wolf from the door. Don't you know of anything coming along which would be helpful to us? I see that you are publishing some stuff by Owen Wister. Is there any way for us to get onto his curves? When I was in England, I heard a good deal about a book by John Oliver Hobbes, and I got an offer on it. I send you by mail a set of proofs. It seems to me that it might be pretty good serial matter. Will you be good enough to look it over and see what you think of it? It is certainly entertaining. If you will let me know about this quickly, I shall be obliged, as I have got to either take it or give it up.

"How much do you pay for serials? Another question I would like to ask you—do you know anything about Mason? And could you use one of his books serially? In my opinion, he is a coming man. 'The Four Feathers' was a great success, and, in fact, all of his books have shown a remarkably strong and interesting side.

"You may not know it, but I have just returned from London, where I spent seven or eight days, and the most interesting thing I discovered there was that the Disraeli memoirs had passed into the hands of Moberly Bell, of the London *Times*. Mr. Bell is a friend of mine, and I spent an hour with him talking about the matter. In March, 1906, the first of these memoirs will be ready for publication. I should be very glad to know if this interests you. Of course, I am anxious to get the book. In London they say that it will be the most important book published for very many years, and they rank it as much more interesting and spicy than the Life of Gladstone. The trouble is going to be to know what to leave in, not what to cut out.

"There is also a posthumous novel, incomplete, and consisting of only twelve thousand words. The London *Times* is going to publish this and has paid a thousand pounds for the right to do it, and Moberly Bell wants to sell the right in this country for an equal sum. I have promised him to do my best to see if such a sum could be secured, but I presume that an amount of this kind is impossible, is it not, for such a work? Perhaps you will be coming over some of these days and we can talk about these things."

The two men talked many times. Out of their conversations came still another Lorimer book, his last. He called it "Jack Spurlock—Prodigal." Cast in novel form, it was published in 1907. "Jack" sold well but never attained the popularity of the "Merchant Letters," although some of those close to Lorimer, and the author himself, thought it his best book.

Of his hero, Lorimer once remarked to Marcosson: "Jack Spurlock is the happy-go-lucky fellow, with no definite idea of what he is going to do when he leaves college; who is educated along the lines of least resistance; whose father is too busy making money to pay any attention to him; and who leaves college with very hazy ideas about life and with the necessity of finding himself in the world. He illustrates one great defect of our academic training, for this training does not concern itself with what a man must do when he is graduated from college."

Like ripples from the proverbial pebble dropped in a pool, the effect of Lorimer's three books spread in ever-widening circles. "Old Gorgon Graham" ran in the Post in 1904 and further stimulated circulation. It also stimulated the interest in business fiction that Lorimer had wanted in the first place; he was overwhelmed with manuscripts in that category, one of which was Frank Norris' great novel, "The Pit," which ran in the Post shortly after the appearance of the "Letters."

There was a cycle of Broadway plays on business themes, and Lorimer was besieged with offers to convert his books into drama. He refused the pleas of three famous playwrights. Roi Cooper Megrue, then in the office of that enormous, cigarette-smoking queen of agents, Elisabeth Marbury, was more persistent. He arranged on behalf of Daniel Frohman an appointment between Lorimer and Paul Potter, who had dramatized "Trilby." Nothing came of this meeting, as far as the dramatists were concerned, but Megrue, Frohman and later Miss Marbury became Post contributors.

Frohman was fascinated by Jack Spurlock and persisted in trying to create a drama based on his exploits. He assigned one of his most talented lady playwrights to the job, but the result did not please Lorimer. "It seems to me that the play as it stands is either too trivial or not trivial enough," he wrote to Frohman in 1911. "I have never been able to see Jack Spurlock except as rather broad comedy. If we had gone at it in that spirit and tried to make every line and situation a laugh, the motive of the play would not have been so important, though even then it was my feeling that we should develop rather strongly the idea of the foolishness of trying to fit a square peg into a round hole. . . . Personally, though I say this with full knowledge that I am not the best critic of the manuscript, it does not seem worth while, for to me the whole thing lacks 'the punch.' "

Frohman would not let the property go, and in 1913 he sold

the movie rights to Famous Players Film Company for five hundred dollars, a substantial figure in those days. Frohman told Lorimer: "This is the price that has usually been paid for well known novels. I rather think that, as in the case of 'The Prisoner of Zenda,' it will also help the sale of the book."

The success of the "Merchant Letters" and their obvious effect on Post circulation compelled other magazine editors to recognize that something new had been added to their business, and there ensued a general reshuffling in the make-up and content of the Post's competitors. Lorimer stayed one jump ahead, however, by virtue of the practice which had brought him more writers than any other. That practice was his rule, made at the start of his editorship, to return a decision on any manuscript within seventy-two hours, and to pay immediately upon acceptance.

It had taken a few months for the effect of that policy to make itself felt; then came a flood tide of manuscripts. Until then it had been virtually impossible for an American writer to earn his living by writing. Aside from a few eminent novelists, and men like Mark Twain, no writer depended on his art for his bread: he had independent means or a job. Without one or the other, he was compelled to live on the rim of starvation.

In the nineties it was not at all uncommon for a writer to wait months before he knew whether his manuscript had been accepted or rejected. If it was accepted, he had to wait for his money until the piece was published, which might be a few months or a few years. Frank Parker Stockbridge sold a story to a magazine in 1891 and got a check for it in 1895. One magazine even told its contributors: "Sending of printed proof sheets is no guarantee of acceptance."

Lorimer was the first editor to pay on acceptance, and young writers flocked to the Post. Even the established writers came along after them, because the Post paid adequate prices and it cost them no more than a week's time to learn whether a story they had written was acceptable to the editor.

Another Lorimer innovation involved the handling of copyrights. Before his time, it was standard practice for a publisher to acquire all rights when he bought a story or article. The Post had a different kind of acceptance slip: it told the author that he was selling only the North American serial rights, and he could have the copyright assigned on everything else upon request. Other magazines soon had to follow Lorimer's example, as to both copyright and payment on acceptance.

These reforms, plus the Post's increasingly good prices and Lorimer's genius for selecting talent, brought new writers to the Post in droves. The rapid turnover of submitted manuscripts inspired Frank Ward O'Malley's contention that the Post maintained a staff in Trenton to intercept submissions and send them back to New York. It was Lorimer, however, who turned the trick. Night after night he read huge piles of manuscripts and unearthed from them the work of an increasingly impressive number of contributors. Often his old newspaper friend from Boston, Frederick Bigelow, who had come down to be an associate editor, sat across the table from him and edited on the spot the manuscripts Lorimer chose from the pile.

Lorimer's private life was now becoming more comfortable. His Post salary was increased from time to time, and royalties from his books poured in from both sides of the Atlantic. With these monies he gratified the urge to get out into the country he loved. The family's first home was a house near the station in Wyncote, ten miles from Philadelphia on the Reading Line. Later they rehabilitated a tumble-down dwelling near by—Alma cleaned it of bedbugs without the aid of professional exterminators—and eventually they moved to their permanent home on Church Road in Wyncote, two miles from the station. Lorimer called the place Belgraeme, a combination of the names of two of his children. By this time he was able to ride behind a coachman in his closed and open carriages, or in a dogcart. Of a Sunday afternoon he delighted to drive a spirited horse himself.

Frequently on a Sunday morning he made a pilgrimage to New York to see his father. The elder Lorimer had left Tremont Temple in 1901 for the Madison Avenue Baptist Church of New York, amid scenes of near hysteria at his old pastorate. It had been said first that he was making the change because of the Temple's bad financial condition, and there had been one Sunday morning when George Claude stood in the balconied auditorium while coins and bills of all denominations showered upon him. The mortgage had been nearly lifted as a result, but the preacher was adamant about going to New York, even though the congregation conducted prayer services to persuade him to stay.

On his last Sunday the scene in the Temple was unprecedented. Dr. Lorimer preached his farewell sermon twice to huge crowds, while thousands milled outside in the streets. Women wept and some fainted. Men cried unashamed. It was a front-page story in the Boston papers.

The two Lorimers were proud of each other. Their Sunday meetings in New York were affectionate reunions. George Horace got to the morning services too late for the collection, but always in time to hear his father's sermon. Then he ate dinner with his parents early in the afternoon and returned home to Wyncote for supper with his wife and children. He continued this practice until Dr. Lorimer went abroad for the last time in the summer of 1904. Death found him at Aix-les-Bains, France, in September.

To his lasting sorrow, Lorimer reached France just after his father died. Then he was faced with the sad duty of bringing the body home for burial. As the ship eased into her New York berth on the return voyage he surveyed the bustle and confusion of the customs with dismay. He was worn out, physically and emotionally, and the task of clearing the coffin, besides his luggage, seemed almost too much for him. But he sighted a familiar figure. It was Bigelow, come to help him. As he stepped off the gangplank Lorimer seized his old friend's hand, and in one of his rare displays of emotion said with tears in his eyes: "Big, I've never been so glad to see anyone in my life."

Except for the excursions to New York while his father lived, Lorimer was at his desk almost constantly. The Post was growing in prestige, and it was gradually taking on its permanent form.

Jack London's "Call of the Wild" ran in 1903. The names of James Branch Cabell, Harold McGrath, Zona Gale, George Randolph Chester, Wallace Irwin, Leonard Merrick, Rex Beach and George Barr McCutcheon appeared between 1903 and 1905. Herbert Johnson's first cartoons were displayed, and the illustrations of John T. McCutcheon, N. C. Wyeth and J. C. Leyendecker ornamented the magazine. The distinctive title and heading type, a Post trademark for so many years, emerged in 1904 from the hand-lettered designs of Guernsey Moore. The type became known to printers everywhere as Post Old Style.

Still more names appeared in 1906–07, names that would later be familiar to all Americans: Arthur Train, Booth Tarkington, Joseph Conrad, O. Henry, Ernest Poole, Brand Whitlock, Stewart Edward White, Corra Harris, Edwin Balmer, Perceval Gibbon and Beatrix Demarest Lloyd.

The kind of fare these writers supplied sent the Post's readership past the million mark in 1908, and the cover bore the legend, "More Than a Million a Week." A few days after that line graced the cover for the first time, the Post announced that it would leave its outgrown old plant on Arch Street, opposite Franklin's grave, and move to the impressive building on Independence Square where it is still published.

Another potent reason for the Post's skyrocketing rise was Lorimer's acquisition of two outstanding reporters who wrote exclusively for him. They were Sam Blythe and Isaac Marcosson, whose names were soon household words. Their kind of political writing was as new to American magazines in those days as some of the other innovations Lorimer made at the expense of established editorial taboos.

More new authors, each one an added stimulus to circulation, arrived at about the same time: Melville Davisson Post, Mary Roberts Rinehart, Irvin S. Cobb, Owen Johnson and Gouverneur Morris. Jack London contributed in 1909 one of his most memorable short stories, "A Piece of Steak."

By the end of that year the Post had taken on, in rough form, the distinctive character it would retain for the next quarter century. And it had become more than the nation's leading magazine: it was an American institution.

People not familiar with the inner workings of the organization sometimes assumed that Curtis, as publisher, was responsible for this phenomenal success. Cyrus always disabused them. He was fond of repeating what he had told Frank Stockbridge:

"I take down some of the profits, but the Post really belongs to Lorimer. I would no more think of telling him how to run it, what to print and what not to print, than I would think of telling Commodore Bennett how to run the New York *Herald*.

"Lorimer is the Post and the Post is Lorimer."

CHAPTER THREE

The Post School of Fiction

Bernard de Voto described the art of writing fiction for the Saturday Evening Post as it was practiced by the "literary" authors who were regular contributors to the little magazines. They would, he said, "toss off a story for the Post" in a mood of Olympian condescension. After the inevitable rejection, another editorial on literary prostitution would appear in the modest periodicals most favored by the late Edward J. O'Brien in his yearly collection of short stories, and young writers would be warned not to sell their artistic souls for gold.

The Post was regularly treated with contempt by the so-called serious novelists, by intellectuals in general, and even by the newspapers. The motive for newspaper opposition was more practical, although no publisher ever admitted it: the Post offered a sometimes damaging competition to Sunday editions.

Typical of the treatment Lorimer's magazine got from its critics was Benjamin Stolberg's 1930 estimate, in the critical periodical, *Outlook and Independent:* "The Saturday Evening Post has done more to develop the technique of the short story as good composition and second-rate literature than any other periodical I know. It is the only magazine where one may find a surprising amount of excellent writing which is not worth reading, except as an index of what the popular mind is allowed for its taste in the best of our mass periodicals."

Nevertheless, as De Voto pointed out, there were only two kinds of writers who did not write for the Post: "Those who have independent means or make satisfactory incomes from their other writing, and those who can't make the grade. Many of the former and practically all of the latter try to write for the Post."

Lorimer's criterion for acceptance was simple: "Will the Post audience like it?" He was uncannily right in his judgment ninety-nine per cent of the time. His own taste was broader than his audience's, and he often turned down pieces he liked himself if he thought they would not please the readers. Explaining his theory of editorial selection to Mary Roberts Rinehart, he declared: "A magazine like the Post has to be like a full meal, beginning with soup, going on to the most important course, which is roast beef, then maybe a salad, and it must have dessert."

As an editorial chef, Lorimer easily outranked any other American editor. No rival magazine so consistently pleased its readers for so long a time. He understood that the magazine had to be edited for a broad middle class of readership, but he wanted to reach the upper level, too, and consequently he deliberately published stories he knew would appeal only to about ten per cent of the audience. They had to be stories, however; he was scornful of intellectuality for its own sake. The formless products of the little magazines were not for him.

He could always be certain that whatever he printed was carefully read. The proof was in every day's mail, and occasionally he got an even sharper reminder, as in the case of John Taintor Foote's "Julie," which ran in the issue of April 27, 1935. Reader response to this story was no larger than normal, yet more than a year later, when Foote decided to use the closing scene of "Julie" as the opening of a new story, "Hellcat," the torrent of letters pointing out the similarity was so great that Lorimer had to have a form letter printed.

Time and again he was right and the experts were wrong. It was said that no popular magazine could print a story about miscegenation, least of all the Post. Lorimer printed one by Charles

Brackett—a story carefully hedged in several ways, it is true, but nonetheless unmistakably concerned with a subject tabooed. In 1909 he published the Potash and Perlmutter series, Montague Glass's satires on the cloak-and-suit trade, in the face of solemn assurances that Jews would be offended by humorous stories about their life, and non-Jewish readers would be bored. Mr. Stolberg thought this series "very funny when our sense of humor is tired," but millions of other less jaded readers gave the stories probably the largest acceptance in Post history. The mail showed that virtually no one was offended, circulation hit a million and a quarter that fall, and Potash and Perlmutter went on to entertain other millions on stage and screen.

Octavus Roy Cohen's Negro yarns passed through a similar experience. Stolberg and other critics argued that these "caricatures of the Negro" were "obtuse and offensive travesties of the American race problem," but unqualified acceptance by Negroes and whites alike kept the series running for years. Cohen had a Negro friend who was regular censor and adviser for these stories. Lorimer's basic theory about this type of humor was proved true even more convincingly when Amos and Andy brought it to radio.

Disappointed aspirants claimed that the Post was a "name" magazine, unfriendly to new writers, but the exact opposite was true. Lorimer constantly searched for and found fresh talent, and the mere name of an established writer, even a famous one, meant nothing to him. The story was the only thing that counted. He turned down a dozen Kipling stories "because they just weren't good." He rejected Willa Cather's "A Lost Lady," although some of her first work had appeared in the Post, because he knew it was not right for his audience, no matter how much he admired its literary qualities. He did not like the idea of "Main Street." Sinclair Lewis was a frequent contributor, but Lorimer accurately surmised that this frank exposition of how his readers lived might not please them. Besides he was indifferent to females like Carol Kennicott. "I'm not interested in the romantic woman in revolt," he told one of his friends. Lewis did not offer his novel to the Post, and Lorimer was saved from making what might have been his major editorial mistake. It riled Lorimer to find that many of the people he met abroad thought all American businessmen were Babbitts and every small town a Main Street.

Most of the time Lorimer's instinct was nearly infallible. He bought the first "Get-Rich-Quick Wallingford" story, the first Potash and Perlmutter, the first Ring Lardner "Busher" letters and John P. Marquand's "The Late George Apley"—all over the dissenting opinions of his editors. He had a lone supporter for "Apley"; the others were unanimous votes against him. Similarly, he bought Walter D. Edmonds' first Post story, "Black Wolf," and Stephen Vincent Benét's "The Devil and Daniel Webster" over strenuous opposition.

In the search for writers, Lorimer relied on three sources. He found Montague Glass, George Randolph Chester and Peter B. Kyne, three of his most popular discoveries, in the unsolicited manuscripts, and the number of names that could be added to this list of resurrections from the familiar "slush pile" would be impressive. Secondly, he scanned the daily press for promising men. In that way he got Irvin Cobb, David Graham Phillips, Sam Blythe and Will Payne, among others. Finally, some writers came to him through his friends among the regular contributors; it was Charlie Van Loan, for example, who rescued Ring Lardner from rejection.

The record shows that Lorimer contrived to get a surprising number of fine writers into a magazine that was sneered at for its catering to the masses. He printed Thomas Beer's "Hanna," Stephen Vincent Benét's "A Life at Angelo's" and his Napoleonic might-have-been, "The Curfew Tolls"; James Branch Cabell's "The Eagle's Shadow," Willa Cather's "Jack-A-Boy," Joseph Conrad's "Gaspar Ruiz," three of Stephen Crane's short stories, Theodore Dreiser's "Free," many stories by William Faulkner and by F. Scott Fitzgerald, several by John Galsworthy, one by Ellen Glasgow, O. Henry's "The Ransom of Red Chief," Jerome K. Jerome's "The Passing of the Third Floor Back," many by Ring Lardner, Sinclair Lewis' "Free Air" and numerous Lewis short stories, several by Leonard Merrick, Rebecca West and Edith Wharton, and Owen Wister's "Lady Baltimore." That is only a partial roster.

Some of these latter-day quality writers, while they were glad to be selling to the Post, clung to the established belief that the magazine's literary history was shady. They were startled to learn that it had published some of the best American writing since the beginning of Lorimer's regime.

Ike Marcosson, the Scott Fitzgeralds, Hugh MacNair Kahler and Lorimer were having lunch in Philadelphia quite early in Fitzgerald's career, and Fitzgerald took the occasion to hold forth at length on the topic of coarse commercialism in the editorial policy of American magazines, after the fashion of cocksure youth. Lorimer listened to him with polite but stony attention, asking an occasional question, offering no rebuttals. At length Fitzgerald worked himself up to his peroration:

"American magazines have always published the work of mediocrities and nobodies. They've taken no notice of real genius. It's a safe bet that nobody in this room ever heard of the most important American writer of the early 1900s. It may be fifty years before anybody, except a few of us, even knows that Frank Norris ever existed!"

The others contrived to keep straight faces and wait for Lorimer. He nodded soberly.

"If that's your considered opinion, Fitzgerald——"

"It is," Scotty said.

"Then maybe I didn't go so far wrong after all when I bought 'The Pit' and 'The Octopus' from Frank Norris and serialized them both in the Post."

With that Lorimer leaned back and his big laugh echoed in the room.

The Post even published superior poetry—the fine early work of Carl Sandburg and Edna St. Vincent Millay, and Alfred Noyes's bitter "A Victory Dance," published in 1920, which became the best-remembered verse ever printed in the magazine.

But it was the writers of broad popular appeal who typified the Post school of fiction developed by Lorimer. Many of them are still writing, and their names are familiar to innumerable Americans—names like Margaret Culkin Banning, James Warner Bellah, Earl Derr Biggers, Katharine Brush, Charles Francis Coe, Edna

Ferber, Joseph Hergesheimer, Emerson Hough, Rupert Hughes, Fannie Hurst, Clarence Budington Kelland, Sophie Kerr, Peter B. Kyne, John P. Marquand, Alice Duer Miller, Kathleen Norris, E. Phillips Oppenheim, Norman Reilly Raine, Mary Roberts Rinehart, Kenneth Roberts, Booth Tarkington, Albert Payson Terhune, Ben Ames Williams, Harry Leon Wilson, P. G. Wodehouse. The list could go on for pages.

It was among these men and women that Lorimer found his friends. With a few he was as intimate as he could ever be; with nearly all of them he was friendly. They in turn regarded him with an affection enjoyed by few, if any, magazine editors. He stage-managed them, treating some with drama, some with humor, others with quiet respect. To them he was always "the Boss," and those who knew him best addressed their letters "Dear Boss." To most, however, he was "Mr. Lorimer"—or "My dear Lorimer," in the correspondence style of the century's first decade—and only a comparative few of his writers ever knew him well enough to call him "George."

Their loyalty to him survived time and temptation. When Hearst's *Cosmopolitan* made its spectacular raid on the Post stable just after the first World War, there were only a few defections, among them Cobb, Lardner and Kyne. Of these, Kyne did his best work for *Cosmopolitan* and other magazines; Cobb was past his writing peak; and Lardner went on to write better stories but not the kind he had done for the Post, which Ray Long, master of the raiding party, had hired him away to do. Cobb seemed the biggest catch at the time, and his departure was the one that hurt Lorimer, because they had been such close friends and because of the manner of his leaving. Lorimer never forgave him. It was not Cobb's leaving which so wounded Lorimer: it was the fact that Cobb signed with Hearst secretly, and then sent George Doran to break the news, instead of telling the Boss himself.

The Boss's enemies (and he had them) were largely disgruntled writers. It is surprising he had no more, considering the fact that he reigned as absolute czar of his kingdom and sometimes showed the weaknesses of all who have such power. But his personality was so strong that he could command respect where he could not command love and devotion. Even those not particularly close to him were often idolatrous. It was said of Conrad Richter, at the start of his career, that he would sit in Independence Square, facing the Curtis Building, and wish that he might be Lorimer's chauffeur or gardener, just to be close to the man.

Only one ironclad rule was imposed on every writer: there must never be an off-color situation, an indecent word or suggestion in a Saturday Evening Post story. The rule was broken twice. During the first World War, Melville Davisson Post contributed a story about a female spy, an otherwise upright and virtuous woman who permitted herself to be seduced by a German officer in the course of obtaining vital information. So strong was the patriotism of Post readers that no one protested.

The second lapse occurred in 1931, when Katharine Brush's "Red Headed Woman" began its serial run. The end of the first installment found the secretary-heroine having a drink with her boss at his home, the boss's wife away and night drawing on. To the profound shock of numerous readers, the second installment began with the two having breakfast, the wife still away, and a significant lapse of time unaccounted for. Lorimer prepared a form letter to answer the indignant mail. "The Post," he said, "cannot be responsible for what the characters in its serials do between installments."

For a long time Post characters were not only continent, for reading purposes, but they did not drink spirituous liquors. When they began to tilt a glass now and then, the complaints were as plentiful as they had been the year the first Post heroine lit a cigarette. Even in 1929, at the height of the jazz decade, a Vancouver woman wrote: "I have read the Post for many years, about twenty-five, but I am through with it now. Too many stories of cigarette-smoking, drinking girls. Of course I know such things are done, so are many other things that I do not care to read about in a decent magazine, or have my fourteen-year-old granddaughter read."

No prude himself, Lorimer never yielded to this constant pressure. The Post did not accept liquor advertising, thereby cutting itself off from a profitable source of revenue; but even during

Prohibition, Post characters continued to drink when drinking was called for, notwithstanding the opposition of ardent drys and church people. One story by F. W. Bronson, "Birthday," in the issue of July 20, 1929, brought forth an unusually vigorous protest. A typical letter, from a St. Louis woman, declared that it was "disgusting to say the least," and added that she could not "understand why the Saturday Evening Post would publish such a story. I am sure many parents feel as we do. . . ."

Lorimer outlined his policy on the whole question to an associate editor, who sent this reply: "The policies for which a publication stands are found in the articles it publishes and even more directly on its editorial page. If you have read the Saturday Evening Post at all closely, you will know that it has consistently and continuously stood for law enforcement, for cleaner living and sounder thinking, and for raising the moral and material standard for all classes and all peoples. As far as fiction is concerned, you must remember that one of the purposes of it is to reflect existing manners and conditions, in short, life as it is. It would be impossible for a writer to describe certain sections of the country and certain types of people of the present without making some reference to drinking, but you will never find in the Saturday Evening Post any story in which drinking or lawbreaking is glorified.

"Some of our fiction is written and printed for the particular purpose of showing up the futility and the danger of certain practices of the moment. 'Birthday' is such a story. There is, of course, considerable drinking in it, and yet it seems to us an eloquent sermon against the foolish doings of some of the older generation today and a story that throws a new light on the younger generation. It may interest you to know that many of our readers have recognized the purpose for which the story was published. Often the best way to correct undesirable conditions is to wake up the public to them. Certainly nothing can be gained or cured by hiding our heads in the sand like an ostrich and not recognizing what is going on around us."

Liberal as it might be in depicting "things as they are" where cigarettes and highballs were concerned, the Post hid its head in the sands of convention wherever sex was involved. It conformed absolutely to the standards of middle-class American morality at a time when a tide of naturalism was rising in American letters and completely engulfing the literary morality which had prevailed up to the turn of the century. The Post's moral standards were about the same in 1935 as they had been in 1900. If they had been any different, there is little doubt that the Post would have ceased to exist. The application of the American novel's standards to a mass-circulation magazine would have been fatal, and Lorimer knew it.

It was inevitable, however, that the Post should thereby lay itself open to the charge of creating an unreal world where romance and morality clasped hands on an equally high plane, where the happy ending and the good clean American life were the prerequisites. It was charged, further, that, having established these artificial standards, the Post compelled young writers to write exactly what it wanted, and at the same time drove up prices on the open market.

This kind of criticism Lorimer ignored when it came from the professional literary critics, for whom he had an enveloping contempt. When it came from the newspapers he was profoundly irritated. Two-faced, he called the daily press: smugly conventional on one side and yellow on the other.

In 1926 the Kansas City *Star* incurred the Lorimer wrath by making exactly these charges in commenting on Sinclair Lewis's refusal of the Pulitzer Prize. Post practices, said the *Star*, were even more injurious than prize offers. Lewis had offered "Main Street" to the Post, it went on, but it was turned down because the magazine did not like the picture of American life presented in it, and Lewis had thereupon sacrificed his serial rights rather than change the story.

Lorimer wrote indignantly to the editor:

> . . . The Saturday Evening Post has, of course, normal and we hope reasonable intelligent editorial supervision and direction. We do not, however, ask or want our contributors to "write down," to write against their convictions, or to do anything except the very best work of which they are capable.

We have never offered a prize either to writers or to illustrators, nor do we tempt writers by paying them more than other periodicals. Though we pay liberally, we are not in the competitive bidding for names. To cite a recent case by way of illustration, *Liberty* put Wodehouse under contract at thirty-five hundred dollars for his short stories against the twenty-five hundred to which we had just advanced him. We do not make contracts with writers as we believe their work deteriorates under the contract system.

Mr. Sinclair Lewis, who is used by your reporter as an illustration, so far as we know wrote exactly what he wanted to write for the Saturday Evening Post and did, we believe, the best work of which he was capable at the time that he was contributing to our columns. The serials of his that we published were suggested by him and his correspondence with us shows that he was a very happy and grateful contributor to the Saturday Evening Post. "Main Street" was not "turned down by the Post."

Mr. Lewis did not submit either the idea for this book or the manuscript of it to the Saturday Evening Post. It was first read by us when it appeared in book form. His two latest serials have been sold in the highest market at prices above those that the Saturday Evening Post has ever paid for serials.

We have no desire either to criticize Mr. Lewis or to question his motives as, no doubt, they are of the highest, but, following the reasoning of your writer to its logical conclusion, the Pulitzer Prize which he refuses to accept is a small affair financially in comparison with the prize money—the term is your writer's, not ours—that he received for his two latest serials.

In our experience, our severest critics are usually men who have been only superficial readers of the weekly and those who have been unsuccessful in their efforts to contribute to it. We do not expect that all men and all classes will like the Saturday Evening Post, and we have no fault to find with our critics, but we expect their criticism to be based on a fair reading of the weekly and a recognition of facts.

That was the essence of Lorimer's philosophy concerning the relation of the writer to the magazine. The editor might suggest a story to an author, saying, "Here's a kind of story we'd like very much to have from you. Would you like to do it?" But all he required of any contribution was that it be a good story and acceptable to the Post audience. Lorimer was the final judge of what was good and what was acceptable. Whether what he chose was "good" will always be subject to differences in viewpoint, but there can be no doubt that he understood what was acceptable to millions of readers.

CHAPTER FOUR

The Post School of Fiction: II

The story of the Post school of writers, and of Lorimer's relationships with them, is a two-part serial divided by the first World War. The Boss drew his inner circle of friends before the war, in the magazine's golden age. In the twenties many of these intimates were either dead or retired, others had moved on to new fields, the Post was entering a different phase of its career, and Lorimer himself was compelled to spend more time with the business affairs of the Curtis Company.

For a man who believed that an editor should avoid personal entanglements with writers—a policy he extended to politicians and foreign countries—Lorimer was generous in making exceptions to his own rule. His best friend was Sam Blythe. Then came the inner circle: Senator Albert Beveridge, David Graham Phillips, Mary Roberts Rinehart, May Wilson Preston, Irvin Cobb, Kenneth Roberts, Joseph Hergesheimer, Edwin Lefevre, Garet Garrett, Hugh MacNair Kahler, Harry Leon Wilson, Hugh Wiley and Charles E. Van Loan.

It was Beveridge who led him to Phillips. These two had been classmates at De Pauw, after which their careers took them far apart philosophically. Beveridge became the champion of imperialism, the defender of big business, while Phillips devoted himself in fiction and articles to attacking the inequities of the American social structure. Beveridge later became as comparatively radical as he had thought Phillips, but no matter how far apart or how near their views happened to be, they remained close friends.

Lorimer and Phillips were even further apart politically. Fresh from his reporting experiences on the New York *Sun* and Pulitzer's *World*, and burning with anger at the injustices he had seen, Phillips spent the last decade of his life recording the social movements of his day in seventeen novels, a play, and innumerable articles. He attacked particularly the evils of business and government. Lorimer was willing enough to attack the government, but when both Phillips and Beveridge were assaulting the entrenched trusts, Lorimer's support was cautious and limited. He went along with Beveridge when the senator embraced Progressivism, and he bought more than forty of Phillips' milder articles, but he was not to be found at the Indiana legislator's side in the memorable Senate fight against the meat packers, and the best of Phillips' muckraking work, particularly his sensational series, "The Treason of the Senate," went into *Cosmopolitan* and other magazines.

Nor could Lorimer stomach the novelist's later work, when he began to examine the changing sexual standards of women, ending with his best-known story, "Susan Lenox: Her Fall and Rise," which was published six years after his death.

In spite of these differences, Lorimer remained close to both men, in a personal as well as a literary sense. Something of the curious working of their relationship can be seen in this exchange of letters between Lorimer and Phillips in November 1909. Phillips wrote:

"Here is the article 'Restless Husbands' and also the assorted pig's feet. Perhaps you have turned down some of the lot before. If so, you can do it again. Don't think because these offerings are stock that they are shopworn—over-iced, or in any way whatever impaired or deteriorated. On the contrary, *our* factory has a secret process by which goods, far from losing with age, improve and become better than when first tinned. Although this is true, still, seeing as we are friends, and you an old customer, the price remains the same, $500 for an article, $1000 for the short stories, except 'Hawk Errant,' which is $750. If the goods are returned, we shall restore them to the shelves cheerfully, and your loss will be our gain."

Lorimer replied: "I am sorry, but under a recent ruling of the Department of Agriculture, the Saturday Evening Post is forbidden to put out any products in which benzoate of soda is used as a preservative. The stories are all good, and all intensely interesting to me personally, but I doubt strongly whether they are Post stories. The article is exceedingly good. Whether we can use it or not depends on whether you care to make some changes in it—not changes that will alter your argument, but that will make the article conform more closely to our style of doing this sort of thing. If you are of an open mind, we can talk it over when I see you next. If not, you can bang the front door of your soul in my face and be ——. [The dash is Lorimer's.]

"In answer to that ad [for a country place] I have had two thirds of the farms in Montgomery County offered to me. They all sound fine on paper, and I'll bet that they will turn out punk when they are investigated. Still, there is a chance for us to spend a day in the open air, sometime during the next fortnight, behind the gentlemanly chauffeur who almost wrecked us last week, if you feel that you can stand another outing so soon. . . ."

They shared a good many outings, and whenever Lorimer visited New York he could be found wining and dining with Phillips; but their tastes differed, even in recreation. When the writer grew weary of New York, his idea was to go to some other great city, Paris or London, while Lorimer spent all the time he could manage in his beloved West. Such differences only sharpened the affectionate exchanges between them. Here is the Boss writing to his friend in 1909:

"My dear Phillips, I'll get as many proofs to you as possible before you sail, and the remainder will follow you, I suppose, to Paris. For, as the scripture so beautifully says, 'The dog will return,' etc. Why in the name of common sense, if your blood isn't up to par, don't you go some place out West, where they make a specialty of red microbes [sic]? Nobody can live near Timberline and feel like the devil. If it doesn't agree with him, he dies in a spasm and the trouble is all over."

The trouble was soon over for Phillips. One day in January 1911 he was shot by a mentally unbalanced musician as he stepped from the Princeton Club after lunch. He was taken to a hospital and died next day. His sister, with whom he lived, heard the news of the shooting from her butcher, who read the story in an early newspaper edition. He called her and remarked, "Those guinea hens you ordered for your dinner party tonight—well, ma'am, I guess you won't be wanting 'em."

Beveridge and Lorimer were among the pallbearers at their friend's funeral, and Lorimer was able to perform still another last service. "The Grain of Dust," on which Phillips was working when he died, was running serially in the Post; his editor finished the job for him.

It was in 1909 that Lorimer met Mary Roberts Rinehart. She became one of those close enough to call him George, and even though she sold her work to other magazines, the Post always had first call on it, with a few exceptions.

The Rinehart career began with fiction. Her first Post appearance was a two-part serial, "The Borrowed House," in 1909, and this was followed by the first adventure of her memorable Tish, in "That Awful Night," published in 1910. The creation of Letitia Carberry, the lovable and amusing spinster, brought instant success to her creator. Mrs. Rinehart pursued Tish through a long series before war came to Europe, an event which altered both their careers.

The war caught Lorimer flatfooted. For once he failed to understand the shaping of events, and his usually observant eye did not register the danger signals during the winter before Sarajevo, when he spent several weeks in Europe. Returning from that trip, he wrote chattily to Mrs. Rinehart in January 1914:

"Salute! As we say in that dear, sunny Italy, from which I have recently escaped. I was not idle while you were having diphtheria as I wound up my spell of eyestrain with a grand set piece in Paris, where one of our most distinguished little oculists took out a superfluous piece of my lower eyelid. Happily, however, neither my figure nor my beauty was spoiled, and I am back in the ring, thirsty for copy, and, with the help of a pair of those impressive Colonel George Harveys—the tortoise-shell-rimmed boys, you know—able to read your masterpieces better than ever. As I hear of you gadding around New York, I assume that by this time your throat is again able to perform its offices on everything from the cocktail to the office. This is a soup-kitchen winter and I need work. Please send me a lot of stuff to read."

By this time the lady was the brightest fiction star the Post had in its firmament, yet Lorimer was quick to see that she possessed the versatility to be a first-rate war correspondent when the intrepid Rinehart became one of the first Post regulars to ask for a correspondent's assignment. Lorimer had sent Richard Harding Davis and Irvin Cobb to the German armies, but there was unexpected difficulty in getting reporters to the other side of the lines. It was understood that to the Allies, in this earliest stage of the war, America seemed pro-German, and the British and French commanders were unwilling to send American correspondents to the front.

Mary Rinehart was the first writer to overcome this opposition. She did it by getting herself made a member of the Belgian Red Cross, a simple act that put her in the front lines overnight. Once established there, she found the going easier. Foch and other Allied leaders became her friends, gave her shelter at their headquarters and untangled the red tape. Early in January 1915 they saw to it that she was issued a gas mask—a strip of gauze to be wet in trench water. Later that month she saw soldiers dying of German chlorine, three months before official war histories record that it was used, and at a time when the German government was denying indignantly that it was employed at all. When she came back to America shortly afterward and made this revelation in her first article, Lorimer edited out that portion of the piece, as he did everything that might contradict the official American attitude of strict neutrality.

Her war articles brought Mary Rinehart more mail than she had ever drawn before, more than she ever received for anything else she wrote in her amazing career. The American people were hungry for news and she had given them information they were not getting from any other source. Besides her descriptions of life at the front, there were interviews with all the important Allied generals, another with the King of the Belgians, and still another with Queen Mary—the first time any member of the royal family had given an interview.

Wherever she stopped, Mrs. Rinehart had been a guest of whatever government was involved and consequently the trip had cost her practically nothing. She had taken a two-thousand-dollar Post bank roll with her for expenses, but it was necessary to dip into it only when the winter proved colder than she had anticipated: Mary bought herself a fur coat.

Back in Philadelphia, she walked into Lorimer's office, wearing the coat, and shocked him by returning twelve hundred dollars of unspent expense money.

"I didn't keep an expense account," she reported blithely, "but I do have the coat."

"My God," Lorimer complained, "you'll throw off the whole bookkeeping department!"

"But that coat was useful," she protested. "It covered many a general's knees."

"With you in it?" the Boss inquired quizzically.

Aside from the coat, the chief product of the trip was her first war book, "Kings, Queens and Pawns," made from the Post articles. It was published by George Doran and marked the beginning of her long association with him.

To relax from the strain of her weeks on the battlefields, and recover the health she had lost there, Mrs. Rinehart spent the winter of 1915–16 in Cuba and other Caribbean spots with her husband and a party of friends. Out of that junket came another significant article. She wrote to Lorimer after her return in March: "My dear George: I want you to know that I am back. We have had a bully time, and I feel more like work than I have for months. I expect to start a new novel almost immediately but there will be some short stories right along. I also think I have a cracking good article on some tarpon fishing we did in the jungle on the Chagres

River with Rex Beach. I have another one in mind also, called 'The Pirates of the Caribbean,' dealing largely with the hotel-keepers of Havana."

Lorimer wanted to keep his star occupied with fiction. He replied: "It's mighty good to know that you are back on the job and feeling well. I am not so strong for the special articles as I would be for another Sub-Deb story. Can't you work one in before you start on your novel? Tish appears this week and the cupboard is bare."

But Mary sent him the "Pirates" article first. It was a knife-edged exposure of the way American tourists in Cuba were being relieved of more dollars than the traffic legitimately should bear, and when Lorimer ran the piece, it upset the Cubans considerably. The State Department protested to the Post and the affair took on all the appearance of an international incident. The net result, however, was beneficial to everyone. With the spotlight of Post publicity focused on her, Cuba could do nothing but make a determined effort to improve conditions, and the Rinehart article proved to be the stimulus that started Cuba toward her eventual tourist prosperity.

The Boss worried lest his favorite lamb be stolen from the fold in the great Hearst raid, and he wrote to her in 1917: "Personally, and without naming no names and without knocking nobody, I don't root for your writing for any other magazine whatsoever." At the same time he gentled her into increased Post activity with letters like this: ". . . Just to notify you that I am in a receptive mood that would be almost melting if I were a lady, so don't delay with the Country Club story and be turning over the first of Bab's adventures for the autumn series. I think she ought to spell a little better in the new series as she will have her hair up and her dresses cut a little lower. . . ."

A month later he was at it again: ". . . I do hope that the Deb is beginning to sizz a little in your head. War stuff is important and there are a lot of people who can write it and are writing it, but there's only one lady who can write Tish and Deb and sich like things, and the country needs them quite as much as the other sort of thing right now."

No one was more appreciative of the Rinehart talent than Lorimer. "Age cannot wither her, nor custom stale the infinite variety of Tish!" he exclaimed in 1922 as he accepted another in the perennial series. "I hope that this story is a symptom and that you are going to break out in a rash of short stories." Again, he wrote in December 1924: "The love story is everything that a love story should be and I got up from reading it feeling that I was twenty-one again."

His enthusiasm was expressed concretely as well: Mrs. Rinehart was one of the Post's highest-paid writers. She got as much as forty-five hundred dollars for a short story and sixty thousand for a serial at peak prices. Yet friendship and her value to the Post did not save the lady from the financial rein that Lorimer held on all his writers. Speaking of a 1917 serial, he wrote: "Now, the story, as I see it and as you tell me you have planned it, will make about five parts. I simply can't go over two thousand apiece for them. That is more than I have ever paid anyone for a serial and the absolute maximum of value that I can see in anything short of the New Testament. . . . I am always willing to go the limit for you but ten thousand is the limit. . . ." The limit was increased as the state of the Post's financial health continued to improve in the lush twenties, and Lorimer's enthusiasm occasionally led him to a small bonus long before that time. "Not as a precedent," he told Mrs. Rinehart in a 1917 letter, "but because the Sub-Deb story is extra long and extra good, I have added two hundred and fifty dollars to the check." Sometimes he would hold out an increase as bait: "I see that the Standard Oil has just granted a ten per cent increase to the help. We would do the same thing if we had a Bab story in the shop to operate on."

In spite of the enormous popularity that earned her such prices and praise from the Boss, Mrs. Rinehart was always hesitant when she submitted a new story or a novel, as were most other Post writers. Often her submissions were accompanied by a half-apologetic letter. With a Tish story in 1919 she enclosed a note saying she had written it at a time when she was feeling sad. Lorimer answered: "If you wrote that Tish story while you were feeling a little melancholy, I wish to God that you would write me a companion piece some day when you are so sad that you can hardly see the lines through your tears. It is one peach of a story. By all means, let us have a love story with a good clinch in the close-up." And as he so often did, he added a few lines about himself: "I had a real kid party, thirty Ogontz seniors for the theater and supper afterwards at the Bellevue. I am getting old enough to do the father act, and to say My dear—if they are that good-looking."

Lorimer did much to overcome the Rinehart modesty, and he was joined in this endeavor by Cyrus Curtis, who was exceedingly fond of the lady in his self-effacing way. Curtis was awed by his magazine's chief fiction property; he approached her as a courtier instead of a king. The Boss was aware of his publisher's proper adoration and he teased Mary slyly about it: "Mr. Curtis told me that he had had a letter from you, but he did not show it to me. He has a secret and very marked weakness for you. I should not be surprised if, even though you have written 'This is farewell forever,' he kept right on proposing to you. . . ."

That was a reference to Curtis' attempt in 1919 to make Mrs. Rinehart editor of the *Ladies' Home Journal*. He used George Doran in the negotiations, and Mary was momentarily tempted before she finally declined. "I wanted very much to be in Philadelphia," she wrote to a friend, "but now that we have opened the Sewickley house it is too difficult to pull up all the roots we have just put out. Also, I am not a desk woman and the prospect of the confinement worried me considerably. . . ."

Curtis was disappointed, but his admiration only increased and within a few months he was asking her to share the speaking program with General Leonard Wood and Congressman Hampton Moore at the annual dinner of the New England Society in Philadelphia. "We do not," he assured her solemnly, "do any of the usual silly stunts, or have jazz music, brass-band noise during the dinner, but we have some diversion suited to the occasion, such as a stage scene representing Plymouth Harbor, and the Pilgrims landing on the historic rock, and some trained voices dressed in Pilgrim costume sing something of old-time music—this comes as a surprise between courses and lasts only two or three minutes—the lights being lowered for each scene. Our dinners are different from the usual public dinners and women fight for invitations. . . ."

It took even more fervent urging, but Mrs. Rinehart consented at last, went to the dinner, and became the first woman ever to address the organization.

The prime example of Rinehart modesty occurred at the Philadelphia opening of her stage version of "The Bat," when she sat in a box with the Lorimers and heard the receptive audience give her and the play a virtual ovation at the end of the first act.

"Oh dear," she said, turning to Alma, "I feel so depressed."

"For heaven's sake, why?" Alma asked, astonished.

"I'm afraid I'll never do anything as good as this again," Mary lamented.

In their working and social relationships, Lorimer showed his fondness for Mary Rinehart in his own reserved way. He expressed his affection in the letters he wrote her, and in subjecting her to his special brand of teasing. She was always partial to big hats, and once arrived at a party with one so large that she made a spectacular entrance by coming in the door sideways. Lorimer stepped forward quickly and took her by the arm.

"This is Mary Roberts Rinehart," he announced to the assemblage. "She wears bigger hats than anyone in the world."

Their friendship was warm and constant. They saw each other frequently, and the correspondence between them became voluminous over the years. Lorimer's letters were mostly urgings and suggestions; Mary's were often intimate glimpses of a writer at work. Out of a period of seclusion at Eaton's Ranch, Wyoming, in September 1926, she wrote to him:

"There is a snowstorm and blizzard raging outside the cabin; six inches of snow so far and more to come, and the temperature sixteen degrees last night! So sitting crowded into the wood fire, I am writing to you. Soon (next week) I shall be at home again and at work. All summer I have been making notes for the story and have even done a little work on it, but it is not very good. The real story is always written second draft. If I can, I want to make the story much bigger than its original conception. No one has written the Northwest of today, with the cattle man, still in his boots and Stetson, raising hay and grain for the cattle, turning farmer against all his instincts and yet raising his enormous herds, rounding up, shipping. The gradual invasion of wheat, the new red grain elevators side by side with shipping pens, the cowboy coming down from the mountains to operate a threshing machine. Always of course I shall tell a story, I hope, but I like the idea. Do you?

"Just when the story will be ready I cannot tell. Around the first of the year, I hope. And you may find it long and want to cut it. Of course that's all right with me. I promise not to kill it with an overdose of local color! I was proud and pleased over the advertising of 'The Gray Goose,' and I only hope I make good on the serial. I am willing to work at it until it is just what you want. You know I don't save myself if I can improve a thing. But I am too close here; I need to get home and get a perspective. . . ."

What her work meant to thousands upon thousands of lonely people was expressed in letters that came to the Post from every corner of the United States. This one, written in 1926 by a lady in Fresno, told the common story: "Each year I have followed the joyous tales of Mary Roberts Rinehart, and to a shut-in like myself, they are like a breath of the great outdoors. The account of the fishing trip in this week's issue was too funny for words, and I surely did laugh at and could almost visualize the 'setting broad jump' at the mention of the snake. What a splendid talent is that of Mrs. Rinehart's, to be able to make us forget ourselves for a while, and to share with her at least in story the many little adventures we can never hope for in actuality."

The Rinehart record in the Post is probably the most impressive compiled by any fiction writer. There was the Sub-Deb series in 1916–17, "The Amazing Interlude" in 1918, "Lost Ecstasy" in 1927, "The Door" in 1930—to name only a few of the best-remembered. Among her fifteen Post serials were such well-loved stories as "The Street of Seven Stars," "The Album," "The Wall," "The Great Mistake," "The Yellow Room" and "Miss Pinkerton." All these and numerous short stories too. She was still doing Tish when Lorimer retired, and as this was written she was contributing to both the Post and the *Journal*.

A variety of factors went into the shaping of her remarkable career, but Mrs. Rinehart believes that Lorimer had the greatest influence on her life of any person outside her own family. She was happy for days if he wrote her an enthusiastic letter. Their friendship survived even such incidents as that in 1931, when Mary sold her autobiography to *Good Housekeeping* without showing it to the Post.

"Why didn't we see it?" Lorimer demanded.

"George, I just didn't think it was the kind of thing the Post would be interested in," she apologized.

Lorimer took a deep breath. "Mary," he said, "I wish to God you'd let *me* edit the Post."

At the time Mrs. Rinehart flourished in the Lorimer circle, the Boss's friendship with Irvin Cobb began. He discovered the Kentucky grampus in 1912, when he printed an autobiographical series, a travesty on all self-revelatory excursions, titled "Shakespeare's Seven Ages and Mine." Cobb's first short story in the Post, "The Escape of Mr. Trimen," earned him a five-hundred-dollar check, and then he went on to write such works of short fiction as his much-anthologized "The Belled Buzzard," "Quality Folks" and "The Life of the Party." From remembrances of his Kentucky boyhood, he created the character of Judge Priest, whose salty adventures, recounted in a long Post series, endeared Cobb to the magazine's audience.

Like Mrs. Rinehart, he was part of Lorimer's fiction school, but he also won national recognition as a war correspondent, working on both sides of the lines and proving himself a great reporter in the course of nearly four years, off and on, at the front. George Doran remarked of him: "His self-confidence in the pursuit of his vocation was phenomenal, his courage—some call it nerve—superb." It was Cobb who got an interview with the inaccessible Kitchener and cabled it to the Post before the British could silence such communications by censorship. With news beats like this one, and inimitable reports like "At the Front of the Front," Cobb became the sensation of the war years in the magazine field.

In Lorimer's inner circle Cobb's wit sparkled as brilliantly as it did in his stories. He was the only man who ever dared joke about the Boss's idol, the Grand Canyon, and he did it with exactly the right touch. He assured Lorimer solemnly: "The Grand Canyon of the Colorado is the Saturday Evening Post of canyons."

Wherever the Lorimer circle gathered in the old days, the globular figure of Cobb could be found, whether at Atlantic City, the Canyon, Philadelphia or Palm Springs. At one party he was strolling amiably about the room when the nearby sounds of a piano became audible. Irvin listened intently, and with obvious admiration.

"Who's that playing piano?" he asked.

"That's Mary Roberts Rinehart," someone informed him.

"Say, I'll bet she could fill a tooth!" Cobb said.

At another party he encountered little Jimmy Preston, the artist husband of another noted Post illustrator, May Wilson Preston, whose work was so inseparable a part of the Rinehart stories. Cobb stood back and surveyed the diminutive Jimmy critically.

"How much do you weigh?" he inquired.

"Ninety-six pounds," Preston said.

"Ninety-six pounds!" Cobb exclaimed. "Why, I've got an aunt in Kentucky has a wen that weighs that much."

This female relative appeared frequently in Cobb's conversation. At an exhibition of modern art he remarked: "My aunt *knits* better pictures than that."

Cobb was frequently one of the celebrants at the parties Lorimer arranged in the earlier days of the Post, when he played as hard as he worked. After one of these affairs in November 1912, Lorimer wrote to his friend: "Got home with a little spare change, after touching O. Carmichael for two hundred dollars in passing. It was a lovely little teaparty, though towards the last of the evening I felt that I was imposing on you very much in the fashion of a country cousin. I don't feel that Thompson, or Carmichael, or, for that matter, George Doran need sympathy. You will remember that the two first escaped in the breeches buoy early in the evening, and Mr. Doran, when last seen, was being taken on board the *Carpathia*."

There was something about the Kentuckian that brought out

the Boss's best correspondence. In 1915, for example, he called upon Cobb for help in this fashion: "I have staved this thing off just as long as I possibly could for you, but She-who-must-be-obeyed will no longer brook delay. Everybody has to come across with one talk before Mrs. Lorimer's Club, and you are absolutely elected for the evening of Friday, May eighth, or Tuesday, May twelfth. The subject is anything you please, just so you are amusing. The length of the talk is one hour. The audience is composed of gentlemen and ladies, and a few of those that you left behind you in Yonkers on the hill. The compensation is one hundred bucks. I know this is a low-down graft, but I am quite powerless. Please make home happy for me by wiring that you will come one of the two days mentioned. That is really the only part of the program which has been left for you to decide."

Cobb accepted but he asked for more details, and Lorimer replied: "You can depend on my doing everything possible to make your last hours comfortable, but knowing, as I do, the character of the young person who has charge of the hog killing, I doubt whether it would be safe to count on anything less than a full even hour. Choose your own subject and move along the lines of least resistance. I don't see why you can't string together some amusing by-product entitled 'Me and Europe,' or a little skit on the old state, which will give you a chance to bring in all the poor white and Negro stories that you know, or a third one on writing the stuff, in which event, we will call on Bob Davis for a few remarks about the magazine end, and George Doran for a burning thought or two about book publishing, thereby scoring heavily on the holy man. P.S. It looks as if the tumbril would be full as I have just written to Doran, offering him the hospitality of the laundry room."

That Lorimer felt a deep affection for Cobb was apparent when the humorist had the appendectomy in April 1915 which inspired his classic "Speaking of Operations." While Cobb lay convalescing, all his friends were concerned that he might not recover. His wife, Laura, kept the Boss informed of her husband's progress, adding small, informative postscripts: "I learned today that Dr. Bainbridge had made a seven-inch incision. Irvin always said they'd have to blast." Later she reported that the doctor had told her that "what they haven't cut away they are going to take away with a diet." Lorimer thought that "very good news. I really do not think that it will hurt him to diet a little." He promised to send "a little line" to push along the good work. This was the little line:

"Dear Cobb: When your wife's letter reached me today, saying that you were to be put upon a diet, I had just finished dictating a note to Delmonico's, asking them to send you a case of Pol Roger, '98, two bottles of crusty old port, and to see that you were served every day with a double porterhouse covered with fresh mushrooms. Of course, I shall have to cancel the order now and substitute White Rock and one of Mrs. Lorimer's dog biscuits. I promise you though that I will not breathe a word of this disgraceful affair to Sam Blythe."

Once it was successfully accomplished, Cobb's operation became a standard subject for merriment in the Lorimer circle. The convalescent transferred the final stage of his recovery to Atlantic City, where he was joined by the Rineharts (Dr. Rinehart was also recovering from an operation), the George Dorans, the Lorimers and other friends. The celebration on Cobb's behalf stretched satisfactorily over an entire long week end.

His postoperative reflections in the Post were illustrated by Tony Sarg—the artist's first appearance in an American publication.

Ray Long's *Cosmopolitan* raid took not only Cobb, Lardner and Kyne, but P. G. Wodehouse and Jack London at the same time. London came back later and offered to write free for the Post, believing that publication there would restore his sales value.

The seduction of these writers honestly surprised Lorimer. In the case of Kyne, for example, he felt that here was a man he had discovered and raised to high popular acclaim in the Post's pages, from "A Little Matter of Salvage" in 1909, through "The Parson of Panamint" in 1915, to the firm establishment of his reputation in 1917 with the Cappy Ricks series. When Kyne left the Post for *Cosmopolitan* in 1919, Lorimer wrote to Van Loan's wife, Emma: "I received a letter from him day before yesterday stating that Ray Long had offered him, in behalf of the Hearst people, more money than had ever before been paid to any author, but that before closing with Ray Long, he would give me a chance for my white alley, and I wired him that Hearst's bid—whatever it is—was high. Good-by Peter. After Van got back from talking with Peter in New York I was quite prepared for some soubretting on his part, but I really didn't think that he would go over to Hearst, because before he sailed for the other side his wife wrote for us a very clever biography of Pete and wound it up with a summary of his virtues, concluding 'and he never worked for William Randolph Hearst.' As a considerate editor, I cut out that last sentence and so Pete's face is saved."

Another Lorimer discovery lost to the Post in Long's attack was Ring Lardner. The honor of discovery in this case had to be shared with Van Loan, who had been a sports writer with Ring in Chicago. Lardner had been writing straight baseball articles for the Post until he sent "You Know Me, Al" for consideration in 1914. It was returned with a note from an associate editor advising Lardner to "stick to the straight stuff." At the time Van Loan was spending a brief period on the Post, where Lorimer had given him a job to rescue him from his recurring financial disasters. Charlie knew the story was in the shop, and when he found it had been returned before the Boss could see it (a rare occurrence in itself), he retrieved the piece from his old friend and showed it to Lorimer, who bought it at once. The yarn was an immediate hit, and Jack Keefe, the Busher, became everybody's friend. Fame settled on Lardner overnight; people slapped him on the back in bars and chortled, "You know me, Al."

More "Busher" letters followed, after which he contributed "Alibi Ike," "Gullible's Travels," "The Yellow Kid" and "The Battle of Texas," among others, before Cosmopolitan put him under contract. He wrote one more Post story in 1921, "Some Like Them Cold," and in 1932 appeared with "Meet Me in St. Louis." As late as 1933 he sent Lorimer an article, "Some Champions," which the Boss printed.

Lorimer and Lardner had a private contract, in writing, which provided that Ring would get five dollars for every word changed in his stories. Lardner insisted this was simple protection, because of the numerous colloquialisms and intentional grammatical lapses in his style which were in constant danger of being changed by readers and copy editors.

His Post stories brought Lardner enormous popularity, but he was ignored by the hyperintellectual critics who scorned the Post and all its works. Most of the scorners have since joined the canonical chorus, praising Lardner as a great American writer. The conversion took place when H. L. Mencken, then bell-wether of the critical herd, remarked in the course of an essay that he considered Lardner among the foremost practitioners of the short story. Lardner's elevation occurred forthwith.

The departure of Kyne and Lardner did not hurt Lorimer personally, as did Cobb's, but the whole affair made him retreat a little more behind the wall which he placed between himself and anything that savored of intimacy. The retreat, however, did not apply to that stout band of piratical antique hunters—Joseph Hergesheimer, Eddie Lefevre, Kenneth Roberts and Hugh Kahler —whose exploits were the subject of innumerable letters.

Hergesheimer had been another of Lorimer's Post discoveries, beginning in 1915 with a short story titled, "The Professional Game," and continuing with the novels which brought him emi-nence—"Java Head" in 1918 and "Balisand" in 1924. He was equally successful with non-fiction. His thoughtful essays on American communities, "Quiet Cities," appeared in 1927, followed the next year by ten articles on "The Deep South," the first time that phrase was used. This series became a book, "Swords and Roses."

Hergesheimer's work was not the kind Lorimer enjoyed most, but he respected it, and he watched it carefully. At one time he became convinced that his friend's fiction was losing its story values under the weight of meticulously drawn background. He suggested to Hergesheimer that this was occurring and they dis-cussed the problem. That was as far as Lorimer would go; he re-fused to interfere further.

When Hergesheimer lived in historic, charming Dower House, in Pennsylvania's Chester County, Lorimer found it an ideal place for relaxation. He went as often as he could to sit in the fine old rooms and talk with his friend on the inexhaustible subject of antiques, particularly the Pennsylvania Dutch variety, which he came to love. Sometimes he sat in silence for an hour or more, soaking in the tranquillity of the house.

The checkreined friendship Lorimer extended to the writers who were close to him was also given, in more practical ways, to those outside the inner circle. It was the Boss's suggestion, for example, that turned Octavus Roy Cohen from the sports stories he had been trying to write, with indifferent success, to the hilarious pieces about the city Negro which brought him fame. There were numerous other instances of such specific acts of friendship, inspired by Lorimer's editorial instincts, but there were almost as many examples of simple loyalty, with no qualifying motives.

A case in point was William Sydney Porter, whose O. Henry pseudonym concealed the fact that he had served a jail term in Austin, Texas. Will Irwin learned of Porter's record through Al Jennings, the reformed train robber whose autobiography Irwin ghosted for the Post. Jennings had been in prison with Porter. He told Irwin that the two inmates had discussed their return to the outside, as they sat together in a cell. Jennings argued that they should not try to conceal their records, that they should disarm their enemies with frankness.

"I can't do that, Al," Porter said. "I'm too sensitive."

Porter was sensitive indeed—to the point of virtual seclusion. He deliberately cut himself off from a society that would have been glad to welcome him. Lorimer was one of the few people he permitted to share his always delightful company. His past was whispered about town, but none of his writer friends ever spoke of it.

By the time Irwin came to write Jennings's autobiography, in which Porter appeared under another pseudonym, the storyteller was dead. Irwin told Lorimer that he intended to use the Porter anecdote in his series on Jennings, but he meant to use a pseudonym other than "O. Henry."

"That's right, disguise his name," Lorimer said. "If Bill had wanted this known, he'd have told it himself."

Lorimer was always proud that in 1907 he had printed one of O. Henry's best stories, "The Ransom of Red Chief." It was for Porter's sake, too, that he broke his rule about payment in advance, the only time he ever did so. Always hard-pressed for funds, the writer had come to his editor one day and disclosed himself as in a particularly desperate plight, whereupon Lorimer advanced him payment for his next two short stories. Within a few days O. Henry pleaded that he was in even worse straits, and said that *Cosmopolitan* had offered to buy up his Post contract and pay him a higher rate. Lorimer could do little but release him; *Cosmopolitan* paid off the Post, and O. Henry died before he could write the stories. Lorimer said the experience was a lesson to him. He never broke his rule again.

The Boss's personal interest in his writers was sometimes rewarded in unexpected and touching ways, as in the case of Booth Tarkington. The careers of Tarkington and Lorimer had begun about the same time; "The Gentleman from Indiana" was a success in the period of Lorimer's early tribulations on the Post. Though the two men saw little of each other during a lifetime of friendship, a profound mutual admiration existed between them. Tarkington was not a regular contributor to the Post, by any means, but the Boss always welcomed his work, and when it appeared elsewhere he honestly rejoiced in his friend's success.

Tarkington's first Post appearance was a two-part serial, "His Own People," followed by his novel, "The Flirt," which ran in 1912–13. After these he devoted himself for a time to the Penrod stories, only one of which ran in the Post. His contributions to Lorimer were infrequent from 1913 onward. In 1919 he collaborated with Harry Leon Wilson on a three-part serial, "The Gibson Upright," and then he was seldom seen until "Presenting Lily Mars" appeared in 1932. A year later he created for the Post the Little Orvie stories, a somewhat pale echo of Penrod. At the time of Lorimer's retirement in 1936 Tarkington had begun the successful series about Rumbin, the art dealer. This subject was suggested to him by Graeme Lorimer, then a Post associate editor, who had been trying hard to think of something for him to write. The old master had been out of touch with the world because of ill-health and a temporary near blindness caused by a cataract. Graeme visited Tarkington to discuss the matter, and while he was driving from the station with Mrs. Tarkington she told him of her husband's recent acquisition of a Velasquez, of his startled delight in the colors he was now able to see, after an operation, and of how she wanted him to have such expensive luxuries if he enjoyed them so much. Graeme suggested that the Velasquez could be paid for by a series of Tarkington stories about art, written from the collector's point of view. Tarkington disagreed; the point of view should be the dealer's, he said. Hence Mr. Rumbin, whose inspiration was an art dealer who had become the writer's close friend.

Tarkington paid his last visit to the Post offices in 1931, at the worst of the depression. He approached Thomas B. Costain, then one of Lorimer's editors, somewhat diffidently.

"You know," he said, "the Boss and I have had an agreement that my price would be boosted to six thousand dollars for short stories and sixty thousand for serials. But it looks to me as though things were going to be pretty bad, and it seems to me these prices are too high. I feel that I shouldn't take so much."

"I think you'd better talk to the Boss," Costain replied, and ushered him inside.

Writer and editor sat talking behind closed doors for a long time, and no record exists of what was said, but at the end of it Lorimer told Costain that they had agreed to go back to the old prices. The new scale had equaled the highest prices ever paid to any Post writer. Shortly afterward Tarkington submitted "Presenting Lily Mars."

In ordinary circumstances Lorimer was adamant on the subject of prices. He set his scale, and if he cared to pay more for a particular story, he would do it. He wanted to feel, however, that the largesse came from him.

Edwin Balmer, editor of *Redbook* for the past two decades, was one of the early Post writers who encountered the Lorimer rigidity in the matter of payment. He submitted a story that he thought was worth more than the six hundred dollars the Boss wanted to pay him for it.

"I can get more from Hearst," he remarked brashly to Lorimer. "Sell it, then," Lorimer said shortly.

Balmer sold the story to *Cosmopolitan* for eight hundred dollars and, seeking stubbornly to prove his point, sent the letter of acceptance to the Post's editor. Lorimer made no answer. He simply refused to buy another Balmer story for six years, although the writer had contributed to the Post since 1907.

Eventually their relationship was resumed, but Lorimer made the peace overtures in his own way. Costain went to Chicago on a scouting trip and telephoned Balmer. "I have a message for you from Mr. Lorimer," he said. "You know those stories of yours that have been running in the *Metropolitan?* Well, he says he would have bought those stories."

"All right," Balmer said, "I'll write him some more he'll buy."

Until he traded writing for editing in 1927, Balmer remained a Post contributor.

The strangest financial bargain Lorimer ever concluded with a writer was a case involving George Randolph Chester. Young and chronically penurious, Chester had broken into the Post in 1903 with "The Castaway Brokers," one of the first business stories to appear after the "Merchant Letters." Thereafter he wrote moderately successful pieces until 1907, when he married a girl so beautiful that she rendered others than the happy bridegroom speechless.

Few men have been as anxious to go on a honeymoon, and few have had as little means to do it as Chester. In a mood of black despair he went to Lorimer and asked for an advance of a thousand dollars for a series of six stories to be written on his bridal journey.

"I can't do that," Lorimer said, thinking quickly, "but I'll tell you how you can *earn* that much and more."

An hour later Chester retired to the Majestic Hotel for a Post honeymoon. Lorimer had provided the happy couple with room and board, on condition that Chester write for his keep. Spurred on by love and need, Chester turned out the stories in six days. His wife typed them, the Post bought them, and the Chesters then went to Europe.

After that episode there were no more requests for money. Chester coined it. He wrote on a slowly diminishing wave of popularity until 1920, when he achieved a renewed fame with his Izzy Iskovitch stories, about a Hollywood agent. Chester's continuing quarrel with the Boss was over wordage. He had trouble keeping the Izzy stories down to ten thousand words, an abnormal length for the Post. After one unhappy struggle with condensation Lorimer wrote him:

"My dear Chester: I don't want to encourage you to write long short stories, but on the whole, I think we should pay you an additional five hundred dollars on 'Angel Child.' This isn't a precedent, though, as I really want them short, and if you do it again there won't be a leaf stirring."

On the other hand, Lorimer had an aversion to stories he thought were too short.

"Nobody can really tell a story in less than three thousand words," he once remarked to Ben Ames Williams.

"De Maupassant did," Williams reminded him.

"De Maupassant's dead," Lorimer replied curtly.

With Chester, as with some of the other old-timers, Lorimer was often more familiar in his letters than he was in his conversation; in them he disclosed tiny facets of himself. Early in January 1924 he wrote to Chester: ". . . For the past twenty years I have spent New Year's Eve in my library and find it a very pleasant place to be on that occasion. There is nothing in the world more sodden and tiresome than the downtown hotel celebrations of the New Year."

A few days after Lorimer wrote this letter Chester died. His wife, Lillian, replied. "He never ceased to express his gratitude," she wrote, "for your encouragement and enthusiastic treatment during this past year—the happiest in his life, for he was writing again, successfully. Your letter, which arrived on the morning of his death, would have made him very happy, for while we were at work on that last night, he said that somehow he believed you would be lenient about the length and that we might go ahead with what he felt certain would be one of the best stories in the entire series."

Chester's success story was matched concurrently by that of George Fitch. In 1906, Lorimer bought the first of his Siwash series. It was the pioneer humorous football story, and "Siwash" became a part of the American language. The president of Knox College, writing in the Post in 1935, claimed proudly that his institution, Fitch's alma mater, was the original Siwash.

The list of writers Lorimer helped in one way or another was endless. Arthur Somers Roche was at his lowest point, after a year in which he made exactly thirty-seven dollars, when he sold Lorimer a serial called "Loot" in 1916, and under the Boss's further prodding, went on to write his way to the top rung. A year later Lorimer gave a start to still another struggling writer when he bought a short story, "The Rescuer," from a young man named Thomas Beer. Here was no popular writer whose work could be guaranteed to boost circulation, but Lorimer was pleased to see that Beer got a strong minority report from the Post's readership. He encouraged his find to write a three-part story, "Sandoval," in 1923, and Beer rewarded him in 1929 by giving him the Hanna articles, which assured the author of lasting remembrance.

In time Beer was writing for two audiences. If only the minority appreciated his best work, the others delighted in the character of Ma Egg, his popular creation. Late in 1927 he abandoned this lady, wrote to Lorimer that he was sending along the last of her exploits, and inquired about Vichy as a place to go for his health.

"We view with sorrow the passing of Ma Egg," Lorimer responded. "She has been especially good in this last series. I have had no experience with any European cure except Spa in Belgium, where my mother used to go when I was a small boy. Mr. and Mrs. Curtis went to Vichy several years ago and both caught the whooping cough, and in the sequel Mr. Curtis almost went under with it in Paris."

About the time Beer came to the Post the Boss acquired another writer of "literary" stories, with whom he had less friendly relations. It would be difficult to imagine a writer further away from the Post's style than Theodore Dreiser. Nonetheless, Lorimer bought a story from him in 1918, titled "Free," and immediately after took another, "St. Columbia and the River." The first brought five hundred dollars, the usual rate for a new writer, and the second, in the Boss's estimation, was worth seven hundred and fifty. When he got the larger check, Dreiser antagonized Lorimer by hinting strongly that he thought it should be more.

"We always feel . . . that every story is a special case," Lorimer replied stiffly, and he asked Dreiser to put a price on his submitted manuscripts in the future. He turned down "Old Ragaum and His Theresa," the next story Dreiser sent him, and returned "St. Columbia" to its author in 1923 without using it.

If he did not get the kind of fiction he wanted, Lorimer created it, as he had done with the first business stories, and he was not above using it to advance his political beliefs on occasion, if that seemed the best medium to start people thinking on a subject. When the inroads of Japanese farmers in California began to disturb him, he persuaded Wallace Irwin to write "Seed of the Sun," dramatizing the idea and informing Post readers of an explosive situation without causing international complications.

His prime creation of fiction occurred in the case of Emerson Hough. This rugged outdoors man was close to the Boss; they shared a passionate love of nature and a zealousness to advance the cause of conservation. Hough had been a regular contributor of outdoors articles since his series on "The Wasteful West" in 1905. Even before that time he had demonstrated that he could write fiction on the same theme, with his first Post story in 1902. By the time war came he was writing both articles and short fiction, besides conducting a column on conservation and the outdoors.

One spring night in 1920 he arrived at Belgraeme for dinner in a mood of blackest depression. "I can't write any more; I'm all through," he told Lorimer. After dinner they went out on the terrace, and the Boss began talking as he sat on the porch swing, right foot curled under him, left foot propelling the swing with an occasional push on the Mercer tiles. It was a characteristic after-dinner pose.

"Your trouble," he told Hough, "is that you don't realize your potentialities. Here you've got the finest fiction material in the world, and it's wasted. I mean that piece on the Oregon Trail you wrote for the column, and the other trail pieces that went with it. There's all the drama any reader could ask for. Why don't you turn it into fiction? Take a wagon train leaving Independence for the Oregon country. You've got all ages, both sexes, all kinds and conditions in such a party. The wagon wheels supply the movement and there's a new adventure every hour—Indians, storm, prairie fire, flood, quicksand, wild animals, thirst, hunger, heat, cold, birth, death, love, marriage. That's your novel. It might be an American epic."

As he talked on, outlining the book, Lorimer got up and paced the terrace; his cigar went out unnoticed. Hough caught the fire of Lorimer's imagination, and shortly afterward he left the Post to go West and write "The Covered Wagon," which was to bring him the belated recognition he would not live to enjoy.

By October 1921 the job was well in hand. "I find here the completed first draft of my novel, which I sent on from Yellowstone Park in longhand," Hough wrote to the Boss from his home. "It runs 380 pages, or above 90,000 words—I could not tell just how much it would bulk until I saw the revise in type. I think we now have this story whipped, or are within reach of that. Would you like to give it one reading by one of the three original readers, in order to get an idea of the new version? Of course, if you say you would want only a certain number of thousand words, I can do the shortening in November. In that case, I might cut out precisely what you might fancy; and I have come to regard this as rather a partnership book anyhow. . . . I have followed the line of your suggestions as closely as I know how, and I think the story has worked out into a good serial. If you do not like the name 'The Covered Wagon,' you might consider 'Oh, Then Susannah!' "

Lorimer replied: "My dear Hough, Miss Neall has read the new version of 'The Covered Wagon' and pronounces it good, though she suggests some minor cuts. I shall read it over the week end with a pencil in hand and suggest where those cuts might be made to advantage."

The "partnership book" appeared as a Post serial in 1922. It was a best-selling novel, sold to Hollywood for eight thousand dollars, and became a film classic. Hough had never sold anything to the movies before, but now he dug out from the trunk all the fiction he had ever written, and a producer paid him eighty-two thousand dollars for the rights to his previous work.

Hough followed "The Covered Wagon" with "North of '36" in 1923, and was on the way to greater popularity when he died that spring. Lorimer wrote an affectionate editorial to mark his passing. This elicited a revealing letter from another Post author, Herbert Quick, whose "Vandemark's Folly" was also a best seller.

"It was a fine thing to give us that editorial on Emerson Hough," Quick wrote in June 1923. "He was, and his memory is, worthy of it. I got to know him well during the war, when he and I were both in Washington. Everything you said of him was and is true. . . . My last good time with him was in Chicago just after 'Vandemark's Folly' was published. He was as generously enthusiastic over the book as if he had been its publisher—the generosity lay in the fact that not only was he not its publisher, but it was rather close to his own field. He spoke of it to an audience of writer-folk, saying that Batcheller had carried the settlement movement to the Mississippi, I had taken it to the Missouri, and he had carried it on from the Missouri to the Coast, and that the three books, though by different men, really made up a trilogy.

"When 'North of '36' was running in your magazine, I was so delighted with it—I think it better than 'The Covered Wagon'— that I wrote him telling him what a good thing he had done. I was just on the point of going to Rochester, Minn., because of the recurrence of my malady of three years ago. He wrote me what must have been one of his last letters. 'Look out for doctors,' said he. 'They almost got me last year, and I am none too well now.' This letter came to me just as I was coming up from the second dip, with two nurses in attendance in Rochester; and in the papers that very morning, or only a day or so afterwards, was the announcement of his death. He went, and I happened to remain. . . ."

Farther on in this long letter Quick posed a question that was also disturbing Lorimer. "While I was laid up, I read a lot of magazine fiction. What's the matter with it? Even yours leads one to ponder what you reject when you accept some of what you print; and when one goes from the Saturday Evening Post to the other periodicals, he finds that you have skimmed the cream of it. Maybe a man who has been carved and is coming back is not in the best mental condition for criticism, but I really believe that we are in a dreadful slump. I am getting at work on a new novel, but I am sometimes tempted to put on paper two or three short stories I have in mind for you. . . ."

That Lorimer was well aware of a changed situation was apparent in his reply: ". . . I quite agree with you about the run of current fiction, but we are doing the best that we can under the circumstances that obtain. The contract system, the moving pictures and easy money have all had a share in bringing about the present condition of affairs. If you can help us with some regular short stories, go to it, but I do not believe that the Russian story [one Quick had previously submitted] is the medicine that we need just now. Frankly, I have never felt that it was up to the mark of the fine work that you have been doing in your recent novels."

It was Quick, however, who wrote "One Man's Life," considered by some Post editors as the best such work the magazine ever carried.

One of the measures Lorimer had taken to adjust the magazine to the postwar situation in fiction was the hiring of several new associate editors. Of these new men, Thomas B. Costain was perhaps the most ambitious, and as contact man in New York, he soon proved himself valuable and a recognized candidate for the Boss's throne. The Boss realized he needed such new blood in his organization. He still depended heavily, as always, on Adelaide Neall, who had been his chief editorial aide since 1909, but the huge size of the Post, his own increasing participation in the business side, and the obvious need for fresh viewpoints led him to distribute some of his burden among the new men, as soon as they could assume it.

Costain had been the editor of *McLean's*, a Canadian magazine modeled after the Post; he had come to that job from seven years of Canadian newspapering. On a visit to the States immediately after the war, he went to Lorimer without an introduction and told him bluntly that he wanted to break into the big league.

"You certainly seem qualified," Lorimer said. "I'll keep you in mind."

It sounded like the usual polite evasion, but Costain was not discouraged. He sent copies of *McLean's* to Lorimer and kept up a barrage of letters. At last he was hired, initially with the idea that he would work for the *Journal*. There was a brief tug-of-war, after which he found himself on the Post. He began by reading manuscripts, then moved up to contact work, first in Boston, later in New York.

At that time the Post was in a momentary slump. In the surge of realistic writing which followed the war, the magazine had lost its bearings. Then had come the boom magazine market of the early twenties and the Post suffered an exodus like the one induced by Ray Long's 1917 raid. By that time, however, Lorimer's leviathan had passed through its worst period. The only circulation recession in its history had touched bottom in 1918, and by 1919 the cover again carried the banner, "More Than Two Million." (Even at its low point, the Post was 152 pages thick, carried $466,-982 in paid advertising, and had a net paid circulation of 1,976,-161.) The quality improved more slowly. Names appeared in the Post which had never been seen before.

Costain's first job, as contact man, was to lure the strays back into the fold—those top-notch writers who had been seduced by contracts or higher prices. One of the first to succumb to the new editor's approach was Alice Duer Miller. She gave him "Manslaughter," which everyone else on the staff except Lorimer voted against. Then Costain went up to Boston and persuaded Ben Ames Williams to return, and in the Williams wake came Clarence Budington Kelland, P. G. Wodehouse and Tarkington.

When he encountered an unrepentant contract writer Costain had a system he employed, as in the case of E. Phillips Oppenheim. This master of international intrigue was no stranger to the Post. His first serial, "The Lightest Way," had appeared there in 1912, and was followed by "An Amiable Charlatan" in 1913–14, "Mr. Grex of Monte Carlo" in 1914, and "The Double Traitor" in 1915. After these he listened to the call of contracts and more substantial rewards, and disappeared from the Post until 1925, when Costain brought him back with the seven stories called "The Channay Syndicate."

Costain's method with Oppenheim was to send him an idea for a story through his agent, with the understanding that the Post would get first chance at the piece if he wrote it.

On the first trial of this system Oppenheim came through with a series of ten short stories. Only one hitch ever occurred in the operation of the method. Costain had given Oppenheim an idea which the writer had turned down, so Tom felt free to show it to Hugh MacNair Kahler, whose 1920 short story "Kwyw" (an abbreviation for "Know What You Want") had started him on a prolific twenty-year stretch of writing for the Post. Kahler liked the idea intended for Oppenheim and indicated that he would do something with it. A few days later Oppenheim and his agent appeared to keep a luncheon date with Costain. Oppenheim carried a bundle under his arm and announced proudly that it was a serial he had fashioned from the idea he had supposedly rejected. Costain tried to conceal his apprehension, made his guests comfortable, and hurried out to a telephone where he could call Kahler, who relieved his mind by telling him that he had not yet done anything about the idea.

In the cat-and-mouse game with authors, the mouse sometimes got away from Costain. Damon Runyon submitted what may have been his first short story to the Post, but Costain sent it back with a detailed criticism. He objected, among other things, to Runyon's use of a hophead cat in an opium den, where much of the story took place. "Make the cat a lush in a saloon," Costain advised. Runyon thanked him, took this and other advice, and sold the story to *Collier's*.

It was a case of turnabout with *Collier's* in the matter of Guy Gilpatric's Glencannon stories. Gilpatric first appeared in the Post in 1929 with "Lulu Was a Lady." The following year he submitted the first of his yarns about the redoubtable skipper to *Collier's*, where he had sold his first stories. *Collier's* didn't care for Glencannon but Lorimer did, and the master of the *S.S. Inchcliffe Castle* lived happily ever after at the Post.

The Boss kept a commanding finger on all the new writers, and at the same time prodded the veterans who were his friends into renewed activity. A few were beginning to drop by the wayside, written out or too old. One of the most durable was Harry Leon Wilson, who had been a Post writer since 1911 and a member of the Lorimer inner circle for almost that length of time. The Boss had met Wilson on an excursion to Lakewood, New Jersey, in 1905, where he and Phillips shared a room adjoining one occupied by Wilson and Tarkington, who recalled that occasion as a time when "we were all very gay. . . ." Lorimer was fond of Wilson, who was always a part of any Western trip he made. To Lorimer and the others, Wilson was "Old Ironface," a nickname derived from his roughhewn features, which were cast in a rugged mold.

This masculine humorist married a woman who was his opposite in every conceivable way: the pink-and-white, rounded, two-hundred-pound blonde confection of a woman who was Rose O'Neill, the artist whose creation of the "Kewpies" made her famous. A few years after their marriage the Wilsons planned a Mediterranean winter and rented the Villa Narcissus at Capri with the Julian Streets, Booth Tarkington and his first wife, and a fourth couple. It was this expedition which created a scene long remembered in the Lorimer circle.

Until the voyage over got under way, Wilson had been captivated by his wife's habitual baby talk. This whimsey did not amuse Street, who was astounded that Harry had ever become enamored of it; he proceeded to give his friend an outside view of the matter. His most effective gesture in that direction did not come until the party had settled in the villa, but then he enlivened the evening meals, which were consumed on a balcony overlooking the sea, by listening carefully to a few paragraphs of "does ums" and "ittum bittums," after which he would excuse himself ostentatiously, hurry to the balcony railing and pretend a realistic-looking nausea. After a time Wilson began to get the idea. He too felt nauseous twinges. "Rose," he remarked one day, "if you ever say 'woses' again, I'll divorce you."

A few days later the entire entourage was breakfasting on the terrace, silently enduring the agonies of a collective hangover. All except Rose. She had been up for hours. Rose was a teetotaler.

Of a sudden she appeared amid the somber gathering, all dewy and fresh from the garden, a huge bouquet in her arms, looking like a character in an English novel. She floated across the terrace to her husband, who seemed momentarily overcome, and thrust the flowers into his nose.

" 'Mell my pitty, pitty woses!" she caroled.

Wilson folded his napkin deliberately, pushed aside his half-finished breakfast, and stood up.

"Rose," he said, "I told you never to say 'woses' again."

Without another word he retired to his room, packed his bags, and caught the next boat to the mainland. He filed suit for divorce soon after.

Tarkington was the only voyager able to salvage anything from this shipwreck. He immortalized Rose as the "baby-talk lady" in his "Seventeen," and he collaborated with Wilson on a play, "The Man from Home," which was a hit for six years.

From the time of his first story, "A Message from the Mikado," Wilson was a popular Post writer. Millions of readers chuckled over "His Majesty Bunker Bean" in 1912, "Ruggles of Red Gap" in 1914–15, "Ma Pettingill and the Song of Songs" (first of a long series) in 1915, and "The Wrong Twin" in 1920–21. By 1922 he had still to write his funniest serials: "Merton of the Movies," in that year; "Oh, Doctor!" the following year, and "Professor, How Could You!" in 1924.

The correspondence between Lorimer and Wilson in the early twenties shows clearly the editor's skill in working with a valuable writer who was also an old friend. Here, for example, was Lorimer in April 1922: "My dear Wilson, How about that rough old woman of yours? She is behaving in a singularly reticent manner. Apparently the Post is a howling wilderness to our readers since Merton passed up and out and the only one that can keep the pot boiling is Ma Pettingill. Tell the old lady to have a heart."

Lorimer was completely honest with Wilson, and less reticent about his private thoughts than he was with some of his other friends. "Ray Long has been making the rounds of the Post men," he wrote in June 1922, "in an earnest endeavor to segregate those whom he considers the key writers; but I am not at all concerned about that as I have a stable full of exceedingly promising young colts. Sam and you are the only two men through whom he could really hand me a jolt, and I have always felt that there would have to be a better reason for it than anything that Hearst has heretofore had to offer. I have been, and always shall be, willing to go along on price except when that particular razor is selected in an effort to cut my throat."

Apparently he was worried that Wilson's renewed popularity might make him dissatisfied with Post prices, for he had written three months before: "Sam tells me that you are home again with your system full of poi, hula hula and yan hok. It seems fitting then that you should move on Ma Pettingill. The price for short stories and specials has moved up with the stock market to twenty-five hundred dollars. Merton seems to be hitting them where they live."

That summer he and Wilson discussed work and prices during a Western trip, and on his return in August he wrote Wilson a characteristic letter which combined friendly chattiness with business, the one sugar-coating the other.

"As I have just written Sam," the Boss reported, "the quietest little piece of wilderness that I found in my travels was the Del Monte golf links at Pebble Beach. The rest of the West, including the National Parks, is simply boiling with trippers. I beat it out of Glacier after three days because I was afraid if I didn't I would be caught there without my winter overcoat. There hadn't been a freight train through Montana in six days when I left and they were pulling the passenger trains every day. Those that were left would drop in anywhere from six to twenty hours late.

"Since my return I have been thinking over our business relations and I feel that under all the circumstances and in the face of the high prices that are being paid by the opposition and one or two of the other magazines that are stringing along with it, we should offer you better terms than any I have as yet suggested, for to be perfectly frank, I value your stories more than any that come to the Saturday Evening Post, or, for that matter, any that are being written. Suppose we say for the present three thousand for short stories, twenty-five hundred for special articles, thirty thousand for full-length serials, and novelettes in proportion? May I, however, ask you to keep these prices absolutely confidential, as in the case of the average writer 'theirs not to reason why,' theirs only to want as much as the next fellow is getting."

In spite of his obvious success and Lorimer's enthusiasm, Wilson was extremely modest about his work. "I am mighty glad you thought so well of the stories," he wrote in December 1922. "Here is another that may be as good, though I never can tell myself when they are so fresh. Your man Thomas Beer is the best thing that has come into the Post since the first Wildcat. I hope you grapple to him with hooks of steel—or some equally effective metal."

The Wilson well had begun to run dry in 1925, not long before his death, but Lorimer did his best to prime it, in the old manner: "My dear Wilson, I hope this letter will find you in a coarsely commercial frame of mind and with your broker demanding more margins, your wife asking for a string of pearls, and your oldest son demanding a sporty roadster, for we need some of your humorous short stories, either about Ma Pettingill or Cousin Egbert or anyone else among your characters and friends."

Tarkington summed up Wilson's character, and the reason it so appealed to Lorimer, in a letter written long after both men were dead.

"He had a grand nature and one of the best minds I ever knew—in some things the best," Tarkington declared. "With that, he completely lacked any self-protective egoism—had little shrewdness in estimating people who touched his sympathies or his admiration, and he would give anybody anything. He had no care of what that did to himself and when it did dreadful things to him, he could take it. Nothing ever got a squeak—not of the briefest or faintest—of self-commiseration out of him. I never knew anyone who more entirely viewed every personal detail of his outwards and inwards from an aloof position and with an unmoved eye. I think that Lorimer's feeling for H.L. was based upon these qualities—and upon the great humor that played over everything. . . ."

Another contributor from the earlier days who went on to increased popularity in the twenties was Earl Derr Biggers. He was not one of Lorimer's best friends, as Wilson was, but he was a man whom the Boss had discovered and brought along carefully, and who rewarded him at a later date than most of the others with some of the most successful fiction the Post ever carried.

Biggers was conscious of the debt he owed Lorimer. At the time of the editor's twenty-fifth anniversary in 1924 he wrote: "The morning paper brought the news of your silver anniversary on the Post. I'd like very much to write you a letter of congratulation—but I can't. For as I sit down to it I realize suddenly: 'He isn't thinking about himself. He's thinking about the Post. That's why the Post is what it is. Consequently what he wants from you is a good short story, and not any flowery words about anniversaries. Well, I haven't got the story about me at the moment. That doesn't mean I haven't been trying. Conditions this winter have not been such as to make composition easy, but they are about to change for the better. I think I can promise that during the period that began so auspiciously today—I mean your second twenty-five years as editor of the Post—but hold, hold, that begins to sound like anniversary oratory. So, back to work. But please enroll my name on the long list of authors who have found you kind and appreciative and just, and who wish you well."

It took ten years for Biggers to hit his stride, after his first Post serial, "The Agony Column," had launched his career. He wrote nothing more for the magazine that was outstanding until "The House without a Key" in 1925, although he had done some of his better work for other publications in the meantime. A year after "The House" appeared he began to write his mystery stories with an oriental background, beginning with "The Chinese Parrot," and he soon became one of the most popular writers in America. He was at his peak in 1928 with the publication of "Behind That Curtain." A man in Folsom Prison, California, about to be hanged, pleaded as his last request that he be given an advance copy of the Post with the final installment of the serial. A reporter wrote Biggers that the condemned man spent his last night reading it, "oblivious to his surroundings and his fate."

It was not the only time the Post got such a request. When four installments of Nordhoff and Hall's "The Hurricane" had appeared, a reader wrote: "I am going to leave next week and where I am going I cannot get the Post. I am very much interested in the story, 'The Hurricane,' and I will appreciate it very much if you could send me proofs so that I can finish it before I go. I wish that I could take Bud Kelland and Norman Reilly Raine and Agatha Christie with me when I go. I wouldn't give a damn if I did go to hell, if I could have them there to tell me stories. Maybe I can read over your shoulders when you are reading manuscripts. If any of you feel a touch on your shoulders when reading a bad, rotten, lousy story and think of accepting it, that will be me protesting. Good luck to both of us."

A week later the writer of this letter was executed at Charlestown Prison, Massachusetts, but not before he had received galley proofs of "The Hurricane."

More common were such letters as this: "I must undergo a major operation on Monday, March 30th, from which I may or may not recover, accent on the latter probability. The next Post will not reach me until Tuesday and I want to know how that Nero Wolfe 'Rubber Band' story comes out. My compliments to Mr. Rex Stout—I can't figure it. So would you please, pul-lease forward immediately by air mail tear sheets of the story or tell where and how I shall get this information? This is genuine and constitutes for me a real emergency."

The Seattle circulation office checked the authenticity of the appeal and the reader got an advance copy. Other impatient readers who tried the same device while enjoying good health got nothing. All such pleas were investigated.

On the night the final installment of Biggers' "Behind That Curtain" was due to arrive at Grand Canyon, the superintendent of the park gave a "Behind That Curtain" party, at which all the guests appeared dressed as characters in the story, and a prize was given for the best guess as to how it came out. No one guessed correctly.

Relaying this news to Lorimer in a letter, Biggers added that he had heard it rumored that Lorimer was about to retire—"a false alarm, I trust." Lorimer wrote beneath it with his heavy black copy pencil, "Very false."

When Biggers died, the Post looked around for someone who could do the kind of stories which had so endeared him to readers. Costain suggested to Ben Ames Williams that he go over to China for a while, soak up the oriental atmosphere, and produce some thrillers of the type Biggers had created. But Williams was busy with other projects and declined, so Costain made the same proposition to John P. Marquand, who took the trip. The result was the Mr. Moto series, which brought delayed recognition to Marquand and enabled him to write his serious novels.

At the time of this episode Williams was well launched on his own writing career, which continues to be spectacular. From the day in 1917 that he sold his first piece to Lorimer, a whaling story called "The Mate of the *Susie Oakes*," he wrote Post fiction that varied from short stories of an absolute minimum length to an eight-part serial, "The Great Accident," which was about a hundred and fifty thousand words long, one of the lengthiest novels the Post ever ran.

"The Mate of the *Susie Oakes*" was his first major sale. He had left newspaper work two years before and begun free-lancing; the results had been a few pulp stories. Lorimer cut the first story, but there were no quarrels about length or editing during the next fifteen years, except for a single instance in 1932, when Lorimer thought a paragraph of explanation was needed to elucidate a technical point in a story about cribbage. A cut in this story unwittingly created another error, which resulted in a flood of letters.

Shortly after 1917 Williams became one of the first writers to hit the movie jackpot and soon he was earning more than a hundred thousand dollars a year. Despite this flow of gold, Mr. Williams was not enamored of Hollywood. Deliberately he changed the pace of his stories from the sharp, staccato tempo which the movie people admired to a gait almost too leisurely for the Post. His movie sales dropped, but oddly enough he was more popular than ever with Lorimer's readers. One day he realized that the Post had bought everything he had turned out for the past eighteen months, without a single rejection. Fearful of being typed and of wearing out his welcome, he changed style again, making his work even more deliberate and plotless. His acceptance rate dropped, but Lorimer raised his price, so that in spite of all his efforts he went on making more money.

Williams sold 162 stories to the Post between 1917 and the end of Lorimer's regime. At one time he was the highest-paid writer on the pay roll. His novels, "Jubilo" in 1919, "No Thoroughfare" in 1926, "Jephthah's Daughter" in 1931 and "Money Musk" in 1932, were his best-known contributions, but a serial in 1928 called "Immortal Longings" brought the largest mail response. Another mail getter, for a different reason, was a short story, "Coconuts," based on a mathematical teaser. The perennial interest in this piece is amazing: Williams still gets letters setting forth new solutions.

Lorimer and Williams were both strong men, not exactly comfortable in each other's presence because each sensed the other's strength of will. Fortunately they were not often together, but even so there were a few disagreements. Lorimer thought there should be more plot in Williams' famous Maine village stories; the author refused to change them. Yet the Boss bought without question a story called "The Rational Hind," which had virtually no plot.

Occasionally there was an actual parting of the ways. Once Lorimer insisted on paying a one-part price for a two-part story because he said it wasn't worth any more. Williams published it elsewhere. Later Williams wrote "Great Oaks," a connected series of short stories about an island off the Georgia coast. Costain read the series at Williams' camp on Lake Winnepesaukee and liked the pieces, but Lorimer rejected them. From a friend Williams heard that the Boss had considered them "too dull for utterance." To the author's satisfaction, the stories became one of his more successful books.

Williams once tried to do a modern story based on Shakespeare. He got as far as making a complete outline of Hamlet, laid in the little Maine village of Fraternity, which had been the locale of so many of his short stories. But the original overwhelmed him and intruded constantly on his own narrative. He complained to Lorimer: "I found Polonius and Laertes and Ophelia crowding in and filling the whole so full of details that no reader would swallow them. It's my understanding that Shakespeare changed the original story to suit needs, took a seed and planted it and let it grow as it would. If a writer could take an idea from Shakespeare without falling under the master's spell too completely, he might succeed in such an experiment as this. But it seems to me the more competent the writer, the more closely he will follow his original, and the more certainly he will fail."

When he was not writing Post fiction, Williams contributed articles—another example of the versatility which seemed to characterize the older members of the Post fiction school. Williams sold Lorimer articles on such diverse topics as color blindness, sleepwalking and buying outsize clothing.

The conversion from fiction to non-fiction, usually the order of succession, was reversed in the case of Kenneth Roberts, who began as an article writer and wound up as a novelist of high repute. With eight years of newspaper work on the Boston *Post* behind him, plus staff writing for the old *Life* of Mitchell, Masson, Martin and Metcalfe, as well as for *Puck* and *Judge*, Roberts went to war in 1917 and served as captain in the intelligence section of the Siberian Expeditionary Force. While thus occupied he inquired of Lorimer whether he wanted anything from that remote part of the world.

"Interested in having Siberian article dealing particularly with social economic political conditions," Lorimer replied by cable. This was his stock assignment in reply to any such query. It became a byword among Post writers, and remains so among Lorimer's old friends.

When he got back to San Francisco, Roberts had a twenty-two-thousand-word story about Siberia, and a one-act play in the bargain, which he had written en route in collaboration with Robert Garland. He sent the article to Lorimer and soon followed it to Philadelphia. Walking into the inner sanctum for the first time, he was greeted affably by the Boss with the news that he intended to use the whole article in one installment. Roberts was almost overwhelmed. He was in a low financial state, and his nervousness over the meeting had not been improved by the presence of Albert

Payson Terhune, who was talking with Lorimer when Roberts entered the office. Terhune obviously resented the interruption.

"Have you got anything else?" Lorimer inquired.

"A few pieces," Roberts said, and named the titles.

"Go ahead and write them," Lorimer invited, whereupon he excused himself from Terhune and took Roberts to lunch.

That was the beginning of a long friendship. Roberts was a companion on antique-hunting jaunts, and the two families visited often at each other's homes. For the Post, Roberts wrote 207 articles, and Lorimer acknowledged every one of them with words of praise, always phrased differently, as he did with Hugh Kahler and the other Post writers who were his friends.

Roberts' first assignment was to strike a series of blows for one of the Boss's primary crusades—limiting immigration. Lorimer was dogmatically convinced that America could not assimilate the South European peoples as it had the Nordics. To prove his point, he determined to send Roberts on a correspondence trip, which he outlined in a letter dated October 31, 1919:

"The prime object of your trip," he wrote, "is to secure a series of articles for us on immigration. Of course, it is not possible to lay out this series in any detail as it will depend entirely on the character and the abundance of the material. It should, however, be approached from two slants: First, you should get in touch with as many aliens recently returned from America as possible and get their reactions on the situation that they find at home and their intentions as to settling down in Europe or returning to America. Secondly, we want to find out to just what extent aliens are planning or hoping to emigrate to America; the causes behind their decision; whether they are going to make a stake with the idea of returning to Europe and settling down there or whether it is their plan to become citizens of the United States. Also, find out whether the larger number of these would-be immigrants hope to settle in the United States or some other country, particularly the direction that emigration from the Central Empire is likely to take and whether they will go in large numbers to Latin-American countries. The character, trades and desirability of these would-be immigrants should be determined.

"The series should, of course, be relieved by anecdotes tending to bring out the points that you are trying to make. In addition to these articles, there should be several light papers on living conditions in European capitals that will give us an insight as to whether Europeans themselves are taking their problems seriously or letting them joyride; whether they are doing their utmost to relieve want and suffering or depending on America, and to what extent. Perhaps you will be able to dig up some new stuff about the increase or the decline of Bolshevism. Anything showing how it has resulted in actual operation would, of course, be worth getting. The same thing is true of business conditions in Great Britain, France, and Italy, especially with an eye to American interests, opportunities and duties. You can always query me by cable about specific developments and make suggestions as to articles that seem important but that are not covered in this plan. The same thing is true about funds if you run low at any time. . . .

"In a sense, you have a roving commission as to the way in which the articles shape up and their number depends entirely on what you find from actual investigation. It is, of course, important that articles be sent to us just as fast as the material for them can be assembled and they can be written. I don't want to do anything in this series unnecessarily to offend the sensibilities or to promote antagonism between the United States and European countries. You will, undoubtedly, be frightfully irritated by a number of small happenings, but you should not let these interfere with handling or looking at your subjects in a big, broad spirit."

Armed with these instructions, Roberts went off to Ireland and made it the subject of his first article. Lorimer responded: "You succeeded in getting a mighty good piece out of Ireland, and a check for it will be deposited to your credit on Tuesday next. Wishing you as happy a New Year as the limitations of your itinerary for the next few months will permit, I remain . . ."

Roberts more than surmounted whatever limitations his itinerary imposed. His immigration series was so thorough a job that it became a potent factor in the maneuvering by which Congress changed the immigration laws. It resulted, too, in the establishment of Roberts as a first-rank correspondent: after that first trip

he covered the world for the Post. "How soon can you go to
Cairo?" Or Shanghai, London, Moscow or any one of the world's
cities. That was the form Lorimer's assignments took, and Roberts
always replied, "I can leave tomorrow." The Boss then took care
of the advance: "Give him twenty-five hundred dollars," he
would say to his secretary. There was never any discussion about
payment, and the rates went up progressively.

Invariably came the Lorimer letters of praise for each article.
They were more than welcome in those early days, when Roberts
was finding himself. Mrs. Roberts recalls how encouraging it was
to get such a Lorimer cable as, "Vienna article received. It's a
bear." The Boss usually appended a characteristic observation to
his letters. He wrote in January 1921: "The articles that you have
done on this trip are the best that you have ever turned out. I
can't say too much about the British booze articles. They are both
corkers. That Folies Bergère stuff sounds interesting from the
point of view of an investigator of social conditions. I investigated
socially, but not economically, last night, as the tickets were $5.50
a throw—a little piece called 'Aphrodite.' If the Paris mode is
nothing but muffs, ours is nothing but diamonds, and they seem to
be unusually scarce and expensive this year."

A few months later he reminded his correspondent: "Please
keep in mind we are running a maximum of 112 pages instead of
224 right now. Thirty presses whirling away merrily today, and
more being made ready. God save the King!"

In August of that year he reported: "You struck twelve and
kept right on striking up to one hundred plus in this last story. It
illuminated my whole evening and reconciled me to my hard life
as a farmer. . . ."

Early in 1922 Roberts scored a news beat for the Post. He took
a trip on the Italian dirigible *Roma*, a type which the United States
was then considering for development. Roberts' article asserted
that the *Roma* was dangerous and that America was buying a
lemon. Before an international incident could be precipitated by
this forthright declaration, the *Roma* blew up and justified his
prediction. Lorimer cabled: "Compliments and regards on the date
of your trip on the *Roma*."

Roberts proved to be equally useful at home. His political articles, and in fact his articles on every conceivable subject, were standard equipment in the Post. In 1922, Senator George Wharton Pepper, who was socially prominent in Phidadelphia, made representations to Lorimer that resulted in the Boss's approval of a Pepper story by Roberts. The resulting article contained a few digs at the senator.

On accepting it, Lorimer wrote Roberts: "If he [Pepper] should by any chance write for a copy of your article . . . you will kindly say to him that it is against the policy of the Post to permit anyone except its authors to see advance proofs of anything that is to appear in its columns. . . ."

The taste of nationwide publicity was highly pleasing to Senator Pepper, who, like many senators of that and every other period, felt that he could occupy the White House to good advantage. Mrs. Pepper thereon stepped to bat, which led Lorimer to write Roberts: "Mrs. Pepper met Mrs. Lorimer last night and said to her that she read a lovely piece in the Saturday Evening Post about Mr. Pepper and wondered who had written it, as there was no signature at the end of the article. Mrs. Lorimer told her. Then she wondered how we could have secured the article, but she supposed one of Mr. Pepper's 'clarks' gave it out. No, Mr. Pepper had not read the article but it was such a lovely piece that she was cutting it out and pasting it in a scrapbook of clippings that she was making for George."

Pepper then came forward with a few suggestions for powerful articles which might benefit the nation and in any case would do no harm to his reputation, but Lorimer was not stirred by these intimations. He wrote Roberts: "We will lay off that noble countenance [Pepper] for the present. In the recent primaries here he lined up with the Vare contractor gang and while the women assumed that he was for Pinchot and reform, he was as organization as Penrose without the late Senator's brains and courage to come out boldly in the open. Incidentally, I see signs of his wobbling on the bonus stand, which was the thing that originally attracted me to him."

Meanwhile, the Boss kept Roberts plugging away at immigration, with results that seemed to please him. He wrote in June 1922: "The Canadian immigration article worked up into a bully piece. Check by the treasurer on Tuesday. We seem to be cashing in on our immigration policy in all directions, but more particularly, at the moment, in our coal fields. I wonder if the employers of cheap labor are going to find that it has them in the end? The kind of radicalism that these fellows are importing and spreading is likely to put a horrible crimp in them before they get through."

Two months later he reported to Roberts: "A fellow made a very cagey suggestion in an immigration article I read several weeks ago. He suggested that we base our percentage law on the immigration of 1890, that being a year when Nordic immigration was strong and the low-grade stuff hadn't begun to come to us in volume. Perhaps you would like to try your hand at an editorial along the lines of Mr. Bradley's letter."

After a time there were fewer immigration articles and Roberts worked in other fields. Lorimer seldom made changes in his copy except for reasons of policy, as in the case of a piece called "Flaming Hollywood," from which he extracted half a paragraph in the opening pages because "printing it would simply result in a year's controversy for you and for me with the Los Angeles Chamber of Commerce."

In the mid-twenties Roberts began developing the articles about antique hunting which became the basis of his book, "Antiquamania." He named the first of these "So This Is Pleasure." The Boss said he thought a better title for it would be "A Tour of the Bottle Fields," and he added: "I see that you took the author's privilege of socking everybody in the eye and treating yourself with great discretion and tenderness. I never so thoroughly appreciated the purity and nobility of your character as I did while reading your story."

By 1929, Roberts had contributed nearly two hundred articles to the Post, and he had nine non-fiction books to his credit. It was not surprising, therefore, that Lorimer viewed his star contributor's turn toward fiction with little enthusiasm. He was encouraging, but he showed no immediate inclination to buy the stories that Roberts now began to fashion. Nor did Roberts expect it. He knew—or thought he did—that his novels were too long for serialization.

Undismayed, Roberts wrote and published "Arundel" in 1930. A year later he had another novel which Lorimer asked to see on Tarkington's recommendation. This was "The Lively Lady," which Roberts, with Tarkington's help, had already whittled from 275,000 words to 150,000 words. That was almost short enough for the Boss, who wired Roberts: "It's a grand book and by cutting in the opening pages some of the privateering stuff and a good deal of Dartmoor Prison we can get a five-part serial out of it. If this is satisfactory and you are willing to trust our surgeon confirm. Glad to have you supervise the job if you prefer." Roberts wired back: "Go ahead but please ask the surgeon to be as merciful as possible. If it will be any advantage to him I will be glad to come over and help." Later Roberts begged Lorimer to make it six installments instead of five, saying he didn't want additional money, only additional space.

"No, no!" Lorimer protested. "What we print we'll pay for! We just haven't got the space! Well, I'll see what we can do. Now don't bother me about this any more, damn it!"

Eventually "The Lively Lady" ran in six installments, cut to eighty thousand words. Lorimer liked the book, but he was still extremely doubtful that the Roberts fiction was meant for the Post's audience. He considered the serial "a departure from our usual policy and more or less in the nature of an experiment."

Tarkington's work with "The Lively Lady" manuscript was not his first collaboration with Roberts. The two men and Hugh Kahler had been the joint authors of "The Collector's Whatnot" in 1923, and Tarkington had illustrated "Antiquamania" in 1928.

"The Lively Lady" proved to be a popular experiment, but Lorimer remained unconvinced of Roberts' conversion from fact to fiction, at least as far as the magazine was concerned. Late in 1931 he was confronted with another Roberts novel, and this time he gave his friend what amounted to a flat rejection.

" 'Captain Caution' has gone the rounds," he reported, "and has finally been read by me, and the vote on the manuscript is unanimous. We all think that it is good, and in some ways a better story than 'The Lively Lady,' but we do not feel that we can run another novel that so closely parallels 'The Lively Lady' for some time to come, at least. We now have on hand at least an eight months' supply of serials. Unless you have an earlier market or decide not to defer book publication, we shall be glad to reconsider 'Captain Caution' six months from now."

Roberts had an ardent faith in what he was doing, and he had need of his conviction now because "Captain Caution" made the rounds of every slick magazine in the United States and was promptly returned by each one. The editors who rejected it offered only the stock reasons. A *Good Housekeeping* editor said it "sagged in the middle." Another periodical complained that there "wasn't enough conflict."

With the other markets closed, Roberts turned to writing "Rabble in Arms," but continued sending "Captain Caution" to Lorimer at six-month intervals. He sent it for the sixth time on a day when he had finished three years of work on "Rabble"; he was broke, tired and discouraged. And this time Lorimer bought it! Now that the struggle was over, and Roberts' belief in his work was vindicated, he was anxious to know why "Captain Caution" had been so hard to sell. When he saw Lorimer after final acceptance of the book, he related his experiences with other editors. How, he asked the Boss, did his book "break down in the middle" and what about the "lack of conflict"?

"The gents who made those criticisms didn't know what they were talking about," Lorimer observed sharply. But he never disclosed what had made him change his mind.

"Captain Caution" increased Roberts' popularity in the Post, and Lorimer insisted on seeing "Rabble in Arms," which finally appeared as a book in 1933. Aside from Tarkington, the Boss was the first to see "Rabble," and he sent it back with a note which might have discouraged any other writer:

"Under separate cover I am expressing back the ten-pound novel. I read it with a great deal of personal interest and I believe that you have done an exceedingly good job, even though, in my opinion, and I believe yours was the same, it is not possible to make a serial out of it. How it will go as a book is, of course, something of which I have very little knowledge, though 'An American Tragedy' and Powys' new novel have both made good at between eight and ten pounds apiece. And you have done such a good job with this that I see no reason why you should not graduate into a short-story and serial writer whenever you feel the urge. . . ."

Although this book, in the opinion of many critics, stands as Roberts' best, and although Lorimer jestingly continued to refer to it as "another American tragedy," he could not be accused of an error of editorial judgment in not taking it, since it was more than 300,000 words long, and too closely knit to be divided or cut to serial length.

Whatever Lorimer might think of his fiction as Post material, Roberts was now firmly established with an ever-growing public as a storyteller, and he turned most of his energies in that direction. Lorimer continued to depend on him for articles, however, as though his career as a Post correspondent had never been interrupted. In September 1935 the Boss inquired: "How about taking a little run up to Aroostook County and talking with the potato growers there? This new potato bill has both an amusing and a serious side, and it would, I think, be interesting to get the views of some of the big potato growers on it." Three days later he cautioned: "Don't start out with any preconceived notions on the potato bill. Take the comment as you find it."

The result of this expedition was an article, "Potato Poor," which required cutting. Outlining that procedure, Lorimer could not resist adding: "If you learn to compress your articles for us, you will probably stop writing those ten-pound books and reduce their weight to one pound as a maximum."

For all that, one of Lorimer's last acts as editor of the Post was to buy part of a Roberts "ten-pound book," and he bought it after he had read only half the manuscript. The book was "Northwest Passage."

Roberts was one of the two outstanding new novelists whose work first appeared in the Post during the last decade or so of Lorimer's reign. The other was John P. Marquand. Unlike Roberts, Marquand served no non-fiction apprenticeship but devoted himself from the first to storytelling. Costain encountered him when both men were at the start of their careers. Lorimer paid the customary five hundred dollars for one of Marquand's first short stories, "The Right That Failed," and its publication in 1921 started the New Englander on his way to literary eminence.

This initial transaction was not accomplished without a piece of jockeying between Post and *Journal*. Marquand had offered Lorimer a novel, "The Unspeakable Gentleman," before the short story had been submitted and the Boss had turned it down. Then came his purchase of the short story, and immediately afterward the *Journal* bought the novel. By the ethics of publishing, that gave the Post's sister publication first call on whatever Marquand might write next. What he wrote was another short story, which the *Journal* bought for five hundred dollars. Marquand promptly submitted a third, and his agents, Brandt and Brandt, set a six-hundred-dollar price on it. The *Journal* refused to expend another hundred dollars, and Lorimer, who was waiting in the wings, seized his opportunity and retrieved Marquand for the Post audience.

"The Unspeakable Gentleman" was lucky to get into print at all. Marquand had lost the manuscript in a New York taxicab, and he had no carbon. Wearily he sat down to rewrite it, and by the time that job was completed the original was belatedly returned.

Marquand was appreciative of Lorimer's encouragement in those early days when he was unsure of himself. He wrote from his home at Curzon's Mill, Newburyport: "After a long summer's financial drought, the news that you like 'The Last of the Rich Men' fills me with great relief and your raising of the price was an unexpected climax from which my head is still spinning in a most welcome way, especially as the house here is being shingled. I wish I were near Philadelphia to thank you without the medium of a letter and to tell you without having recourse to my bad handwriting how hard I shall try to keep my work up to the standard your kindness has set. By the by, I wonder if the publisher of 'Lord Timothy Dexter' sent you a copy, because if nothing else, it certainly is a proof that I have been loyal to the old home town, as you suggest. In fact, I think I have worked off a whole lifetime of local loyalty. P.S. I am starting today on a new story—largely autobiographical—about an infant's nurse's effect on a quiet household."

Another modest report from Curzon's Mill said: "Thank you for sending me the letter from Australia. Much as I fear he has overestimated the situation, it is tremendously pleasant and surprising to think that anyone cares enough about anything I have written to send word of it halfway around the world—and I am writing at once to thank him. Today I am just finishing up a story which I shall send on. I am sorry not to have completed it sooner, but I never realized the demands put on anyone who has to move into a house four miles away from anywhere. Now, however, that the furnace is running and the garden is covered and the wood is cut and the storm windows are on, and I have a guest room and a stove, here alone in our deserted grist mill, I have every hope of turning out a decently impressive amount of work. Also I expect to be coming down to New York one of these days soon, and if I do, I am looking forward to running down to make a call in Philadelphia, provided you are there and not too busy."

Later Marquand found it necessary to move to the city, and even in the midst of what was to him a shocking experience he found time to write: "Only the horrors connected with moving a country-bred baby to the city, and I found they preclude nearly everything, have prevented my thanking you for your note about the last story. Few things that I remember have been pleasanter than your letter, and it makes me hope that sometime I'll deserve to have you write me again. In the meanwhile, it gives me new courage because I know that if you think I'm getting somewhere there is hope, and my motto is more and better stories for the Post."

There were more, and they were better—such novels as "The Black Cargo" in 1924, "Warning Hill" in 1929, and the Bill Rice series about blockade running in the Civil War, in 1934. Then Marquand made a profitable switch to oriental stories, with "Ming Yellow," and climbed to new popularity with the creation of his Chinese detective, Mr. Moto.

From such slick thrillers he turned abruptly in 1936 to the biting social commentary for which he is celebrated today. Lorimer was the first editor to read "The Late George Apley." He passed it on to Adelaide Neall for a second reading. Both thought it was a Post serial, but the others on the editorial board were unanimous in dissent; they thought it too local.

Marquand himself had been doubtful of its acceptance. At lunch in Philadelphia with Lorimer and Miss Neall, he had talked about the novel before he submitted it and remarked that he did not think it was the kind of thing the Post would want to publish. Carl Brandt, Marquand's agent, was present and agreed with his client; he implied that no one's feelings would be hurt if Lorimer chose not to consider it at all. But the Boss was stubborn. He had lived in Boston, he said, and he thought he would enjoy reading it, whether he bought it or not.

He enjoyed it so much that, over the objections of everyone on the staff except Miss Neall, he bought three long excerpts for the Post. The novel did not lend itself to serializing, and the excerpts did not even run in consecutive issues. Nonetheless, Lorimer's instinct was correct: Post readers enjoyed the tasting they were given. One reader who did not enjoy it was a Boston lawyer, who identified himself with a crooked attorney in the book and brought suit against the Post, without result.

In handling Marquand as a writer, Lorimer's technique was obviously quite different from the one he had to employ in dealing with Roberts. He had a still different method for such problem children as Hugh Wiley, who was one of the Boss's closest friends in the latter days of his career. This lovable, improvident man had gone to the war in charge of a Negro labor battalion and come back to write the yarns about Negro crapshooters which Post readers enjoyed. It was the only kind of story he knew how to write, and he wrote it over and over with variations. The spontaneous crap-game chatter he reproduced was hilariously funny to his audience, but it did not come spontaneously to its author; he sweated it out in long hours of concentration. When he was actually shooting crap with Sam Blythe and Harry Wilson, he had nothing at all to say beyond the usual clichés.

"Wildcat," as everyone called him, was habitually broke, but he was generous with whatever he had, to the point of sheer exaggeration. This trait was well known to his friends, but it sometimes came as a shock to other people. Once, when Lorimer had made him a member of the Post staff for a brief time to save him from financial disaster, Wildcat strode into the Curtis Building on a spring morning with a new hat which, he boasted, had cost him twelve dollars. Wesley Stout, then an associate editor, offered appropriate admiring remarks and Wiley forthwith insisted on giving the hat to him. He got a little huffy when Stout declined, and stalked over to Pete Martin's office, where he again showed off the hat. Martin also expressed his admiration, and the Wildcat again made his generous offer, and again met with a modest but firm refusal. This time Wiley was not only hurt, he became definitely hostile as well, and Martin was so intimidated that he had to take the hat.

Wiley did not stay long at the Post. He enjoyed the companionship, but he found the work confining. Lorimer made him welcome as long as he wanted to remain, however, because the Boss had the same affection for him that he had given Charlie Van Loan. He had, in fact, a predilection for talented, congenial writers like these men, who he must have known would never be particular stars.

There was only one popular writer developed by Lorimer in the Post with whom the editor did not become friendly. That exception was Clarence Budington Kelland. There was an intangible, mutual antipathy between the two men; they treated each other politely, but there was no cordiality. Several points of actual friction existed between them. After his introduction to the Post with a seven-part serial, "Sudden Jim," in 1916, written while he was working in a sawmill, Kelland had created his famous Scattergood Baines character the following year, and contributed twelve consecutive stories based on this cracker-barrel philosopher. Then, to his utter astonishment, Lorimer made him stop. "You want to stop a series while the readers still want more," he advised the outraged Kelland, who immediately began selling his work to the *American Magazine* and to *Collier's*.

Lorimer could never understand why a writer would leave the Post after a turndown. To him the Post was the greatest thing in the world; he believed a writer should wait patiently until he got back into the magazine again. He understood Kelland's departure no better than he had the others, but he did welcome back the stray in 1922 with a serial titled "Backbone." After this, however, Kelland wrote no more for the Post until 1932, when he produced in rapid succession three of his most popular serials: "Footlights," "The Great Crooner," and "The Cat's Paw."

Some Post editors thought that Kelland, in an odd fashion, was afraid of Lorimer and that that was the reason they had never become friends. This theory might have been true, but it is more likely that hostility arose because of Lorimer's scarcely concealed distaste for Kelland's work. Obviously he felt no closer to a Kelland serial than he did to its author. He was convinced that Kelland deliberately wrote down, that all his characters talked alike, and that he told the same story again and again, a fault he readily excused in Wiley. But in spite of these convictions Lorimer had an excellent reason for publishing Kelland: the public liked him. A Kelland serial could be started in the Post with the absolute assurance of a circulation jump. Notwithstanding such popularity, Lorimer refused to pay the prices Kelland commanded in the twenties, which accounted for the writer's ten-year absence from the Post.

If it appears that Post popularity was confined to Kelland, Marquand, Roberts and the other male writers, it seems so only because Lorimer was closer to the men. As a matter of fact the Post had a surprising number of women writers for a publication considered to be primarily a man's magazine. The Boss's natural reserve prevented him from forming any close friendships with most of the women who wrote for him but he did not neglect them by any means. He encouraged their work, as he did the men's, and he enjoyed their company.

It was Lorimer who bought Eleanor Mercein Kelly's "Basquerie" after it had been turned down by another magazine. Mrs. Kelly had brought the manuscript to Adelaide Neall, with a letter from Helen Walker, an ex-associate editor of the Post. After the publication of that notable story every magazine wanted her, including the one that had rejected it. But Mrs. Kelly went on writing for the Post the stories about the Basque country and the Spain she knew so well. An exchange of letters in 1928 indicates how carefully Lorimer guided her progress. There was still "a surplus of scenery" in her last story, he told her, and she replied from her Louisville home, The Barn, on Edgehill Road, "It's hard to get away from the scenery in Spain because it seems to make the people."

To that, Lorimer replied: "After all the first thing in a short story is the story, and important as the background and color is it must take second place. There is, I know, always a temptation where one has accumulated a gorgeous amount of material to use it as much as possible, but one then falls between stools, the short story and the descriptive travel article."

Lorimer sent Mrs. Kelly to Spain, to get more material for her stories. The expense account she submitted lists $700, "my third of the expenses of automobile and chauffeur, including hotel bills, for six weeks"; $120, the "cost of Spanish expert (engaged to show me the sights I would have missed otherwise)"; and $180, "extra cost of the expert, for hotels, etc., also 'specials' I would not have done for my own pleasure, such as various types of the bullfight, special performances of gypsy dancing, and others. . . ."

A closer association than that with Eleanor Kelly was Lorimer's friendship with Sophie Kerr, whose first Post story, "Values," in 1918, was the beginning of a long list of short stories and serials, whose end is not yet. Miss Kerr, or more properly, Mrs. Underwood, may have been the only writer who got a raise from the Boss by asking for it. Her asking was done in a feminine way that amused him.

"I see they're wearing checks larger this spring," she remarked as they were riding out to Wyncote one afternoon.

Lorimer laughed, and she knew he had understood. Her next check was larger.

On another occasion, as they were driving together, the antiquity of the car became evident as it groaned over some rough roadway, and Lorimer turned to her half apologetically.

"This is an old car," he began, "but——"

"I know," she interrupted, "you're going to tell me it's an old car, but it has a wonderful engine."

For a moment the Boss was taken aback. Then he laughed his hearty laugh, amused as she was at the joke on himself.

As he did with the others, Lorimer guided Sophie Kerr's progress. "Write more about this character," he would tell her, and she always listened to his advice. There were few who did not. "Everyone stopped, looked and listened when he even came into a room," Mrs. Underwood recalled. Another writer thought "he used up all the oxygen."

There were many other ladies whose literary ambitions Lorimer helped to realize. Temple Bailey got her start with the Post in 1919, Margaret Culkin Banning appeared in 1925, Katharine Brush wrote her two most successful books, "Young Man of Manhattan" and "Red Headed Woman," for the Post, Edna Ferber appeared as early as 1911, Zona Gale in 1905, Ellen Glasgow in 1923, Helen Hull in 1905, Fannie Hurst in 1912, Fanny Heaslip Lea in 1921, Kathleen Norris in 1913, and I. A. R. Wylie in 1918. Agatha Christie's first Post mystery, "Murder in the Calais Coach," appeared in 1933.

On one occasion a lady was assisted to fame by Adelaide Neall. In 1931, Katharine Dayton came to Miss Neall for advice about her career. She had appeared on the Post's humor page frequently, and now she wanted to go to Geneva and try her hand at political humor.

"Why Europe?" Miss Neall inquired. "Geneva has been overrun for years with American reporters, sob sisters and earnest souls. Why not Washington? Our own politics certainly are important and interesting enough these days to keep anyone occupied."

Miss Dayton took the advice. She went to Washington, armed with an introduction to David Lawrence, and got herself a job on his *United States Daily*. After an immersion in national politics, she began to produce for the Post a noteworthy series of satirical sketches on the Washington scene. One of these was a skit titled "Mrs. Democrat and Mrs. Republican." Lorimer suggested that she carry these ladies onward into further adventures, which she did, thereby attracting the attention of George S. Kaufman, who suggested collaboration on a play about the Washington scene. The play turned out to be a Broadway success, "First Lady."

Few if any of the Post's ladies could match careers with Frances Noyes Hart, whose father was president of the Associated Press for many years, whose husband was a noted lawyer, and whose own life was fabulous. She wrote from a background that included residence in the far corners of the world, but her best novel was based on a trial she covered in the United States, the Hall-Mills case. This book, "The Bellamy Trial," was serialized in the Post in 1927 and brought her more acclaim than anything else she ever wrote. It was a highlight in Post history and afterward emerged on the screen. While it was running serially, every issue of the Post was swept off the newsstands in record time.

One of the finest pieces of writing Mrs. Hart ever did was a long autobiographical letter written to Adelaide Neall. It was intended as material for the department about Post authors, and only a small part of it was published. It was prefaced with an apology—"I'm afraid that, like happy countries, I have no history" —and then it went on to picture the kind of life millions of American women wished they had lived.

"I was born," Mrs. Hart wrote, "on my grandfather's farm in a little place in Maryland called Silver Spring, about eight miles out of Washington. Being a handmaid of truth, I must admit that it wasn't one of those farms that all the nice gaunt interesting people in the prize-winning novels live on; my grandfather informed me once that he never acquired a potato that cost him less than an orchid, and I'm afraid that there was quite a long bowling alley, and a playhouse apiece for a reasonable number of grandchildren, and a black pony called Minnie and a white pony called Snowball, and a gray donkey called Trilby. The big dark rooms inside smelled agreeably of all the things from India and Japan that lurked in their corners and there were tiger skins instead of rag rugs, and sandalwood screens instead of patchwork quilts and a great piano instead of a melodeon, and a whole room full of books instead of the family photograph album. Shelves and shelves of them—if I close my eyes now I can hear the katy-dids singing outside and see the small person prone on the floor, investigating the contents of the lowest one near the fireplace. . . .

"No, it wasn't a really orthodox farm—but it was the best place in the world to be born. And, besides tiger skins, it had every-thing else. A stone dairy, forever cool, with water running across the paved floor—meadows, full of agreeable brown cows and daisies and bees and red clover and sunlight—nights full of fire-flies and stars and the smell of locust and honeysuckle. Haystacks and threshing machines and a great long house filled with golden corn and small gray mice—baby ducks and ancestral turkeys, a pine wood and a brook and oak trees planted a hundred years ago by someone who knew exactly how they should be arranged for a really superior game of Puss-in-the-Corner. Its name was Alton Farm; I loved it very much.

"Where have I been to school? Oh, almost anywhere. To danc-ing school in Washington, in a sash bluer than any skies I've ever seen and white silk socks, and black patent-leather slippers; to Chicago, led sedately down the Lake Shore Drive by a very tall coachman pursued by shouts of derision, while my teeth chattered with cold and rage in spite of all that blue reefers and scarlet beret and mittens could do; to Florence, where I was just beginning to be old enough to eye the officers in their gray-blue cloaks and Duse in Monna Vanna's black velvet one with respectful adora-tion; to Farmington, where through the pretty New England street the bells went ringing all day long—sleigh bells and church bells and bells to tell you when to rise and when to sleep, when to work and when to play; to the gray walls of the Sorbonne and the Collège de France, where I learned about Roland and Euripides and Pascal and Molière—and where I learned how lovely learning was; to the grayer walls of Columbia, where I learned something about writing; oh yes, I'm the only writer, living or dead, who believes that something about writing can be taught—or am I the proof that it can't be? Is that enough about schools? . . .

"Where have I lived? Oh, almost everywhere. I was born near Washington, and came out there, and was married there, but it doesn't seem to me that I can have lived there much. There are too many other places. There's Chicago, of course—and a big house outside of it between a golf course and a wheat field—there's an army post in Texas where I learned to think that Taps was the loneliest sound in all the world until for years and years I didn't hear it, and that was lonelier still; there were two enchanted summers of golden days and silver nights in a villa on Como—and a heavenly autumn of cloudless skies and dancing leaves in a Normandy château; and a winter on the Left Bank in Paris, where windows looked out on a walled garden, and for a franc you could keep the copper bowl on the desk filled with violets—where in the gray afternoon the fire in the grate burned like a nest of golden eggs— and in the evening in the big salon you played a nice game called Poisoned Handkerchief with grave members of the Academy and the Cabinet who suddenly became exceedingly amiable lunatics. Being twenty in Paris is probably better than anything else. Unless it's being seventeen in Oxford—and having afternoon after afternoon on a green river, and evening after evening in a green garden where at nine o'clock you could still see clearly enough to read 'Evelina' and 'Kenilworth' and 'Jane Eyre' aloud—and at eleven you could still smell the wallflowers and the lavender.

"And there was a room in Nice, filled with sunlight and flowers from November until May. And years in Maine—and years in the Adirondacks—and all those apartments in New York—and that house in the Westchester Hills—and those are just the places that I've lived in—not the places that I've stayed in for days or weeks or even months at a time. I haven't said a word about China or Russia or Hawaii or Jamaica or Nassau or California or Korea or Austria or Costa Rica or Greece or Japan or Bermuda or Cuba or Switzerland or Panama or—oh well, maybe I didn't live in Washington after all. I don't see how I could possibly have found time for all those years there without being Methuselah's great-aunt. . . ."

That was the kind of almost unreal world Lorimer himself lived in, for he was, as one of his closest friends put it, "a swell for all that." On the other hand, he was not spoiled by money. He believed that the chief value of having a lot of money was that it could buy independence, or as much independence as could be found in this world, and even when he became a millionaire he was still the same Lorimer who wrote in "Old Gorgon Graham": "It's good to have money and the things that money will buy, but it's good, too, to check up once in a while and make sure you haven't lost the things that money won't buy."

Fragments of the dream life of the very rich frequently pervaded the Post's pages, because Lorimer understood that this was the pleasant vision of millions of middle-class Americans, who yearned first for the good things they saw in the Post's advertising pages, and second for the lucky break that would project them into the world of yachts, beautiful women and champagne.

Meanwhile they stuck perforce to their meat and potatoes and beer, to that vast complex of American business life which was guaranteed to make the dream a reality—if and if. That was the life most of Lorimer's writers depicted in fiction, mixed generously with the romance that made reality bearable. If the critics carped, as they did, that Lorimer showed middle-class America its face in a mirror designed to reflect its imagined best, like the Wicked Queen in the fairy tale—well, the Boss could say that it was a representation of the nation's average life. Not the hard, bitter struggle of the proletariat beneath, nor the rarefied atmosphere of social posturing and intellectual conflict at the top, but the huge amorphous segment in between.

If the fiction that Lorimer published—the mirror of average America—seems today even more unreal than the life of Frances Noyes Hart, it is because the face of the nation and its people have changed.

The nation changed and the Post did not. It was Lorimer's tragedy that he retired still unable to accept, intellectually or emotionally, what had happened to the country he grew up in, and to whose life he had so faithfully held up the mirror. In 1936 the magic mirror no longer said, "You are the fairest one of all."

CHAPTER FIVE

The Post as America's Interpreter

At the heart of the Saturday Evening Post for the thirty-seven years Lorimer edited it was the editorial page, and at the core of the page were Lorimer's own editorials.

For years these columns were a sounding board for the Boss's continuing crusades. There he argued in his crisp, incisive prose for "the extension of our national parks, the protection of wild game, the conservation of our national resources." There he demanded "drastic reforms in the administration of justice." There he fought against the cancellation of war debts, and for the ever tighter restriction of immigration. There he preached the fundamental isolationism of Washington's Farewell Address. And there, finally, in the last four years of his tenure, he fought the New Deal, and lived to see his page become the rallying point for a majority of Post readers, who had grown up with the magazine and with Lorimer—grown as much as he had and no more.

The Post's critics were often loudest in their attacks on the editorial page. To Benjamin Stolberg, one of the sharpest appraisers, the editorials were "either tritely idyllic or calmly orthodox, and almost invariably dull." He thought they were "apt to lapse into pithy and cocksure reaction. The cocksureness parades as hardheaded realism."

Whatever faults the page had as a whole, and however much one might disagree with Lorimer's opinions, it could scarcely be said that his editorials were dull. Lorimer was almost incapable of writing a dull sentence, and his touch was so distinctive that his unsigned editorials stood out from the others like lighthouses. A Lorimer editorial always provoked a huge mail.

The page itself was loosely put together; it was never well organized. Sometimes the other editors wrote simply to fill space. Lorimer never dictated what the subject matter should be, but naturally no one wrote contrary to Post policy. An editor informed the Boss what he wanted to write about, and the Boss told him to go ahead. For himself Lorimer reserved the important topics, and no one else ever wrote a policy editorial, until Garrett occasionally did so in later years.

The Boss performed his editorial chore wherever he happened to be. In the early days he often wrote at Atlantic City during the week end. At other times he would spend an afternoon tramping over the acres of his King's Oak farm and then set down a first draft before dinner. For years the editorials were written on the expense sheets he sent every week to the accounting department, with one week's purchases of editorial material itemized neatly on them. His secretary, Margaret Davies, ordering a new batch of these forms, had asked by mistake for more of them than Lorimer could use in a lifetime. Rather than waste the excess pads, he used them as editorial copy paper.

No dish on the Post's menu got more loving prepublication care than a Lorimer editorial. It appeared first in the Boss's firm, broad longhand (he never learned to type), written with a black copy pencil, edited and re-edited. These sheets were typed and edited again, after which the editorial was ready to be set and galley proofs run off. Lorimer edited the galleys, sent them back, got revised galleys, and edited again. After these were returned the page proofs came along, beginning with the roughs and continuing through two revises. Nor was the job concluded with the final page proof. The Boss edited that one, too, and even insisted on a revised final, which he often sent back with a correction or two. Only mechanical limitations prevented him from editing his work until the presses began to roll. As it was, no one but an editor as powerful as Lorimer could have trifled so with a composing room.

Lorimer regarded his editorials seriously; he considered them guideposts to America as he desired it. They reflected his basic attitudes. For example, as far as he was concerned, only employers of cheap labor were opposed to immigration restriction. Strikes and "revolutionary radicalism" were the logical result of imported labor, he believed, and therefore the Post's fight against it seemed to him a sound business program. ". . . We have been almost alone among the periodicals in our campaign," a Post promotional pamphlet (probably written by Lorimer) declared, "although there is really an overwhelming, enlightened sentiment behind us. . . . We are not crusaders or uplifters or muckrakers in our editorial policy, but we are trying to follow the dictates of ordinary business common sense and to work for the best interests of all America over a term of years."

Branching out from both sides of the editorial page was the solid structure of the Post's substance, fiction and articles. The articles were divided roughly into political and non-political, and probably the most effective belonged in the former category, where they existed as potent extensions of the editorial page. Through the years of Lorimer's editorship these articles followed faithfully the rise and fall of administrations in Washington, the ebb and flow of public opinion.

Even the non-political articles had purpose and direction in most instances; there were few with no other purpose than to entertain. The influence of Post articles was remarkable. Sometimes it was difficult to tell where interpreting America left off and telling America began. In the first World War, when it seemed strategic for the high command to let the American public know about the attempt to brigade our troops with the French and British, with the idea that an aroused public opinion might prevent it, no other medium than the Saturday Evening Post was even considered.

Again, when the veteran Chicago publisher, H. H. Kohlsaat, who had a lifetime knowledge of media, decided to publish a series of reminiscences titled, "From McKinley to Harding," he told Lorimer he wanted the articles to run in the Post regardless of price.

Occasionally the fiction possessed influence too. Publication of "The Covered Wagon" inspired a mass meeting in Pocatello which led to a petition asking the legislature to change the name of the Idaho Pacific Highway to the Old Oregon Trail.

There were frequent and impressive examples of reader response to Post articles. Lorimer was on vacation in the summer of 1934 when a manuscript called "Schoolhouse in the Foothills," by Alvin Harlow, turned up in the mail. It told, with names disguised, the story of a primitive mountain school at Shady Grove, Tennessee, and of its teacher, Ella Enslow.

The staff disagreed on the article. Some thought it a dramatic commentary on a passing phase of American life; others doubted its appeal. According to practice, and at the particular insistence of Bruce Gould, a new associate editor, the manuscript was held for Lorimer to read when he returned. The Boss settled the matter by voting a decisive yes. His instinct was correct. It seemed that no Post article had ever moved so many readers. They were stirred by memories of their own schooldays and by the tragedy of this particular Tennessee schoolhouse. For the burden of Harlow's article was that the struggling little school was doomed by the waters of Norris Dam and that its population was about to be scattered into a doubtful future.

Another kind of flood engulfed Shady Grove. Clothing and gifts of every description poured in, to the Post as well as the tiny town. More goods came than the schoolhouse families could ever use. Shady Grove's railroad station and freight house were jammed to the doors and Miss Enslow had to see that it was distributed to neighboring school districts. The work and excitement gave her a nervous breakdown, and Harlow took over. The Post supplied him with stenographic help to answer the mountain of letters, many of which contained checks or money orders.

Miss Enslow did not defeat the enemy that the public power project represented to her schoolhouse. Remembering the admonition of her own schoolbooks, "If you can't lick 'em, jine 'em," she recovered from her breakdown and married a TVA employee.

The Shady Grove story was typical of Post articles, and indicative of how far removed its non-fiction pages were from the success stories and inspirational pieces which cluttered other periodicals. Lorimer avoided such hackneyed items even in the twenties, when the *American Magazine* was able to exceed Post circulation by building a periodical on that general formula. The Post leaned heavily to biography and autobiography. As its promotion remarked, "Much is to be learned between the lines of an autobiography as well as in the lines. More from an actual record of life than from deliberate and deadly attempts to tell the young man to be good and he will be happy."

Thus the Post ran Calvé's autobiography, depicting the great singer "toiling up with incredible labor through hardships and rebuffs to triumph," and at the same time showing "her human weaknesses." In Kohlsaat's articles political idols were shown saving not only the nation but their jobs as well. Augustus Thomas' autobiography was presented as "a typical American life."

Toward inspirational articles the Post took the same view, oddly enough, that its critics took toward the magazine: "There is in all so-called 'inspirational' literature," said the Post, "a Victorian blinking of facts, a Pollyanna point of view that disgusts any young man of this day whose intelligence is greater than that of a child. . . . Pollyanna does not write our advertisements; neither does she contribute to our editorial columns."

This declaration was printed five years after Lorimer had given his famous newspaper interview, in which he declared that "what this country needs is more professional Pollyannas."

Along with politics, biography and autobiography, Lorimer filled the Post's pages with pieces on health, medicine, sports, popular science and the more practical arts. These articles were like the fiction—faithful representations of what average people were thinking and talking about, or of what they aspired to think about.

Perhaps the most notable interpretations of American life in the

Post were its covers, those familiar portraits of homely people and situations which were literally mirrors. These covers were easily the Post's most distinctive feature, its most popular single item and its greatest sales asset. They were not changed until after Wesley Stout had resigned as editor.

Lorimer picked the covers as a weekly routine, with the same unerring judgment that he exercised on the editorial content. Fifteen or more cover candidates would be lined up on the floor, leaning against the wall, and the Boss would walk past them like a general reviewing troops. As he made his rapid progress he would stab at them with a finger and keep up a running monologue: "Out, out, out, maybe this one, maybe, out, out, this one." He went through the same process with the story illustrations, and he also sat as censor on the advertising art. If he thought there was too much feminine leg in a picture, he would order it retouched. He meant to keep the Post a family magazine, right down to the smallest illustration.

His genius for picking covers was affirmed time and time again by the evidences of their enormous popularity. In some Midwestern communities there were groups of readers who maintained betting pools on the topic of the next week's cover. The bettors had only to go over their own everyday experiences to make guesses, because it was from such experiences that the artists drew their material.

Once a cover by Orr showed a man priming a frozen pump with hot water, which had dripped on a dog who was jumping away. More than one reader wrote vehemently, protesting this cruelty to animals. Examining the picture, Lorimer noted that Orr had forgotten to paint in any steam, and he told the protesters that the dog was just surprised, not hurt; the water couldn't be hot because there was no steam.

Norman Rockwell was the outstanding Post cover artist; his work became a national institution, like the magazine itself. One of his most memorable canvases depicted a situation understandable to millions of people. It showed a motorist in a Model T Ford, or a reasonable facsimile thereof, passing a high-powered luxury car on a hill. The whole country chuckled over the driver's expression of mingled tolerance and pride, and the ill-concealed looks of triumph on the faces of his wife and small son.

It was Rockwell, too, who produced what is probably the best-remembered Post cover—one in 1929 which depicted an old family doctor holding his stethoscope to the chest of a doll held by a grave little girl.

Sometimes cover ideas came from the readers. One idea in particular resulted in a cover that brought letters for years afterward, requesting copies "suitable for framing." The idea originated with an electrical engineer in Portland, Oregon, who saw on a street corner an overalled small boy accompanied by a huge St. Bernard. Boy and dog wore expressions of pathetic sorrow. Two other touches told the story: the boy's patched and bedraggled overalls, and an awkwardly lettered sign attached to the dog's collar—For Sale. The engineer described this scene vividly in a letter to the Post, and Angus MacDonnall, a discerning artist, drew it, adding an effective touch of his own by facing the boy against a brick wall, his head bowed upon an uplifted elbow.

Another source of supply for the cover artists was the editorial staff of the Post. One editor who returned from a week end at Atlantic City told J. C. Leyendecker, an artist who ranked in popularity with Rockwell, about a fat woman he had seen on a beach, a lady in a ruffled bathing suit, blowing up with sublime confidence a pair of water wings which looked pitifully inadequate for the job. The nation chuckled again over that one.

On infrequent occasions Lorimer used the cover for policy purposes. An example was the New Year cover—always a Leyendecker canvas and uniformly beloved by the Boss. The one for 1923 showed the New Year Kid (a regular starter) as an American statesman. Approaching him with the caricatured crafty gestures of a foreign diplomat was the Old Year. The American Statesman New Year Kid was telling the Foreign Diplomat Old Year, in effect, to leave the United States in the splendid isolation which Lorimer desired for it.

Other popular magazines used the pretty-girl cover as though it were a badge—it was standard equipment on *Cosmopolitan* and *McCall's*—but the Post scorned the good-looking female unless she were a legitimate part of the story told by the cover. Coles Phillips was the artist most often entrusted with portraying American womanhood as something more than pictorial, until Neysa McMein's covers injected a more familiar note.

A Post cover girl was once boosted into Hollywood by her appearance on the magazine. Every noted illustrator in New York had begged the movie executives to give one of their models, a beauty named Mardee Hoff, a screen test. No one listened. Then in March 1936, Norman Rockwell's cover showed Miss Hoff as a movie star on tour, surrounded by reporters and photographers. On the day the Post hit the stands three movie companies wired the Post for the model's name. Twentieth Century-Fox got there first, and by the end of the following week Mardee Hoff was on her way to the Coast under contract.

"Why haven't we heard of you before?" one of the Fox executives asked her, with the simple wonderment of Hollywood.

"You have," said Miss Hoff politely. "I'm the girl Mr. Rockwell and Mr. Patterson have been telling you about for two years."

Inside the magazine, Post stories used the talents of the country's best magazine illustrators to carry out the idea of realism—Post variety—in the picture accompaniments to fiction. The artists were specialists, and their work was authentic.

F. R. Gruger, for example, could draw the interior of an Italian palace exactly as it appeared because the picture would be a replica of something he had seen in Italy. Henry Raleigh's illustrations for stories involving Parisian life were based on his own observations, recalled from his life in France. Anton Otto Fischer's dramatic pictures of full-rigged ships, inseparable from any Post sea story, were accurate because Fischer had spent much of his time on ships. When one story used Sherry's Restaurant in New York as a locale, Lorimer sent an artist there to make realistic sketches. H. J. Soulen drew pictures of life inside steel mills, and in poking around the great plants he was more than once mistaken by company detectives for a spy from a rival firm. Soulen also frequented the Chinatowns of several cities, and out of that experience produced the paintings which characterized the Post's oriental stories. For humorous stories, Lorimer relied for years on

Tony Sarg's work; animal stories inevitably called for Charles Livingston Bull; and the political cartoons came from Herbert Johnson's pen. Other favorite illustrators were John Sloan, Rollin Kirby, Arthur William Brown and May Wilson Preston.

The Post came to the use of photographs much more slowly than other magazines, because of Lorimer's resistance to change. During the war he used stock photographs of public personages to illustrate articles, and about 1921 he began to print detached photos as filler material—scenes showing America's beauty spots pointed up his editorial drive for the conservation of national parks. But it was not until the latter part of his career that the Post began to make really effective use of photographs.

Post art, on the cover and inside, was hampered for years by the mechanical limitations of the two-color process, for a long time the limit of high-speed presses. In 1926, however, the magazine bloomed in full color and the covers took on new values. Rockwell's work gained most by this innovation.

It was Lorimer's insistence on verisimilitude that characterized his magazine's art work, as it did the editorial content. What Bernard De Voto had to say about the Post's brand of fictional accuracy was equally true of its articles, covers and illustrations: "Its realism, though light and shallow, is frequently quite as good as any in the contemporary novel. You will not encounter realism about homosexuality, let us say, or strikebreaking or adultery, but you will find superb realism about women at matinees or literary clubs or the A. & P., men in the locker room or the bar or the commuters' car, married people worrying about expenses or the children's diseases, adolescents adjusting themselves to the high school world. . . . The historian is going to recover the surface of American life—at least of middle-class life—much more fully and with less distortion from the slicks than from the novel of our day. The slicks render the surface more honestly, more accurately, and with greater respect. The slick writer, unlike the novelist, is penalized if he loads his dice."

The kind of realism Lorimer gave his readers is evident in an analysis of the Post's content for a typical year, in this instance 1922. That year the Post printed 272 short stories and 269 articles,

20 serials and 7 two-part stories. The serials were excellent examples of Lorimer's taste, his ability to touch American life at fundamental points. They included "Merton of the Movies," "The Covered Wagon," Irvin Cobb's "J. Poindexter, Colored," Frances Noyes Hart's "Less Than the Dust," "Laughter, Ltd.," by Nina Wilcox Putnam, "Tumbleweeds," by Hal G. Evarts, and "Backbone," by Clarence Budington Kelland. Two-part stories included F. Scott Fitzgerald's "The Popular Girl," "Pobble & Co.," by Ruth Burr Sanborn, and "The Road to Casualty," by Ben Ames Williams.

In its important 1922 articles the Post was America's interpreter to an even greater degree. There was Eddie Lefevre's "Reminiscences of a Stock Operator," the Augustus Thomas autobiography, Kohlsaat's articles, Eleanor Egan's exploration of Russia, and the two series by Isaac Marcosson, "Europe in Transition" and "The Changing East." There were also Lorimer efforts to make foreign situations simultaneously real and palatable to the American reader, embodied in Philip Gibbs's "Miss Smith of Smyrna" and "The Beggar of Berlin," short stories in form but essentially articles in their effect.

Lorimer was at his best as editor when he dealt with domestic situations. In 1922 he had Forrest Crissey engaged in dramatizing transportation, Kenneth Roberts arguing the Boss's side on the immigration question, Sam Blythe directing his barbs at Prohibition —which Lorimer nonetheless insisted should be enforced until it was repealed—and Emerson Hough in solemn discussion of the American spirit and conservation. These were supplemented by strong editorials on war, debts and disarmament by Garet Garrett, George Pattullo, St. John Ervine and Lorimer himself. Other article writers dealt with farm prices, taxes, radicalism, the sad state of the theater, moving picture censorship, crime and the courts, free ports, town building, highways, floods, the Ku Klux Klan, Boy Scouts, currency problems, and yellow journalism.

The parallel between the subject matter of those days and of ours is painfully obvious.

Articles on business and finance were the backbone of the Post's non-fiction side, but the magazine undertook also to advise its readers on a variety of other subjects, including how to settle an estate, buy a home, get out of debt, bring up children, take care of babies, and collect antiques. It rehearsed the problems of traffic cops and telegraphers, explored the mysteries of radio and of balanced work, exposed disease carriers and speculation, argued about the price and distribution of milk, revealed the hotel business from the inside, praised life insurance, assailed the high cost of theater tickets, and rejoiced in the small-town home.

All this in a single year. No more comprehensive picture of middle-class America could have been found than in the Post's editorial content during that or any other year, before progress overtook it.

Another staple item was Lorimer's great outdoors, and he utilized some of his best writers to advance the interests of that department. In 1922 a dozen or more pieces on the subject included Will Irwin on motoring to Pike's Peak, Sam Blythe on golf, "Common Sense Vacations," by Floyd W. Parsons, a piece on mountain motoring by Courtney Ryley Cooper, and Nina Wilcox Putnam's "A Jitney Guide to the Santa Fe Trail."

The smallest percentage of the magazine's pages was devoted to articles of particular interest to women—such 1922 pieces as a lively examination of current reforms in dress and diet, a profile of Mrs. Gifford Pinchot, and a discussion of "Our Official Family," by Mrs. Josephus Daniels.

That the Post's coverage of American life was not so topical as to be completely transitory, like the daily papers, but was concerned with subjects of continuing interest is shown by the studies Lorimer made of the "life" of single copies. These studies indicated that the Post enjoyed a longer existence than any other American periodical, that every copy was passed along to many other readers, and was mailed frequently to friends at home and abroad. Each day's mail at the Curtis Building brought inquiries about, or requests for, copies from as far back as the turn of the century. The requests came from all over the world. Even today readers ask for copies of the three articles Albert Beveridge wrote in 1907, on "The Bible as Good Reading."

The Post made no effort to encourage circulation outside North

America, but world travelers found it to be as ubiquitous as the Standard Oil can. Mrs. William Hard wrote to Kenneth Roberts from Rumania in 1927: "I am on a train somewhere near a station called Fetesti, with three Italians and no other American, and I have been disgracing myself, I fear, in their eyes, for they stop to look inquiringly at me as I laugh till I cry over your satire in the Post of May 28, which I picked up in Beirut. So I have to send you this little note of thanks for it, and to thank the extraordinary sales staff of the S.E.P., which made it possible for me to have this cold drink in a dusty train, as it were. . . ."

Of all the article writers who helped Lorimer interpret America to itself and the world, none was more prolific and few were more popular than Samuel George Blythe. For thirty-five years, from 1903 to 1938, he was the most regular of Post contributors. His wordage easily surpassed that of any other writer, and what he wrote was, in the main, more consistently worth reading. Unfortunately much of it was so topical that its life was short. For Blythe was Lorimer's Washington man, an astute and cynical, often acidulous man, who saw successive administrations from McKinley to the second Roosevelt pass through the White House, and who commented on all of them with penetration and wit.

It is not too much to say that Blythe was the best-informed and best all around political writer American journalism has ever seen. Even when he was wrong he was informative, and he was always entertaining.

Born in Geneseo, New York, in 1868, Blythe began his working career on the Buffalo newspapers, where he rose to be managing editor of the *Courier* and *Enquirer* in 1897–98. He moved briefly into the magazine business in 1899 as managing editor of *Cosmopolitan*, but a year later he had found his true home in Washington as chief correspondent for Pulitzer's New York *World*. He served the *World* there for seven years, after which he became the Post's observer in the national capital for the rest of his working life.

Blythe began writing for the Post in 1903, as a sideline to his *World* job, contributing acid portraits of current political figures. In that year, too, he and Lorimer began their lifelong friendship, the most intimate the Boss was to know. By 1907 Blythe was so much a part of the Post that his permanent move to the magazine was inevitable.

His first work as regular Washington man was a department titled "The Senator's Secretary," forerunner of his famed "Who's Who and Why" series, which soon followed and were a continuation of his earlier personality sketches. Then Blythe began the more concentrated work which established his reputation—pieces like his examination of Thomas P. Gore, "The Man Who Talks," and his three-paneled portrait of Taft, White and Bryan. Nearly all these were unsigned, but with his profile of "Hughes—A Potential President," in March 1907, his by-line appeared for the first time and became as much a Post trademark as the magazine's masthead.

His output was prodigious. It fills three card-index files in the Post's archives, and besides these contributions he wrote sixteen books between 1909 and 1929, some on politics, a few indifferent novels, and others on health.

In the twenties Blythe began to slow down. Sometimes his copy was not at all to Lorimer's liking, and as editor the Boss was compelled to throw it back to his close friend. As a writer who had for many years seen every line he wrote accepted unquestioningly, and who had worked more closely with Lorimer than with any other person, Sam could not understand such refusals. They led to a gradual estrangement between the old friends. There were exchanges of rather strained letters, such as Blythe's complaint in 1930, saying he wished he "might have had a better position break for the old Washington story. Judging from the applause that is coming in, even with its secluded situation in the book, it would have gone over big a little further front. However, I am too old a bird at this game not to take what comes with equanimity." And Lorimer's somewhat tart reply: "My dear Blythe, Every now and then we have to sacrifice someone for the good of the cause, and use him after the editorial page in order to strengthen the number at the last minute. As a matter of fact, I think that this position is more underestimated by the writer than by the reader."

Blythe disappeared slowly from the Post, like a venerable

Cheshire cat. He wrote more and more from his home in California, as ill-health and age began to sap his vitality, and often his copy was only a wordy, pale reflection of his former artistry. He made his last Post contribution in 1938, and afterward slipped into the invalid's solitude, until he died at his Monterey villa in July 1947.

The men who worked with Blythe over the years paid him the highest compliment any reporter, political or otherwise, can merit. James Wyman Barrett, the *World's* last city editor, summarized what all of them felt: "Blythe never betrayed a confidence, never suppressed news, never manufactured gossip."

Next to Blythe, the most prolific and important of Post article writers was Garet Garrett, who served the magazine from shortly after the first World War until Lorimer retired, and thereafter until Stout resigned. Garrett had been executive editor of the New York *Tribune* before the war. On a dull night, while he was holding that position, he happened to read a copy of the Post and sat down to write a letter to Cyrus Curtis. "The editorials in the Post are rotten," he told the publisher. According to the traditional success story, Garrett should have been hired immediately as chief editorial writer, but in this case Curtis simply passed the letter to Lorimer, who was writing many of the editorials at the time.

Lorimer never mentioned this letter to Garrett, but neither did he forget it. Five years later, when Garrett was working for him, the Boss got back at him in his own way. Looking carefully out the window, he remarked, "I think you should write some editorials." Garrett declined respectfully; he understood that this was Lorimer's method of disposing of the letter. Later, of course, Garrett wrote numerous editorials for the Post.

When the war was over Garrett went to his New Jersey home, where he settled down to wait. For the kind of top job he would have to get in the newspaper business, to equal his prewar status, he might have to wait two years, and he was prepared to do so. Until something he wanted came along, he turned to writing. He wrote first a book called "The Blue Wound," which was published with moderate success. Then he tried a short story and sold it to the Post. Soon after he submitted a piece in the form of a letter to Lord Balfour, answering the Balfour Declaration, and Lorimer sent for him.

The Boss appeared surprised that his correspondent was a small man. He looked down upon Garrett's scant stature and told him, "If you'll write this letter as a straight article we'll take it." Garrett did so, and followed it with two or three others on the same subject; from that point on he was a Post staff man. There was seldom a lengthy discussion of ideas. Garrett would outline an idea briefly, and the Boss would say, "All right, that's good, do it."

The two men were having lunch one day when Lorimer inquired abruptly, "What do you think we should do with the Philippines?"

"I think we should give them up," Garrett answered.

"So do I," Lorimer said, "but you'd better go out there and have a look at them first."

As soon as he could arrange it Garrett sailed for the Philippines and spent three or four thousand of the Post's dollars making a firsthand investigation. When he got back he reported to Lorimer: "I'm not so sure we should give them up."

The Boss was not dismayed by this reversal. "All right," he said, "write it as you see it."

One of the most provocative articles Garrett ever contributed was "That Pain in Our Northwest," printed April 12, 1924. It was a candid examination of the bank failures, foreclosures and other financial disturbances that were upsetting the economic structure of the Northwestern states.

Both author and magazine were deluged with letters, proclamations, and every conceivable form of indignant protest. The newspapers of North Dakota, South Dakota, Minnesota, Montana, Iowa and Nebraska were in full cry. Various organizations took up the battle. More outraged than the others was the South Dakota Development Association, of Sioux Falls, which sent out a clarion call, asking the formation of six district congresses to formulate a counter-campaign. This proclamation was a masterpiece of civic prose.

"South Dakota and the Middle West were crushed by the collapse of a War Structure, which, in the name of world democracy, we were besought to erect," it began forthrightly. "In the crash went farm, business, home and bank. Bleeding, mangled, maimed, and yet smiling, we were extricating ourselves, when the Goliath of the press (the Saturday Evening Post), fat and sleek, from some of our feeding, wielding a club which our money helped buy, crept up on us and dealt us a cruel, crushing, unwarranted blow. There is not one extenuating circumstance. . . . What then can be the motive for this uncalled-for assault? THIS IS THE QUESTION WHICH THE SPHINX ASKS and nobody answers. What is the remedy? Know South Dakota and the Middle West and see to it that every vale and hamlet in America knows the truth. To this task we dedicate ourselves. The South Dakota Development Association accepts the challenge of the Goliath and The Little David girds himself for the fray. . . ."

The Little David of South Dakota was joined by numerous recruits. The Montana Association of Commercial Organization Secretaries leaped to battle; dozens of prominent bank officials in the affected states wrote to demand an apology or a retraction; and R. A. Nestos, the Norwegian-born governor of North Dakota, wrote an angry letter, followed by a more conciliatory one after Garrett had sent him an explanation.

Apparently one paragraph in particular had got under the skin of Governor Nestos. It ran: "They [the original North Dakotans] were followed by settlers mostly at first Scandinavians imported by the railroads that had Federal land-grant acreage to sell. They are a strange, unaccountable people, both credulous and suspicious in morbid degree, with the brooding fatalism of a one-crop mentality, a Nordic belief in imitative magic, and no sense of humor."

The substance of the reply Garrett made to all complaints was contained in the answer he gave to a particularly critical Ipswich, South Dakota, banker. In this letter Garrett demonstrated indirectly how closely Lorimer tied his articles to political maneuvering in Washington, and how such provocative pieces as "That Pain in Our Northwest" were developed.

"I beg leave to say," Garrett wrote, "that in all this criticism you are holding your sight on the wrong target. Consider: the President of the United States in a special message to Congress had proclaimed the existence of a grave crisis, not in the country as a whole, not as to agriculture at large, but in your Northwest. At the same time hundreds of your Northwestern people were coming to Washington with requests for Federal aid to save the country from ruin. Mr. Hoover had called a conference of businessmen, farmers, bankers, railroad officials and others to devise ways and means of withholding the Northwest from the brink."

(At this point in the story's development, Lorimer had sent Garrett on an exploratory tour of the Northwest, and he had reported: "As far west as Chicago I found bankers fearful lest the Northwestern disease should spread eastward.")

"Well," the letter to the Ipswich man went on, "after all this the Saturday Evening Post decided to look at the Northwest. And what did it say? It said the Northwest had been on a credit spree, that it was not ruined, that the acuteness of the trouble was marginal, not fundamental, and implied that the people had the courage and resourcefulness to work themselves out of the hole in their own way. If that is dealing you a cruel, unwarranted blow, as your Development Association says, we are simply not thinking in the same language. Why did you support the propaganda of ruin at Washington? It was much worse than the truth, and yet nothing was done to stop it, except what we did. And it is our opinion that since those articles you complain of were printed, a much saner view of the Northwest prevails in the East. Everybody can understand the truth. It is an old truth, of which we have much traditional experience in this land. But the legends of impending ruin which had been widely spread from Washington, perhaps for political purposes, could not be understood at all."

Logic was on the Post's side, but nonetheless the article and its author were denounced by at least three fourths of the newspapers in the six states. One South Dakota organ advised, "No true South Dakotan should purchase this bunch of paper." Eventually the furore died down, but before it did, a revealing picture of the Post's effect on its readers was provided by the secretary of the

Rapid City, South Dakota, Commercial Club, who had been one of the original complainers.

"I wish to thank you for your courtesy in replying to our letter to the Post," he wrote. (Garrett and Lorimer had undertaken to answer every complaint.) "Undoubtedly a view from your side of the fence does clarify our conception of the Post's efforts. However, the general idea is that nobody believes any of the bunkum spread from Washington any more [this, the reader must remind himself, was in the Hoover administration] but to attract attention in the Post or other national institution we must be in a bad way.

"We all go out and get lit up and probably the women talk it over at the Aid Society, but we like to keep out of the papers. That's our view. We don't mind a local to the effect that we have returned from Dwight, Illinois, and that the business outlook is fine, but we do mind their chanticleering the fact that we have been down to the Keeley Cure. But it's all true. Won't you come out and look us over again sometime? We have some nice golf courses if you like golf, saddle horses to any degree of fineness, a lot of mountain streams full of trout (hungry), cool nights, and a few philosophers. No mosquitoes. If you have many replies to make to the rest of us patriots, you will need a rest, and this is an invitation to take it here. And we might get better acquainted. We'd like to. . . ."

Another Garrett article that stirred up an even more widespread reaction was "The League of Debtors," a castigation of those who wanted to cancel the war debts. Thousands of copies of this article were reprinted and distributed in pamphlet form. The Post encouraged the response by building up the demand for weeks through editorials, references in articles, and pieces on allied subjects.

As in most successful collaborations between writer and editor, Garrett and the Boss thought much alike. Perhaps more than any of the other article writers, Garrett shared Lorimer's deepest convictions, as is shown by this letter, written while he was working on a story involving a favorite Lorimer topic:

". . . The naturalization story will come first and I expect to get to the writing of it Wednesday or Thursday. It is more complicated than you might think. And as always, government unobserved gets in the way of doing strange things. What do you think of a Bureau of Naturalization, Department of Labor, having citizenship classes in penal institutions? Throughout there is a confusion of two matters. One is the individual's economic and social participation; the other is his political participation. Why should aliens be solicited to participate politically? Here is the Metropolitan Life conducting *citizenship drives* in places such as Passaic, New Brunswick and Norristown. When I ask them why they are so anxious to convert what at worst is a police problem into what at its least is a political riddle, they say: 'We are primarily interested in their welfare, in their education, but you have to hang it on something.' They hang it on citizenship, therefore. They cannot sell the alien education; they *can* sell him the vote."

By such identity with Lorimer's views, both Garrett and Blythe emerged as the brightest stars in the Post's galaxy of article writers. A more remote planet, because he wrote on non-political subjects, was the fabled Isaac Marcosson. He was remote by choice. Marcosson cast himself in the role of the great interviewer, and he lived the part. He was seldom seen in Philadelphia, but he became a Post trademark as he traveled about the world, having breakfast with this statesman in London, chatting amiably over after-dinner coffee with that world figure in Paris, forever sitting at the feet of the mighty. He was as peripatetic as Elsa Maxwell, and he had O. O. McIntyre's trick of conveying to the reader the sense of "I was so close I could almost touch him"—except that Marcosson imparted a feeling of complete intimacy with his subjects. He appeared in his own stories as the interpreter who stood between the world's great and its eager masses. Few interviewers were willing to spend so much time in travel, and consequently Marcosson had his particular field almost to himself.

As an interviewer of great men, Marcosson began with a serious handicap: he stuttered badly. By virtue of will power and practice he became an accomplished public speaker, fluent in three languages. Meanwhile he developed an interviewing technique, and he began to build up a card index on everyone he met; eventually he could tell a man all about himself when he met him a second time.

Ike's career began on *World's Work*, where he was one of the mainstays in Walter Hines Page's modest but influential publication. Looking around in 1907 for a larger and more national audience, he chose the Post as the obvious medium for his talents. He admired Lorimer, who seemed to him "a man of affairs, who interprets the absorbing romance of business in fact and fancy," whereas he had looked upon Page as a "seer and scholar."

Lorimer set his new writer to work on one of the most troublesome aspects of his program to popularize business. The subject of finance was seldom discussed in periodicals of that time. Only experts wrote in a field which affected directly the lives of millions of people, and they wrote in the unintelligible jargon of experts, as though they were writing for each other. It was Lorimer's idea to set up an unsigned weekly department in the Post, devoted to popular investment and written in simple language. The fact that Marcosson knew nothing about finance only made him the more eligible for running this department, in the Boss's view. He would be compelled to write in simple terms because he would have to learn all a lay reader needed to know about a complex subject before he could lay his fingers on the typewriter.

"Your Savings," the departmental result of this idea, was the longest consecutive series of articles ever to run in the Post. Its 124 pieces were spread from 1907 to 1910, beginning with "The ABC of Investment" and ending with "Saving for a Home." To get the material, Marcosson became a habitué of Wall Street. He made friends and acquaintances everywhere, many of whom helped his interviewing career at a later time. And Lorimer was always at his elbow. "The trail of most of my adventures in interviewing began at Lorimer's desk," Marcosson wrote.

A by-product of the new department was a series of eight interviews with the giants of the Street, men like Frank D. Vanderlip, Thomas Fortune Ryan and John W. Gates. Almost at once, in developing this series, Marcosson got what amounted to a major news beat. The story centered on Standard Oil, a company which had not given any kind of interview in thirty years, notwithstanding the fact that it had been a primary target for attack. John D. Archbold was head of the corporation. He was regarded as the most inaccessible of all the financial titans. When Marcosson suggested the idea of an Archbold interview to another Standard official, he was told: "Mr. Archbold has never been interviewed. The Standard Oil Company does not believe in such things."

But Marcosson worked up through the chain of command, with his habitual persistence, and one day found himself in the directors' room, facing Mr. Archbold, who was flanked by members of his Board. They looked expectantly at the Post's man.

"The policy of silence is a mistaken policy," Marcosson told them. "The time has come when the Standard Oil Company should tell its own story. The longer you wait the harder it will be to change the public's mind about you."

There were other meetings, and the net result was in some ways better than a conventional interview. The company gave Marcosson a "statement and a defense," signed by Archbold himself; it was the first time the company had ever given out a signed statement for publication. Lorimer gave it a huge advertising campaign, and the statement was reprinted widely, to the pleased astonishment of Archbold. As a reward, he gave the dauntless reporter the highest favor he could conceive: an invitation to have lunch with the directors of the company.

Marcosson got another beat with his story on Thomas Fortune Ryan. There was a preliminary meeting at which Ryan sized up his man. Then he invited Ike to spend a day in the country with him. They traveled around Westchester County in Fortune's car, while the financier talked rapidly and freely on everything that came into his head. Marcosson was unable to take notes, but his agile memory recorded the conversation and he reproduced much of it in "Thomas F. Ryan, His Personality and Point of View." It was the first interview Ryan had ever given.

James R. Keene gave the indefatigable Ike an interview on speculation, at a time when the governor of New York was fighting to put an end to the practices by which Keene made his living. Marcosson could get into Keene's Broad Street offices only by means of a countersign which let him past successive guards in successive rooms, until at last he reached the inner chamber where the "Market Maker" stood with the ticker tape running through his fingers, a financial soldier of fortune who fought bitter, secret battles for competing corporations.

It was Marcosson, too, who saw the exciting possibilities in an autobiography of Daniel Frohman. He persuaded the eminent theater manager and producer to set down in 1910 the three articles which ran as "In the Days of the Old Lyceum," and later were expanded into a book, "Memories of a Manager," which Frohman dedicated to Marcosson.

When war came, Marcosson applied his talents at Lorimer's direction to the aspects of the struggle that he knew best. He wrote about the supply of the British Army, and a year later performed a gigantic interviewing task with a similar story about the Services of Supply in the AEF. He also wrote a significant article on the part businessmen played in the British conduct of the war. In compiling these and subsequent articles he not only had the formidable prestige of the Post to smooth his way, but the British government gave him a circular letter of introduction and recommendation, signed by the Prime Minister on a No. 10 Downing Street letterhead. This letter opened to him the Empire's private doors all over the world and, combined with his own and the Post's reputation, guaranteed him any interview he might desire. The interviews were supplemented by articles on foreign trade which proved exceptionally valuable to American businessmen.

Everywhere he traveled Marcosson saw the imprint of Post influence. At the French front one day he was the teatime guest of a French general at corps headquarters. As he told the story in his "Adventures in Interviewing": "I cannot remember the name of our host but his personal quarters were a large dugout bored into the side of a hill. Like most quarters of this kind, the earthen walls were supported by heavy timbers. I noticed, as was frequently the case, that these timbers were covered with magazine covers and illustrations from periodicals. The first cover that I saw there that day was torn from a copy of the Saturday Evening Post. As a matter of fact, the favorite decorations in most dugouts in France were magazine covers. This would not have been surprising in the American Army, but long before we were in the war Leyendecker and Fisher 'cover girls' smiled down on the war-wearied officers and men far up on the fringe of the inferno."

In the late twenties Marcosson's stories began to be more and more superficial, the inevitable result of constant digging in the same mine for two decades. Ike was finding difficulty in following the old techniques. It had always been his custom to appear anywhere in the world, announce grandly, "I am Isaac Marcosson," and find the welcome rug unrolling at his feet. Now the rug rolled far less frequently. There was increasing resistance on the Post to running his interviews, but Lorimer insisted on publishing him because he had once been so popular—another indication of the Boss's unwillingness to change. Lorimer did admit that Ike ought to do better.

The last time anyone sat at the feet of a great man, in the old-fashioned manner of uncritical interviewing, was Marcosson's interview with Ivar Kreuger, who gave him a story that would have done credit to a Rotary Club inspirational speaker. While this interview was running on the press, Kreuger killed himself and the facts of his ignoble career were exposed. A page was re-plated to carry a lame alibi, to the effect that this was an example of the kind of thing a man could say when he knew he was lying.

That story marked the beginning of the end of Marcosson's career. Harold Ross's *New Yorker* began to develop the profile, a superior method of accomplishing a word picture, Alva Johnston introduced the technique to the Post, and then came the depression, which cast doubt on the word of great men in general. Marcosson's kind of interviewing was gone forever, and the profile succeeded it.

Another veteran reporter, of the Marcosson-Blythe-Garrett school, was Will Irwin, whose term on the Post was shorter but in some respects more exciting. In July 1914, Lorimer had advised Irwin to write more of the short stories he had been selling to the Post spasmodically, and Irwin retired to the country to carry out the advice. While he was writing at the Connecticut home of Jane Peyton, later Mrs. Samuel Hopkins Adams, war came to Europe. Few believed that it would last more than six months, and

Irwin decided at once that he would go over long enough for one campaign and then return to America. He telephoned Lorimer in Philadelphia and got the discouraging news that the Post's war coverage was already arranged. He got, in the bargain, Lorimer's view of the war, which was the most profoundly mistaken estimation the Boss ever made.

"I'm going to play this war hard for six months," the Boss told Irwin, "in case it lasts as long as that, and then I'll drop it. By then the American people will grow sick and tired of reading about it."

Lorimer had revised his estimate by 1915, and Irwin was at the front for *Collier's* and the *American Magazine*. His work attracted the Post's attention, and Lorimer proposed to him that he should be "the Post's man" by a special arrangement which would give the magazine first call on his fiction and his article ideas, and put him on call to cover stories worked out in the Post office. If Irwin would agree not to write for any other magazine, Lorimer said, he would raise the prices. This agreement was made; it lasted for the next seven years.

Before he returned to Europe for the Post, Irwin married another writer, Inez Haynes Gillmore, a popular novelist. "Don't quarrel over who gets the plot," Lorimer advised the bridegroom. He told Irwin that he was not interested in the front lines. What he wanted was the background of the war—articles about business conditions or such specific topics as the organization of the French Army. "Send copy on the front line only when you can get some new angle," he ordered. Irwin followed directions and produced several excellent articles. The one that pleased Lorimer most was an interview with Edouard Herriot, concerning postwar opportunities in France for American business.

If he had been mistaken about its beginning, Lorimer at least anticipated the end of the war. He wired Irwin: "Drop military affairs and rush copy on reconstruction." The message reached Irwin while he was occupied with the British advance through the Hindenburg line, but he hurried immediately to Paris, where, according to his memoirs, he was "the only American in Europe who celebrated the false armistice of November 8."

After the war Irwin continued to cover Europe for the Post,

but he was beginning to find his connection with the magazine irritating. He differed sharply with Lorimer on political matters. The Boss opposed the League of Nations; Irwin was for it. Lorimer supported the Republicans in 1920; Irwin wrote campaign literature for the Democrats. By 1923 the wartime alliance had dissolved quietly by mutual consent and Irwin was writing for *Collier's* and other magazines. The parting was amicable. Lorimer wrote to Irwin: "I have never wanted anyone to continue with the Post when he felt that financially, or in any other way, he would be happier with another periodical. The men in this office are all your warm friends and have a great liking for you personally, but we do not expect you either to make a financial sacrifice or to change your point of view in any respect on that account. . . ."

The note of friendship was one Lorimer sounded often, even when he was not particularly close to a writer, because he wanted the men and women who wrote for the Post to feel themselves part of the family of which he was the paternalistic head. Women responded to this approach even more readily than the men. A case in point was Corra Harris, a writer little remembered today but one whose work captivated the Post audience for two decades, beginning in 1910 with "The Circuit Rider's Wife." Lorimer bought the manuscript after it had been rejected many times because he knew how much religion meant in the homes of so many Post readers. In that five-part record of mingled adventure story and spiritual testimony, Mrs. Harris established herself as a unique personality. She continued her autobiography with another series, "An Old Woman and a New One in the Old World," which ran in 1911-12. Then followed, one after another, further leaves from her memory book which told, with a curious kind of intimacy, the life of a semi-genius. Corra was divided equally between spirituality and sensuousness. Hers was a particularly sharp response to people and things.

Post readers were enthralled by the Harris story as it unfolded year after year—"In Search of a Husband," an eight-part series in 1913; "A Circuit Rider's Widow" in 1916; "My Son," another six parts, in 1920-21; "My Book and Heart," a nine-parter which was nearly as popular in 1923 as the original "circuit rider" series; "As a Woman Thinks," 1925; "The Happy Pilgrimage," 1926–27; "Obsolete Womanhood," 1929; and finally, "Last Leaves," in 1930. She wrote a few more articles after that consideration of old age, but with the story of her life told at such length, she had little left to say.

Corra Harris' correspondence with Lorimer was as voluminous as the printed record of her life. Her letters to him would make a long book in themselves. His replies were seldom any longer than customary, but he occasionally unburdened himself of his own philosophy, primed by the fact that Corra's letters were invariably philosophical. The Boss handled Mrs. Harris like a movie director, going along with her moods, checking her with the rein where it was necessary, and extracting from her piece by piece the peculiarly fascinating history of her existence.

In one of her serials the lady, who was always frank, had some uncomplimentary things to say about her deceased father. Lorimer edited them out, remarking: "Corra Harris can say those things about her father if she wishes, but she won't say them in the Post."

After "The Circuit Rider's Wife," Mrs. Harris wrote a few short articles, introspective and full of sweetness and light, somewhat out of the usual run of Post material. Lorimer reported that "we are getting some kicks from the heathen but on the whole it is calling out a remarkably fine bunch of letters. Like you, however, I am a little uneasy because every now and then someone says that it is literature, than which there is no surer sign that it ain't. Literature is never discovered until it has been a hundred years dead and there is nothing but the bones of it left."

As her early popularity increased, Mrs. Harris considered taking on an agent, but she consulted the Boss first, as she did before making any important decision. He replied: "I am not quite sure whether your last letter is the outgrowth of a case of colic or conscience. Sometimes the terms are interchangeable. Still, there is no reason why you shouldn't coquette with brokers if you can get a thrill from them. They make love to an authoress very much like other men. One of them will try to win you by promising you diamonds and motorcars and suppers at the Ritz-Carlton. Another will look soulfully at you and tell you that you are the sweetest little authoress ever, and that his sole ambition in life is to handle your heartthrobs—at so much per throb. Ourselves, we think it highly improper of brokers to make love to women who are married to good steady magazines, and it is only fair to tell you that you can never get a divorce from us. We are good Catholics in that respect."

With the publication of "My Book and Heart," Corra reached the second peak of her writing career. As she submitted the manuscript piecemeal, Lorimer reported that he had thoroughly enjoyed the first two installments, "partly because there was so much about your beginnings as a writer, and partly because there was so much perfectly good human nature in it. I have cut very little in these two installments, and that mostly knocks about the brethren. I struck out the stuff about myself, except for the reference to your visit to the Editor of the Saturday Evening Post and so much of that visit as was needed to put the 'Circuit Rider' manuscript into the Post. You can say it with flowers at my funeral. Incidentally, I have a rule that my name shall not appear in the Post except on the editorial page. And now what do you think your life is worth in terms of dollars and cents, for I know it is priceless on any other basis."

The kind of reception this book met from Post readers may be judged from Adelaide Neall's report to Mrs. Harris: "One girl here in the company told me at lunch today that she and her mother had read the first installment over twice, and that her mother had put the copy of the Post away safely so that she could read it again. . . ."

More strait-laced readers, however, were dismayed by Corra's frank outlook on the relationship between church and congregation. In sorrow and anguish she wrote to Lorimer, enclosing an indignant, sarcastic letter from one of these dissenters, and Lorimer consoled her:

". . . You shouldn't let a letter such as the one you enclose get on your nerves. There are a certain number of lice in the world who love to write that sort of thing. Such people seem to think they exalt themselves if they can drag down others to their level. Every few days I get a letter of this sort either about myself or about the Post and I am getting fat and sassy with them. Even if the writer sincerely felt as this fellow claims he feels, the mere fact that he has put his thoughts on paper and sent them to you proves him a trashy, worthless kind of fellow. The nearest waste-basket or spittoon is the place for him. Personally, I prefer the spittoon but I have none in my office."

After the publication of "As a Woman Thinks" in 1925, Mrs. Harris wrote that she was bored and restless and thought a trip around the world might do her good. Lorimer's response was typical of his impatience with anyone who thought he could find consolation of any kind outside the United States.

"I should say that if you can't find happiness except by going around the world for it that the quest was a more or less hopeless one," he wrote. "I am inclined to think that you will find more of it right here in the United States than in any other quarter of the globe. Anyway look over our beloved country first. . . ."

Corra took the Boss's advice, as she usually did, but in planning her itinerary she stepped on another of his prejudices and brought from him this impassioned statement: "I sincerely regret that you will miss the Grand Canyon. One cannot have had a fully rounded-out life until one has seen it, nor can one be thoroughly happy, even though one may believe that one is, without a night spent in its depths under the stars that it brings down almost within the grasp of an outstretched hand."

Of the innumerable letters Mrs. Harris wrote to her editor, the one that amused him most was her report of a meeting with Ed Howe, the venerable Kansas editor, who had stopped at her home in Rydal, Georgia, on his way up from Florida. Corra found him "a delightful plain wise old man, whose only affectation is sim-plicity, and the only rationalist I ever saw who believes and aspires to live and think honorably and decently, which of course convicts him of being an idealist."

Howe told her he had stopped to discuss his autobiography, which he was planning to write for the Post. They repaired to her study at the edge of the woods on a cold morning and discussed

the matter before a cheerful blaze in the fireplace. The elderly
editor crossed his legs, tucked his chin in his collar, and remarked:
"I want to know how frank I can afford to be in writing this
thing."

"That," Mrs. Harris replied, "would depend upon how good
and how bad your life has been, the amount of conceit you have
in your virtues and the sense of decency you have in choosing
which of your sins or crimes or weaknesses you would choose to
dramatize."

"Oh, I've lived a remarkably decent life," Howe protested.

"And yet not a dull one," she agreed.

"Full of adventures!" he exclaimed.

"And entirely good and decent," she agreed again, politely.

At that point, Mrs. Harris reported, Howe for some reason became suspicious and "he began to tell me very insistently what a
lifelong struggle he had made to be decent. I do not doubt it, still
it was funny seeing that I am a woman and know that he would
not have dwelt so ardently upon this point if I had been a man."

Howe's insistence finally nettled Mrs. Harris and she felt
obliged to defend her own reputation, since he seemed to think
his decency so remarkable.

"As to that," she observed, "I am a very good woman myself
and remarkably decent but it has been a frightfully hard struggle."

"That's it!" he exclaimed. "How did you interpret that struggle
in your autobiography?"

"I left the reader to do that," she said, "by substituting his own
struggles."

"But you didn't tell everything?" he inquired.

"Only such things as would redound to my glory," she replied,
"and excite the sympathy and admiration of the reader."

"But you told the truth?" Howe insisted.

"Absolutely," she declared. "And only the truth—but not
everything."

"Still," he insisted, "you have written several autobiographies."

"Yes," she agreed, "but not one life of myself. That would be a
gross and indecent sacrilege which even the most vulgar modern-
ist could not afford to commit. The cleanest life cannot be put in

print without seeming vulgar and commonplace. An autobiography is only where the light strikes it. The rest of it belongs not to darkness but to unspeakable silence. No man can write out his life. It would be as bad as blaspheming. The best and worst of us can never be told."

After she had made that declaration, Corra wrote in her letter to Lorimer, Howe "sat a long time regarding me with a strange sort of curiosity, no doubt wondering what unspeakable sins this woman with such a good countenance had committed, but not wondering, I'll be bound, what unspeakable victories she had also achieved upon the heights of that thing which we call the human soul.—So are we made, forever tempted to look for that which is dark in each other when the true glory of mind is to discover that which is bright with goodness. This stare ended the interview but we all fell very much in love with Dr. Howe and I believe he will write a wonderful autobiography."

Her prediction was fulfilled. Howe's autobiography was one of the memorable Post stories, and Lorimer continued to share with Corra Harris an appreciation of the essential human values that went into both her work and Howe's. It was, in fact, a mutual admiration between the lady and her editor. As Corra put it in her emotional way: ". . . There is a sort of hard-fisted, sensible righteousness mixed with the furious ardor of mortal men in mortal circumstances back of the editorial policy of the Post which has always commanded my respect and my admiration. . . ." And Lorimer returned the compliment: "Nothing that you write sounds like foolishness—in fact, I don't know anyone who has fewer foolish thoughts than yourself. . . ."

A similar admiration existed between Lorimer and William Allen White. The two men were friends from the day in 1899 when Lorimer, freshly come to the editor's chair, commissioned White to do an article or two for the Post, and the friendship continued until Lorimer's death. In those three decades and more the Kansas editor contributed numerous stories, articles and editorials to the Post. Most noteworthy in the long list was undoubtedly his 1921 article, "Why I Am a Progressive."

Only once did White ask Lorimer to print a specific piece. In the early years of the century the Kansan was stirred by the works of Herbert Spencer, and when that philosopher died he wrote an account and an appreciation of Spencer's life and works. He wanted it in the Post, and Lorimer made no objection. At the same time White was writing stories about Emporia and its people for the Post and *McClure's*, most of them character sketches of politicians. A little later, in 1904, he struck a different vein, and as he recalled in his autobiography, "I began writing a series of short stories reminiscent of my life around a newspaper shop. Each story was complete in form, yet they all strung together as an account of country newspapers in the eighties and nineties. When I sent two or three to Lorimer, he wrote eagerly for more and paid well for them, a thousand dollars each for most of them. For one story he gave me twenty-five hundred—the most money I had ever received for an article."

Lorimer felt a special kind of kinship with such interpreters of American life as White. He had the same feeling for Emerson Hough, considerably enhanced by their mutual love of the outdoors; they were partners in the crusade for conservation of wild life and natural resources. Long before he wrote the novels which Lorimer inspired him to create, Hough had fought the conservation battle, beginning with his 1905 articles on "The Wasteful West." As conductor of the Post's Out of Doors department during the first war, he became the mouthpiece Lorimer used to inform and entertain the public on what he considered a vital subject.

Hough and the Boss were ardent conservationists, but they were also hunters and fishermen, Hough much more so than Lorimer. That fact sometimes put the Post in an embarrassing position with animal lovers. Once, in 1920, it even precipitated a minor crisis. The affair began with a letter from Minnie Maddern Fiske, the actress, written on stationery of the National League to Conserve Food Animals. Glancing at the names on the letterhead, Lorimer may have been somewhat startled to see that the League's incorporators included Booth Tarkington, Charles Hanson Towne and Edward Bok.

"I am sure I don't exaggerate," Mrs. Fiske wrote, "when I say that I speak for thousands of other devoted friends of the Post in this letter. Thousands of Post devotees beg you to cut out these revolting articles on hunting, as they appear from time to time in the Out of Doors department. Intellectually and spiritually, the trapper and hunter belong to the Dark Ages. We don't want either of them in the pages of our beloved Saturday Evening Post. . . . Cruelty is an unpardonable sin. . . ."

Lorimer turned the letter over to Hough, with a note written on the margin: "Please take a shot at the lady." Hough's shot was a long, conciliatory letter, in which he cited his own record of forty years in outdoor journalism as a protectionist and conservationist, noting that this was also the Post's policy. He closed with a paragraph of adroit diplomacy:

"I do not know whether Mrs. Fiske wears fox fur or that of sables. I have seen a sable in a trap, half frozen, curled up in a round, furry ball, hardly able to move after two days in the steel trap. The best it could hope was that someone would kill it and give its skin to a woman to wear around her neck. I did not set the trap, and have never believed in trapping of any sort, but I know how trapping is done better than women know and I wish to say to you that of all the ghastly cruelty you ever dreamed that is the worst. It is worse than killing an animal outright—ten times worse. Men do not do that for sport, they do it for money. It is women and only women who pay them that money—through the fur traders and the shops who retail furs to women. . . . We have to write in this department to please some of the five million sportsmen of America. There are five million of them; and—well, after all, there is and can be but one Minnie Maddern Fiske!"

That ended the incident; there was no reply from Mrs. Fiske.

After Hough left the Post to concentrate on his fiction he prodded Lorimer to continue the conservation fight, although the Boss scarcely needed prodding. In a 1921 letter devoted to the plight of the antelope Hough remarked, "I believe the Saturday Evening Post is about the only branch of the government which is going to be of much use in saving the wild animals and the outdoor sport of America. It comes to rather a hopeless fight, of course, but I never yet saw a man who went into this thing that ever pulled out of it, or who ever was sorry he took a hand. Of course, I am not unmindful of your own tremendous responsibilities, and I don't suppose there is much money in crusading, but look what a walk the old Crusaders had for their money!"

Hough shared Lorimer's intense love of country, but in his case it verged on outright chauvinism. In 1919 an old-timer from the West wrote to him, correcting a supposed error in an Oregon Trail piece, and then went on to deplore the attitude of American workingmen, particularly what he termed their pro-Russian sentiments. "They have no more idea of what the real people of this country are," he wrote, "or what they will do if it comes down to cases, than so many animals. The only way they can be taught anything is to hammer it into them, and it is my opinion it has to be done, and at no distant date. . . . As a matter of fact, the conservative leaders and element are trying to hold the lid down, but one edge or the other bobs up all the time. Every meeting of a labor union or labor council is the scene of a row nowadays, often of a free-for-all fight between the radicals and the conservatives; and the radicals gaining strength every day. So keep a gun handy, for you may need it awful bad someday. You bet that I do."

Hough made this startling reply: "What you say about the lack of Americanism is too sadly true. There is trouble ahead in this country. I look for the old-time Americans to put it down, one way or another, with gentle or hard hand as the case may require. As for myself, I also keep a gun handy. It is a frontier six, and last summer, resurrecting it for the first time in years, I took five shots at a big ace of clubs, put four in the black and cut the edge of the card with the other. Just about as far as across a saloon. I think I am able to entertain any really bloodthirsty Bolsheviks."

In spite of such talk, Hough was actually a rather gentle man. He was a prime favorite in the Lorimer circle, and when he died in April 1923 the Boss wrote to his widow: "He meant more to us than a contributor. We loved him like a brother."

It was men like Hough, Garrett, Blythe, Roberts and the others who contributed most to the Post's interpretation of America, but Lorimer ranged far and wide in search of additional writers who could portray authoritatively any aspect of American life, or who could tell Americans what he, the Boss, thought they should know about events abroad. Nor did he hesitate to print articles with whose philosophies he profoundly disagreed, a particular case in point being six articles by Leon Trotsky on the Russian Revolution.

Time and again he sanctioned the use of Post articles as propaganda, but he was utterly sincere in viewing these distributions as entirely legitimate. Thus he granted George Eastman's request to reprint in pamphlet form, so that they could be distributed to Eastman Kodak employees, four articles on the income tax situation, which ran from December 1923 to January 1924.

He would not, however, open the Post's pages to patent special pleading for political and economic cure-alls. For that reason he turned down Huey P. Long as a contributor in May 1921. Long was then in Shreveport, a partner with his brother Julius in the law firm of Long and Long. Huey's letter, outlining his proposal, referred flatteringly to a 1917 Post article, "How Rich Are We?" and an editorial in 1919 "disclosing the necessity for preventing the swollen fortunes of the present day." Long asserted that he had been working for six years to find a workable solution for the problem of the "swollen fortune regime." His remedy, which he proposed to expound in a Post article, was an inheritance law which would require a testator to distribute his fortune equally among his children at his death; this, he argued, "will solve the whole problem and do no injustice to anyone."

An associate editor turned down Huey politely. In the early thirties, however, the Kingfish appeared in the Post under different auspices. Lorimer was the first to introduce Long full length as a new phenomenon in American politics, in Hermann Deutsch's "Hattie and Huey," a superb reporting job on how Huey made Hattie Caraway a senator from Arkansas.

As he covered the wide range of his magazine's interests, Lorimer did not spare expense to get what he wanted. His control over rates of payment was rigid, but he was exceedingly generous in giving writers what money they needed for expenses. A random collection of Post expense sheets shows the relatively low cost of article writing in the old days as compared with present magazine budgets. George Pattullo, who roamed the world for the Post from 1908 to 1936, submitted an expense account of $446.75 to get material for a 1922 series of five articles on "The Inside Story of the AEF." Nina Wilcox Putnam, in Hollywood from July 29 to September 9, 1921, contrived to spend only $1679.29 during the entire expedition. In 1921, Marcosson worked three and a half weeks in London, four weeks in Paris, two weeks in Brussels, four weeks in Germany, three weeks in Austria, Hungary and Czechoslovakia—expenses from Philadelphia to Philadelphia inclusive: $2600.

Entertainment for most contributors came to more substantial sums. Lorimer often had his writers as guests at Wyncote or at King's Oak, and he also had luncheons for them in the directors' room of the Curtis Building. There were sometimes three or four of these luncheons a week. Always an affable host, Lorimer put most of his guests at their ease. This was a handy attribute because a few came to the throne of the mighty with trepidation. The Boss was aware that, to some of the writers visiting Philadelphia for the first time, he was a remote and powerful figure. That impression was enhanced by the austere character of the Post's offices. Yet over luncheon with Lorimer and his editors, the visitors recovered quickly from their stage fright and went away converted to the clan of Lorimer admirers.

An exception to this happy rule were the comedians Weber and Fields. They had been invited to luncheon at the time their reminiscences were to run in the Post, the result of a double ghosting job by Felix Isman, an ex-real estate operator, and Wesley Stout. Lorimer put one of the comedians on each side of him, and he was secretly amused to note that Joe Weber, for all his assurance on the stage, was obviously frightened of the Post's editor. It happened that Lorimer had spent the week end at the White House with President Hoover, and in an effort to disarm his guests, he began an account of the week end in his wry, humorous manner. It was an unfortunate choice of topic. Weber shrank down still farther in his chair. He could hardly eat his lunch.

If that particular luncheon was not a success, the gusty story of the honored guests, when it ran in the Post, more than made up for it by rejuvenating the comedians' languishing career. They returned to the stage from virtual retirement and were soon drawing down five thousand dollars a week on the vaudeville circuits.

A luncheon guest of a different stripe was Arnold Bennett, who came to Philadelphia on a sort of royal progress during a visit to America. Lorimer arranged an elaborate luncheon for him at the Bellevue-Stratford and invited several prominent people. The affair was scheduled for one o'clock. At noon Bennett called and told Lorimer he would be an hour late because he was about to start on a visit to the Widener Galleries.

"You can come at two if you like," Lorimer informed him, "but the luncheon is going to begin at one."

Mr. Bennett arrived promptly.

The luncheon was planned carefully to consist of famous American dishes, among them diamond-back terrapin. When this course arrived Bennett tested it gingerly and asked for details.

"It's terrapin," someone told him proudly.

"Turtle?" Bennett inquired coldly, and laid down his spoon.

Promptly at two, and before dessert had been served, Bennett pulled out his watch and said he must leave for the Widener Galleries, where, he added, he would doubtless have to endure the boredom of bad pictures. He stalked from the room.

His brief appearance and the manner of his departure cast a momentary gloom on the party. Then Irvin Cobb restored everyone's spirits by rising to his feet and proposing a toast: "To Arnold Bennett, our late but not lamented guest, whose presence has made us all the fonder of his absence."

When he returned to England, Bennett sent a form bread-and-butter letter to everyone who had entertained him during his trip, explaining at length that he could not thank everyone personally who had been nice to him. The explanation did not satisfy the Boss, who was incensed by the form letter. It only enhanced his critical view of the English.

A frequent English guest was F. Britten Austin, who made more or less regular trips every two or three years and expected to be entertained like a visiting relative. Austin came, however, as a valued contributor, unlike Bennett, whose four Post pieces, con-

sisting of three articles and a short story, "Claribel," had scarcely
been representative of his best work. Austin was a prolific contributor from 1917, with his war correspondence from the
Hindenburg line, until 1930. His most significant work appeared
in 1927 and 1930. In each of those years he wrote a twelve-article
series, the first a dramatic, condensed English history for Americans, the second a series of short stories which would, as Lorimer
put it, "reflect . . . dramatic moments in history through the adventures of one or more fictitious characters whose lives and fortunes were involved in the events going forward at these historic
moments."

Perhaps the most welcome guest at the Post luncheons was Will
Rogers. There was no question of putting Will at ease. When he
came for lunch everyone would be exhausted after listening to
him for two hours, but Will would be as fresh and full of energy
as when he started. Lorimer had trouble getting a word in, and
abandoned his customary role of genial host. He was content to
sit back and laugh until he was weak.

Rogers' world-tour series in 1926, "Letters of a Self-Made
Diplomat to His President," was one of the most popular the Post
ever ran, but Lorimer did not hesitate to discriminate in sepa-
rating Will's wheat from his chaff. A year after this series he
wrote: "My dear Rogers, You may remember from your boyhood
that stuff in the Bible about the two women grinding at the mill—
how one was taken and the other was left. That's the way it is
with these two articles. The flying stuff is fine and we are glad to
have it, but, with the greatest possible admiration for Henry and
his new car, I cannot escape the conviction that it should appear
next to pure reading matter instead of *as* pure reading matter.
Otherwise it would seem that we ought to go on with a snappy
series on the Chevrolet, the Buick, the Packard, the Pierce-Arrow,
etc., ad infinitum."

Of all the visitors Lorimer entertained at the office or at home,
there were only two who gave him any difficulty. The first was
Enos Mills, whose outdoor articles appeared in the earlier Post.
When he came to Philadelphia on a visit he proved to be even
more of a rugged individualist than Lorimer. Alma invited him to

a dinner party at Wyncote, given in his honor, but Mills assured her dogmatically that he wouldn't come if he had to wear evening clothes. Alma promised that he could wear what he liked, but his insistence had irked her. She had her revenge. When Mills appeared at the party, dressed in a neat business suit, he discovered that the Lorimer place had been made up inside to look like a ranch house, and the other guests were attired in Philadelphia's idea of Western costume. Mills found himself decidedly overdressed.

The second doubtful guest was Dorothy Parker. It would be difficult to imagine two people more opposite in every respect than Mrs. Parker and Lorimer, but her week-end visit to Wyncote was innocuous enough. She exhibited none of the famed Parker poison wit. In fact, at the time (1922–23) she was a valued contributor and Lorimer was amused, or appeared to be, by the poems, short pieces and short articles she submitted. Most of them appeared on the "Short Turns and Encores" page, in which Lorimer had less interest than in any other Post department.

Even the correspondence between the two was amicable enough. Mrs. Parker, in May 1922, complained that a certain piece would not "turn out funny," perhaps because she was holidaying with her New England in-laws—but she would send it on anyway, expecting the worst.

The Boss replied: "Dear Mrs. Parker, It's here and it's a good piece. Check by the treasurer on Tuesday. My sympathies are all with Auntie. Next time you come to Philadelphia we'll play bridge and do a little tatting, in addition to a ride through the suburbs. I assume that you are hard at work on our visiting British cousins. . . ."

This and other amicable exchanges were followed a year later by the lady's appearance in Philadelphia, come to do a little tatting at Wyncote. The result was disastrous. Lorimer escorted her proudly around his acres, at the house and farm. As a friend remarked, "He showed her his broad horizons." The view only strengthened Mrs. Parker's already dark opinion of capitalist monopoly, and when she returned to New York she reviewed the week end for some of her friends with the delicate bludgeoning for which she became so conspicuous. Samples of these remarks trickled down to Philadelphia and the name of Parker disappeared quietly from the Post.

To Post veterans, it was not surprising to see the name of Dorothy Parker or anyone else in the magazine. The list of article contributors to the Post through the years was even broader than the fiction list in its infinite variety. As America's interpreter, Lorimer left no aspect untouched.

At the beginning the accent was heavily on business and politics as the magazine established its character, but it was not unusual to see something like George Ade's "Tales of a Country Town" tucked in between pieces like "Brokerage as a Business for Young Men" and "The Government and the Trusts" in 1903.

A popular 1907 symposium had a familiar ring to those who remembered it in later years: it was a compilation of opinion on the question, "Is Roosevelt a Menace to Business?" Lorimer had concluded that he wasn't, but he wanted to approach the subject from an impartial standpoint. He followed that policy more faithfully at first than later. When he might have been supporting his friend Senator Beveridge in the fight against the packing trusts, for instance, he made the Post available to J. Ogden Armour for a series of three articles on the packers in their relation to the future, to the people and to the cattle men. But no one ever saw a pro-immigration story in the Post when Lorimer was well embarked on that crusade.

Although he did not particularly rely on the business prophecies of Roger Babson, the Boss made that financial sage's advice available to Post readers from 1910 to 1924. Babson discussed the mistakes of investors, when to buy stock, the cost of living, war and business, moneymaking ideas, railroad receiverships, the coal industry, the farm problem and American self-sufficiency, among other topics. Probably the most remarkable article Babson contributed was one in 1915 with this significant title: "The War Will Not Be Over for Fifty Years."

Early in Post history Lorimer began the "inside" stories—of political battles, of celebrities' lives, and straight-from-the-source predictions of things to come. As early as 1901, Herbert L. Bridgman was disclosing "How Peary Is to Reach the Pole." In 1911, Senator Joseph L. Bristow told Post readers the inside story of the fight for the direct election of senators. From the start, too, Lorimer gave space to his political enemies. He was far from believing in Bryan's politics, but the Great Commoner contributed five articles to the Post, ranging from "The Attractions of Farming" in 1904 to his reminiscences as Secretary of State in the Wilson Cabinet. He appealed strongly to the Post's subscribers in 1906 with his dissertation on "The Moral Awakening: Simple Life vs. the Present One."

Lorimer's interest in the stage and its figures, presumably inherited from his father, was also reflected in the Post. Mrs. Patrick Campbell revealed as early as 1902 what occurs "When the Unexpected Happens," and in 1909 Billie Burke was discussing "The Actress and Her Clothes." A year later George M. Cohan contributed his thoughts on "The Actor as a Businessman."

Occasionally there appeared an article which shocked Lorimer's friends. In 1904 his business associates were amazed to see the workingman's side of the open-shop question argued fervently by Clarence Darrow.

Even before "Post luck" became a stock phrase in the trade, it seemed that Lorimer had an uncanny gift of prophecy, with such articles as Harry N. Atwood's "The Coming Atlantic Airflight," written in 1914. The Post was a better business than political forecaster, however, if one excepts the 1912 contribution by Albert Bushnell Hart, "The Third Term Ghost," and it was on far safer ground with articles like David Starr Jordan's 1900 discussion of "The College Man's Advantage in the Coming Century."

The Post was usually well ahead of the citizenry in understanding American life. As early as 1908, Waldemar Kaempffert, now the distinguished science editor of the New York *Times*, was writing about "The ABC of Flying," and he followed that piece with many forward-looking articles concerning aviation and radio. Guglielmo Marconi told in the Post for the first time in 1902 the details of "How I Thought of the Wireless Telegraph." Joseph Medill Patterson, then in his Socialist phase, speculated optimistically on the future of the nickelodeon in 1907. Theodore

Roosevelt was perturbed about "The Deceitful Red Herring" in 1912, and in the same year Woodrow Wilson advised America to "Cut Out Privilege."

During the years of the first World War, Lorimer concentrated on his pages some of the brightest names in journalism and diplomacy. When the subject was just beginning to be debated, he had Norman Angell writing frankly, "Suppose America Declared War on Germany," and a year earlier Arnold Bennett and Georges Clemenceau had stated in the Post the case for their respective countries. Lorimer assigned star reporters like Cobb, Mrs. Rinehart, Davis and Blythe to the actual fighting, and he had such roving reporters as Eleanor Egan writing from Serbia, Vienna, Turkey, India, Russia, Canada, China and the Philippines. As the war developed, Lord Northcliffe analyzed for the American public the lessons to be learned from the mistakes made by the French and British, and H. G. Wells contributed his series titled, "What Is Coming," later published as a book, and another series called "How People Think about the War."

America's participation in the war was covered with equal thoroughness in authoritative articles from Washington like Newton D. Baker's account of "The War and the War Department"; articles addressed to prospective soldiers, like Frederick Coleman's "What You Will Find When You Get to France"; and such singularly prophetic pieces as Admiral Peary's "Air Power in the United States," written in 1917.

After the war came the anomalous period in which the magazine momentarily floundered. For some observers it was a period typified by Edward Bok's 1920 Post article, "Where America Fell Short with Me."

With the arrival of new editors on the staff, the postwar era of "big names" dawned in the Post. Celebrities of stage, screen, radio, sport and government paraded through the magazine week after week. Most of this flood of reminiscence was ghostwritten. First of the personality stories, setting the pattern for the others, was James J. Corbett's "The Roar of the Crowd." Costain obtained the story through George Putnam, and it excited immediate controversy on the Post staff. Before that time the magazine had done sports only in fiction, but Lorimer cast his vote with Costain, and the Corbett series was a huge success. Corbett himself, as a result of the publicity, became one of the most sought-after lecturers and after-dinner speakers in the country.

Sports articles were subsequently so popular that, when Harry Kipke celebrated his Michigan football team in the Post, opposition stands at games away from Ann Arbor during the season were heard to chant, "Stop that Saturday Evening Post!"

In this new era of the magazine Costain even persuaded Lorimer, the ardent hater of all kinds of card games, to let him get an article on bridge from Hal Sims. The Boss especially deplored the bridge craze, but he realized that Post addicts were probably also bridge addicts, like Costain himself.

Wesley Stout, who was to succeed Lorimer, did much of the ghosting for the personalities whose stories he and Costain obtained. He rewrote the Weber and Fields reminiscences from Felix Isman's original copy, and then performed a similar service for DeWolf Hopper. The Weber and Fields series had become a book, and Hopper announced that he wanted a book too. He offered Stout a half interest in the projected volume, and the writer accepted. To make the Post series last long enough to warrant expanding it to book length, Stout had to persuade Lorimer that the one- or two-article length planned on would be inadequate. Against his better judgment the Boss stretched the series to six installments but he was prodded more by necessity than conviction: the Post's issues were so large at the time that they needed a quantity of material to fill them.

When Stout came to do Jack Dempsey's autobiography, "In This Corner," a feature of 1931, he found the Mauler "a nice guy" but unfamiliar with the ethics of literary production. The suitable reward for services rendered was a standard part of Broadway life, and although thoroughly honest himself, Dempsey found it inconceivable that a man would come from the Saturday Evening Post to write the story of his life and expect nothing in return from him. When the proofs of the story came back to Stout from their prepublication reading by Dempsey and his managers, a hundred-dollar bill was attached to them. Stout returned the money and explained the ethics of the writing business, but still Dempsey felt obligated. He sent Costain, who had been involved in the deal, a fancy cane made by a convict, and this the editor kept.

One of the most unusual ghostwriting arrangements in the history of that fabulous era occurred in 1927 when S. S. McClure returned from a trip to Italy and told Lorimer that he had been in consultation with Benito Mussolini's former mistress, Margharita Sarfatti, who had agreed to act as go-between for the purpose of getting Il Duce's autobiography. A go-between was necessary, Sam explained, because no one had ready access to Mussolini except Sarfatti, who saw him more often than most others. A ghost writer was needed because ex-journalist Mussolini was not accustomed to writing for American publications, and besides, he was occupied with the affairs of the Fascist party. However, he was willing to collaborate for forty thousand dollars —collaboration came high at that time—and McClure asked for fifteen thousand dollars, payable in three installments, for his offices as agent on the deal. Lorimer agreed.

Looking over his stable, he picked Roberts to do the ghosting, since Roberts had written two series of Post articles on the beginning of the Fascist party, and had many influential friends in Rome, among them Salvatore Cortesi, head of the Associated Press in Italy, and Arnaldo Cortesi, head of the Rome Bureau of the New York *Times*.

Roberts, who was in Florida working on a series of articles, was recalled to Philadelphia, though Lorimer well knew that Roberts would not relish being assigned to a ghostwriting chore, even for Mussolini.

It took all the Boss's persuasive power to convince Roberts that he was elected. The doomed man protested violently that he did not want to do ghostwriting, that he viewed the whole proposition with extreme distaste, but in the end he agreed and went to New York to consult McClure, who was to act as entrepreneur in the getting and writing of Mussolini's "inside story."

McClure was in his eighties, and Roberts found him "garrulous, over-optimistic and vague" about the manner in which the story was to be obtained. The "contract" was written on a single sheet of note paper. It was merely a statement that if McClure would furnish a book Mussolini would sign it if he found it satisfactory. The statement was signed by both Mussolini and Sarfatti. Since Lorimer had instructed Roberts specifically that the Post didn't want the story unless Mussolini himself was willing to give plenty of time to it, Roberts telephoned Lorimer from New York and reported that he thought McClure was in his dotage and that the outlook, in his opinion, was dark, sour and smelly. He added that, since he had started, he'd keep going, but he didn't propose to travel on the same ship with McClure and be exposed to endless hours of drivel: he'd jump the *Conte Rosso*, which sailed the next day, two weeks ahead of McClure's ship.

"All right," Lorimer agreed, "but don't let them put anything over on you."

In Rome, Roberts lost no time getting in touch with Sarfatti, whom he found "a dumpy, hard-voiced, coarse-skinned bleached blonde from North Italy."

His interview with this lady confirmed his worst fears. When he pointed out to her that he would have to be allowed to have several personal interviews with Mussolini in order to do the right sort of job, Sarfatti explained that this was impossible. Mussolini was a busy man, engrossed in affairs of state. He had no time to waste on a book! The book, she said, must be compiled from a volume which she herself had written on Mussolini, from a collection of speeches and newspaper articles for which Mussolini was supposedly responsible, and from hitherto unpublished material written by Mussolini's brother Arnaldo. Moreover, when the book—eight installments of ten thousand words each—was finished, it would be thrice edited: first by McClure, then by Sarfatti, and finally by Il Duce.

Roberts snorted. Sarfatti looked offended and asked coldly how *he* thought he should be allowed to proceed. Roberts replied that he should be given at least forty personal interviews with Mussolini, of at least half an hour apiece—one interview at the end of each two thousand words of manuscript—and that he could do with considerably less editing.

Sarfatti was outraged. Roberts, she said, did not know what he was saying! Let him imagine the situation reversed! Let him imagine that she herself wished to write similarly about President Herbert Hoover. Let him imagine her, with her imperfect knowledge of English, requesting forty personal interviews with Mr. Hoover! Ha-ha! She would be ejected forcibly from the United States!

Not at all, Roberts told her. If the situation were reversed—if the United States were in Italy's position, that is, with a government open to criticism, as was the Fascist government, and wished to be placed in a favorable light before the world in a magazine as influential as the Saturday Evening Post—Mr. Hoover would see that Signora Sarfatti had not only forty personal interviews with him, but eighty if necessary, in addition to being supplied with all necessary interpreters and facilities.

That ended the interview and terminated any hope of a rapport between Signora Sarfatti and Mr. Roberts. The gentleman from the Post ignored the Roman finagler's penetrating glares and retired to his hotel, to await the coming of McClure.

Sam arrived and emerged white-faced from his first session with Sarfatti. He reported to Roberts, with masterful understatement, that the lady had assured him they had "got the wrong man." McClure urged Roberts to be reasonable, but Roberts continued to repeat Lorimer's instructions—that the story wasn't wanted unless Mussolini himself would give it his time and attention. The story, Roberts insisted further, was to be Mussolini's, and not a secondhand biography compiled from the works of brothers, ex-mistresses, press agents and special pleaders.

In desperation McClure offered to turn over to Roberts the last five-thousand-dollar installment of his Post payments if the story were handled as he and Sarfatti wished it handled. It was the only time Roberts had been offered a bribe in his entire experience as a correspondent.

To escape Italian censorship, Roberts went to Monte Carlo and filed a cable to Lorimer: "McClure says impossible get story way you outlined. Material necessarily got through Sarfatti; Rossoni, former editor American Socialist newspaper; Mussolini's brother

Arnaldo; various officials; sundry books on Fascism; Mussolini's speeches, and Fascist press bureau. Says impossible follow your wishes as Mussolini would never agree to personal co-operation, and might revoke contract if crowded. Neither Sarfatti nor McClure dares put proposition squarely before him. Thinks with phenomenal luck might have few moments with him once a month but never his assistance in preparing material. Declares six months shortest time doing story McClure's way, subject triple supervision, maybe longer. His opinion everything handsomely covered using his methods. He will donate last 5000 installment toward expenses man writing story. Believe delays connected with McClure's method extremely trying and material far removed from your outline. Do not agree with McClure it would be Mussolini's inside story. This cannot be delivered by Sarfatti or anyone else. By time McClure and Sarfatti finish editing and Italian translation made for Mussolini's approval, story might have flavor cheese: not Mussolini. Also doubt Sarfatti able hold Mussolini in line if decided book or method of writing undesirable."

Roberts caught the next boat home. When he reported to the Post he found Richard Washburn Child, one-time ambassador to Italy, conferring with Lorimer. The Boss called him in to give Child a firsthand account of his experiences with McClure and Sarfatti, since Child felt that his own personal knowledge of Italy and the Italians might prevail on Mussolini to write his real "inside story." Roberts insisted that any Mussolini story would be instigated and supervised by McClure, Sarfatti and Arnaldo Mussolini, and must inevitably be worthless as inside stuff and duller than ditch water.

A week later Child sailed for Italy on the same assignment, and in a remarkably short time Mussolini's "inside story"—slightly edited translations of articles by Arnaldo Mussolini—appeared in eight installments which bore titles characteristic of the Fascist dream: "War and Its Effects upon a Man," "The Death Struggle of a Worn-out Democracy," "The Garden of Fascism," "Toward the Conquest of Power," "Thus We Took Rome," "Five Years of Government," "New Paths" and "En Route." Two years later another pair of articles collectively titled "My War Diary" were published. The series was received with only mild interest by the Post audience and, published as a book by Scribner's, was a dismal failure.

The Post "regulars"—seasoned correspondents like Blythe, Cobb, Irwin, Roberts and Marcosson—frequently grumbled discontentedly among themselves over Lorimer's occasional weakness for "specialists" who had been diplomats; but they never suffered long. "Specialists" such as Child and Norval Richardson were unable to work as carefully and arduously as trained reporters, and inevitably, after writing a series or two for Lorimer, they vanished permanently from the Post's columns, thereafter to be referred to by the Boss as "soubrettes."

Like Herbert Hoover and other distinguished but unobservant Americans, Lorimer admired Mussolini's efficiency. He did not take him seriously. Similarly, when Hitler came to power he thought the Fuehrer a clown. He did not believe there were either villains or heroes in Europe.

Consequently he presented stories from abroad to Post readers with the simple intention of keeping his public informed, and strange names appeared in the magazine. Franz von Papen was represented in 1933 with "Germany's Place in the Tropical Sun." George Sylvester Viereck wrote in 1926 a relatively innocuous article setting forth "Kaiser Wilhelm's Views on Love and Marriage," but he chose to be anonymous in 1929 with his own views on war propaganda, in a five-part series. Lorimer despised Viereck personally, but he printed the man's articles because he intended them to be an antidote for what he considered British propaganda.

Dorothy Thompson contributed one of the few politically aware articles in the disturbed years after the Great Crash. Her 1931 piece, "Something Must Happen," subtitled "German Youth Demands a Different World," was ominously accurate.

Aside from politics, however, the Post was filled in the twenties and early thirties with the names that were bright and familiar to Americans in that era. A surprising number of them are already forgotten. They were all, whether overnight sensations or permanent fixtures in the national scene, quite humble about getting in the Post. Richard E. Byrd wrote to Lorimer in November 1927,

after the Boss had accepted his first article, "The X in Exploration," and declared frankly, "It has been the height of my ambition to get an article in the Saturday Evening Post."

Lorimer was impartial where fame was concerned. He accepted
the work of known figures like Byrd, but he was also willing to
read and publish the exploits of unknowns like Richard Halliburton, twenty-two years old and just out of Princeton, who wrote
from Barcelona in 1921, enclosing a nine-thousand-word article
on "Andorra, the Doll Democracy." Halliburton explained his
submission modestly: "I feel a narration of this experience not un-
worthy of the Saturday Evening Post, for though I undertook the
trip not as a correspondent but as an adventurer, the season, the
observations and the interviews were of such an unusual and interesting a nature that I felt it would be selfish not to share them
with the reading public."

Reading the files of the Post in that last decade or so of Lorimer's editorship is like viewing a cross section of what America
was doing and thinking in an era which now seems like ancient
history. There was Alexander, the Grand Duke of Russia, writing
about "Tight-Rope Walking as Practiced by Royalty," and Roy
Chapman Andrews spinning yarns of his adventures in the Gobi
Desert. Bugs Baer wrote the gaudy history of Madison Square
Garden. Princess Marthe Bibesco gossiped in print about royalty,
and the Earl of Birkenhead preceded a long procession of his
visiting countrymen by taking a British view of America. Artur
Bodanzky discussed his fourteen years at the Metropolitan Opera
House. Evangeline Booth asserted in 1928 that "Some Have
Stopped Drinking." The life stories of Fanny Brice and Luther
Burbank were almost cheek and jowl. James M. Cain, on the eve
of more profitable sex and slaughter, wrote wittily of Frank Mer-
riwell. Red Cagle contemplated his football glories and Uncle
Joe Cannon lectured the faithful on party discipline. Eddie Cantor
recalled his career as an entrepreneur of musical comedy and
children, while Frank Carideo mulled over the kind of quarter-
backs produced by Knute Rockne. Maurice Chevalier disclosed
"How I Got That Way."

Dr. A. S. M. Rosenbach's articles on rare books brought a flood of mail as Post readers ransacked their attics for hidden fortunes. A man in Port Chester, New York, found a Button Gwinnett signature, that scarcest of all Declaration of Independence signers, and it brought a reported fifty-one thousand dollars. In the same vein, a short article in 1925 by Vincent Starrett titled "Have You a Tamerlane in Your Attic?" was a question asked only half seriously because just five copies of this rarest American first edition were known to exist. A Worcester, Massachusetts, housewife read the article, poked around in her attic and found a sixth copy, now in Owen D Young's library.

Then there were Richard Washburn Child's ten articles on crime in 1925, intended to shock the American public into action and at the same time establish Childs as Marcosson's successor. The first purpose was successful in the most startling manner. Child's first article hit the stands on the same day that five bandits shot up the Drake Hotel in Chicago, thus beginning the legend of "Post luck." Even with such a spectacular beginning, Childs was unable to fill Ike's peripatetic shoes.

The parade went on. Christopher, Prince of Greece, figuratively took off his shoes and sat down in a rocker to chat comfortably with Americans about "This King Business." Winston Churchill for the first time projected a United States of Europe, in 1930. Glenna Collett argued the merits of women's golf games, and Josephus Daniels was even more vociferous in behalf of a big navy. Mr. Daniels was soon under the heavy fire of Billy Mitchell, who appeared bluntly in 1925 with "Aircraft Dominates Seacraft" and "How Should We Organize Our National Air Power?" Elmer Davis wrote a thoughtful piece titled "Radio among the Ruins" in 1923, but Lee de Forest was more optimistic by 1928 with "Radio Comes of Age." Paul de Kruif temporarily forsook medical popularizing in 1933 to chronicle the story of Boss Kettering, while Sir Henri Deterding told in the same year all that could be told about the life of an international oilman.

Still they came. Jack Donahue tapped out the record of a hoofing career. Will Durant asked soberly whether our civilization was dying and whether democracy was doomed, but Americans were more interested in reading Lieutenant Commander Edward

Ellsberg's dramatic submarine story, "On the Bottom." Geraldine Farrar and Bud Fisher confessed the sins of singing and cartooning at about equal length. Henry Ford was inspirational in "The Modern Opportunity" and appeared at numerous other times, solo and in collaboration; nearly all his Post efforts, no matter how signed, were written by Samuel Crowther, who was in effect the official chronicler of the Ford empire.

It was comforting, in a sense, to find both Gatti-Casazza and Rube Goldberg reminiscing in the Post, jointly offsetting a consideration by Eugene Grace of "Distributed Property." John Gunther appeared inside a Viennese restaurant in 1933, exploring the processes of preparing "Cabbages for Kings." Eamon de Valera was the subject of an article by Francis Hackett, so authoritative and expert a study that Lorimer picked it to lead an issue. And Hermann Hagedorn reported what Teddy Roosevelt had talked about with his physician.

Ralph Ingersoll was still an obscure laborer in the journalistic vineyard in 1925 when he wrote "The Magic Disk," an article about radio; Jeritza and Elsie Janis were old and tired celebrities at about the same time. The magic of the stage was further rehearsed by Leslie Howard and Sol Hurok. Hugh S. Johnson traced the flight of the Blue Eagle from egg to earth, and wrote to Lorimer: "I hope the ants-in-pants episode will give you eight sellouts." It did.

Alva Johnston introduced the art of profiling with a sideview of Fiorello H. LaGuardia, and Sir Harry Lauder was found appropriately "Roamin' in the Gloamin'." Lindbergh told what it felt like to fly the Atlantic. Vachel Lindsay was outspoken about "What It Means to Be a Poet in America." Harold Lloyd spoke of his career as "An American Comedy." Rear Admiral T. P. Magruder anticipated most of his gold-braided colleagues with an article on aircraft carriers. The lives of Marie, Queen of Rumania, and Groucho Marx bore oddly reversed titles, Marie's being simply "My Life" and later "My Life as a Crown Princess," while Groucho recalled the time "When I Was Young and Charming."

The lives of Graham McNamee, Helen Wills Moody and Charles Paddock were immortalized in type. Drew Pearson had not yet acquired his crystal ball, but he was turning in excellent reporting from Havana and way points. Nor had Westbrook Pegler yet learned the financial advantage of kicking other people in the backside from behind a typewriter, and in 1924 he was so retiring that his article on "Bums" appeared anonymously. George Rector conducted a gastronomic tour of Philadelphia, New Orleans, Boston, California, Mexico, France, Italy, Austria, Germany, Normandy and England.

Vincent Richards anticipated the *Reader's Digest* in 1926 by condensing the history of tennis into three articles. History of another variety was made in the Post contributions of Carl Sandburg and Edna St. Vincent Millay. Al Smith and John Philip Sousa summarized their careers, and Henry L. Stimson pondered heavily on American policy in Nicaragua. Mark Sullivan was lost in contemplation of the unfortunate proximity of Herbert Hoover to the world depression.

It was the day of Norma Talmadge and the rising star of Hendrik Willem van Loon, and of Alexander Woollcott's batch of whimsey which brought the story of Irving Berlin's career to a date approximately midway.

Nearly all this fare came easily to the Post table, but there were difficult exceptions. One of the most difficult was a tasty dish indeed—Ike Hoover's reminiscences as White House chief attendant, published in 1934. Costain had visited Ike intermittently at the White House for five years, trying to get a commitment from him. Ike had told him many stories, and intimated that much of his life was already in writing, but he gave no promises. Then one day he was dead and Costain went to Washington to see his widow. He found her in the humble semidetached house in the suburbs where the couple had lived for years. It was an odd contrast to the splendor of the White House: Ike had been a part of that splendor so long that the world he lived in away from it seemed incongruous.

Mrs. Hoover told Costain that her husband had left his literary notes in an old hatbox upstairs, which she showed him willingly. The Post's man made her promise that she would not show the notes to anyone else until he could send someone down from

Philadelphia. He returned and Lorimer dispatched Stout to investigate the possibilities of the hatbox. In two days he wired back: "This is a gold mine."

The Post offered twenty-five thousand dollars for the notes. If Lorimer had offered five thousand dollars he could have had them without question, but the high price was a giveaway of their value and there was some hedging and talk of other offers. In the end the original price was agreed upon, and Stout did the articles.

They made a memorable series, but some of the best stories did not go into the articles nor into the book they made. Ike had been overly frank in his conversations with Costain, and voiced opinions he would never have committed to paper. He told Costain that he hadn't liked Taft, despised Coolidge, but adored Wilson. "You know," he said one day, "I don't think Mr. Wilson ever signed those bills they sent over that went back with his signature. He was too sick a man. When a delegation of congressmen was expected to bring over a bill for his signature, or to see him, they'd prop him up in bed and put some artificial color in his cheeks so he'd last long enough for a short interview." Who did sign the bills then? Costain asked. Ike winked and let it be known that he thought Mrs. Wilson had signed them.

In fashioning the Post pattern, it was Stout and Costain and the others who gathered up the threads of American life and brought them into the office, but it was always Lorimer who did the weaving—selecting here, encouraging there, until he had the rich fabric he wanted.

One of his last editorial acts at the Post in 1936 was to buy a series of articles by Gertrude Stein on the subject of money, a topic he had hitherto entrusted only to economists, financiers and top-drawer reporters. The rest of the staff was in solid opposition to this purchase, but Lorimer prevailed.

"Why did you buy that stuff, Boss?" one of the editors asked him later.

Lorimer seemed surprised.

"Because it amused me," he said.

That was as much the answer in 1936 as it had been in 1899.

CHAPTER SIX

The Post and Politics

Ed Howe wrote: "I often think a thing is not really published in the United States until it appears in the Saturday Evening Post."

That opinion was shared to some extent by nine Presidents of the United States, who wrote for the Post and saw the issues of their administrations argued in it for the benefit of a powerful section of the electorate. The Post had a threefold connection with the White House: first, by opening its pages to the Presidents; second, by virtue of Sam Blythe's pre-eminence as a Washington correspondent; and third, by reason of both Lorimer's and Blythe's friendships with several of the Presidents.

The Post-reading public was given the feeling, and an accurate intimation it was, that the magazine was close to the core of government, that its political analyses were based on something far more concrete than speculation. Not until Franklin D. Roosevelt entered the White House did this familiar magic fail, and the failure, when it came, seemed all the more striking because Lorimer and the Post had been closer to Roosevelt's predecessor than to any other President.

Much of what the earlier Presidents wrote for the Post was

superficial. Few of the eighteen pieces Grover Cleveland contributed after his return to private life were more than innocuous
reflections on the pleasures of sportsmen. Some of them, like "The
Mission of Fishing and Fishermen" and "The Serene Duck
Hunter," appeared in 1906 as a book, "Fishing and Shooting
Sketches." Others were historically important—"The President
and His Patronage," "The Cleveland Bond Issues," and "Strength
and Needs of Civil Service Reform"—and these were published
in 1904 as a book called "Presidential Problems."

Ghostwriting had not attained its popularity in the public
service and Cleveland wrote the articles himself, a fact made self-
evident by the commonplace quality of his prose. It was difficult
work for him to write, but Lorimer's checks for twenty-five
hundred dollars per story were undoubtedly a stimulus to his
literary efforts. Tempting offers to write his autobiography were
refused, however; Cleveland felt safer when he was dealing with
ducks and broad issues.

Benjamin Harrison appeared in the Post after he left the White
House with a postscript to his philosophy called "The Obligations
of Wealth," a respectable and uninspiring piece of work. Mc-
Kinley, who succeeded him, wrote a Post article before his elec-
tion but it was on the unassailable topic of "Washington as a
Statesman," and was not published until he was securely in
Washington.

Theodore Roosevelt was another who wrote after the expira-
tion of his term, but his 1912 article, "The Deceitful Red Herring,"
attracted wide attention. A year later he gave his views on the
Progressive fight to H. B. Needham in an exclusive interview.
The Post was deeply involved in that conflict, having stood in
substance with the Progressives. The most important piece on the
subject came from the other side, on October 19, 1912, when
President Taft argued his views on "The Supreme Issue," an
article written, published and paid for while Taft was still in the
White House. Later Taft wrote seven more Post articles, on such
subjects as the relation of the courts to the Progressive party, an
argument for economy and efficiency in government, military
and naval defense, votes for women, the future of the Republi-

can party, and his autobiographical "Personal Aspects of the Presidency."

Woodrow Wilson's single contribution to the Post, his eloquent article, "Cut Out Privilege," which appeared shortly before his election, made his political philosophy clear. It was not the philosophy of Lorimer, and the split between the two men widened, more particularly in the second term. Initially there had been close co-operation. In the May 23, 1914, issue there appeared an article by Sam Blythe, "Mexico: The Record of a Conversation with President Wilson." This was a statement of presidential policy on several vital points. Wilson had planned a message to Congress covering the points in the interview, and he promised to delay it until the Post had appeared with Blythe's article. He kept his promise.

After the war Warren Harding gave what he appeared to consider an important interview to A. R. Pinci, and it was printed in the summer before his election as "The Conscience of the Republic." It made more interesting reading later on than it did at the time.

Calvin Coolidge did not write for the Post while he was in office, but he contributed three articles to the *Ladies' Home Journal* which were delivered on January 30, 1929, and paid for immediately. They were published in the April, May and June issues, and it was understood that Coolidge had purposely delayed their publication until his successor was in office. Later, at Lorimer's suggestion, Coolidge wrote three articles for the Post, in 1931–32, designed to inject some enthusiasm into the failing Republican party. But Mr. Coolidge's pronouncements on debts and taxes, "Party Loyalty and the Presidency" and "The Republican Case," convinced only those who were already convinced.

The Post's support of Herbert Hoover, which was more intense than for any other occupant of the White House, took the form primarily of articles and editorials rather than emanations from the man himself, since Lorimer was well aware of Hoover's limitations as a self-publicist. The Post was, in effect, Hoover's public relations counsel, and if it failed, the fault lay more with the client than the counsel. Hoover's Post articles were written long before his election and were concerned primarily with post-war readjustment. Even then Lorimer was preparing his man for high office.

Franklin D. Roosevelt appeared only once in the Post, discussing through Donald Wilhelm in 1920 the question, "Can the Vice-President Be Useful?" He suggested other articles to Lorimer in the twenties but met with a polite refusal. In 1934 the Boss made his single gesture to Roosevelt as President when he invited him, through Louis Howe, to explain his intentions in the Post. Mr. Roosevelt refused, but Howe contributed a fine article on the President's personal qualities.

Lorimer's approach to politics was pragmatic. His only ideal was America first. In a 1926 interview with John B. Kennedy in *Collier's*, he put his whole philosophy into a paragraph of quotation: "Early in my years as an editor," he told Kennedy, "I suffered from the common delusion of young idealists, and of many older idealists, that the organized action we call politics could bring about improvement in our national life before the people could be brought to demand improvement. That is an error quickly discerned. Sound ideas must be infiltrated through persistent education, which is a function of constructive journalism. Our country owes its first duty to itself. International amity is good, international co-operation for peace is good, but I oppose the League of Nations not because of its promises but because of its failures to perform. . . ."

Lorimer was against Henry Ford's Peace Ship on principle, but the manufacturer he so much admired in other respects nearly alienated him forever by an egregious error in his telegram inviting the Post's editor to join him in the 1915 expedition to end the war. The wire was addressed properly to the editor of the Saturday Evening Post, then it began, "Will you not, as manager of the largest woman's magazine in the world, be my guest aboard the Oscar II . . ." To be confused with Bok was more than Lorimer could bear.

As much as he opposed the League and the means Wilson proposed to achieve world peace, Lorimer showed no inclination to be led down the private paths of the League's most ardent enemies,

even when the issue was no longer paramount. The friends of
Lodge and Knox did their best, however. This was the letter Senator Medill McCormick wrote Lorimer in April 1923, at a time
when he was chairman of the committee on expenditures in the
executive departments:

"I wonder if you will feel it consistent with your policy to publish some philosophic comment by an American politician upon
our ingenuous attitude toward the international Tammany which
manages or mismanages Europe? As you know, I shared the late
Senator Knox's opinion regarding the Treaty of Versailles and
the League of Nations; regarding the outlawry of war and the
horrid legalization of war. The legal luminaries and literati who
generally grace the State Department do not know European
politics. It happens that I know them very much as a City Hall
reporter knows Philadelphia, New York, or Chicago politics. It
happens that I learned French as a baby. Thus, at the instance of
my parents, I have been able to talk the lingo of the political bosses
of Europe. To do business with them, a man should be able to
carry the river wards, and to do his mathematics in French. He
ought to be a mixture of Jim Reed and George Wickersham,
shaken well before using. I am for altruism, but sophisticated altruism. Do you think an article along these lines would be acceptable?"

Lorimer wrote "file" across this letter. There is no record of
his answer.

At the same time, he never hesitated to fight by whatever means
possible any threat, real or imaginary, to the kind of America he
loved. In 1921 he lent the Post's support to all sorts of super-
patriotic schemes for combating what the frightened conservatives believed was a Red plot to seize the United States, a nightmare that had been haunting them at intervals for decades.

The Boss had the support of respectable public figures in this
minority hysteria, which has since been amply documented.
Thomas A. Edison wrote to him in February 1921, commending
the work of the Better America Federation of California, which
was conducting a "campaign in California by opposing Bolshevik

propagandists on their own ground and in their own way by soapbox orators." Edison had recently advocated this technique in newspaper interviews. He went on: "I am informed that the Federation . . . has been in communication with you, asking you to aid in furthering this project through your tremendous circulation, and trust that this simple means of combating Bolshevik propaganda will make a sufficient appeal to your imagination to warrant your manifesting an interest in the subject."

Lorimer replied: "Some weeks ago we printed an article dealing with this matter of meeting the Bolshevist soapbox campaign with one of the same nature and it was enthusiastically received. I expect to do something more along the same line a little later."

It was in the twenties and thirties that the Post earned its reputation for ultraconservatism. At the beginning of Lorimer's regime it was on the fence, as Lorimer was, concerned more with the discussion of public issues than with taking sides. It rarely published critical articles in the early 1900s.

Lorimer was drawn into the political arena through his two friends, Sam Blythe and Albert Beveridge. Once involved, he quickly assumed the role of behind-the-scenes manipulator and the Post was in politics up to its ears from that time onward.

The relationship between Blythe, Beveridge and Lorimer was a curious one. Blythe was the complete cynic, Beveridge the fiery idealist, and Lorimer the catalyst between the two. When Blythe was the New York *World's* Washington man and Beveridge was beginning his crusade against the big-business domination of Congress, there was a natural enmity between them. Blythe continually needled Beveridge in print, and once, in conversation, was so bitterly scornful that he came literally to the point of spitting in the senator's eye. Recalling that incident many years later, Lorimer remarked briefly: "Sam was justified."

The Boss's attitude toward Beveridge was an odd mixture of warm friendship and an aloofness that sometimes bordered on contempt. The trouble between them was Beveridge's fundamental liberalism; the bond between them was the Indianan's passionate love for America.

As the *World's* correspondent, Sam Blythe had been hostile to

Beveridge, but when he switched to the Post he found himself writing about a man who had long been a friend of Lorimer's and he began to see some good in the senator. Fortunately the growing split in the Republican party gave these three disparate men an issue which united them. The rock upon which the Republicans began to split was the tariff issue, and both Lorimer and Blythe approached that question from a broad business point of view. They saw in a more practical way what Beveridge perceived from the standpoint of fundamental justice: that the high-tariff policy of the Payne-Aldrich bloc would benefit the big-business combines but that it would inevitably have an adverse effect on the nation's economy.

Aside from politics, Beveridge and Lorimer were in complete agreement on the enjoyment of living, even though the senator lacked the Boss's sense of humor. They loved the outdoors and long hours of conversation. Where Lorimer's play hours with Sam Blythe were on the convivial side, those he spent with Beveridge were concentrated at Wyncote, on the broad acres of King's Oak, and amid the friendly pleasures of the senator's Massachusetts farm. When Beveridge came to visit, the Lorimer household was not unaware of his presence. His usual state was the heat of argument and he pounded the table at breakfast, luncheon and dinner until the dishes jumped. By contrast with his intense, vital manner, Lorimer appeared even more calm and judicial. The Boss enjoyed the contrast and he had an intense respect for the scholarly side of his friend. It was Lorimer with whom Beveridge discussed his monumental life of John Marshall, and later his unfinished life of Lincoln. Lorimer read this last work as it went along. Beveridge sent it to him in fragments, with such comments as, "In these chapters you will find color—yellow and green, and streaks of scarlet, but no purple and gold as yet."

The two men met at the start of Lorimer's magazine career, through their common friend, David Graham Phillips. Beveridge had risen in the world of politics almost as rapidly as Mr. Curtis' new editor had climbed in the world of journalism. Five years older than Lorimer, he had been sent to the Senate by his native Indiana at the age of thirty-six. Phillips, his roommate at DePauw

University, introduced him to Lorimer soon after and the friendship between the two was as instant as it had been with Phillips and Beveridge. This meeting took place in the early spring of 1900. Beveridge had just returned from a trip to the Philippines, where he had observed the fruits of America's expansion at first hand. The Boss asked him to write six Post articles on his experiences, and Beveridge grasped the opportunity eagerly. It would be an important blow struck in the cause of the new American imperialism, of which he was the chief advocate, and it would certainly advance his political fortunes. Besides, it was necessary for senators and other needy public servants to write for magazines in those days, otherwise they would be short of funds for the vacations they needed.

Despite these great expectations for the articles he prepared, Beveridge was pleased and astonished by their reception, which far surpassed anything he had dared hope for them. He wrote to Lorimer: "Nothing has appeared in any magazine this year which has received the liberal and favorable newspaper notice that has been accorded the American soldier articles, and I hear from them on all sides."

The Philippines trip was followed by another, this time to Russia and the Orient. Beveridge proposed to finance the trip by writing for the Post, and possibly for other magazines. He had declared that while he was in the Senate he would never "buy or sell any stocks or anything of the kind," consequently he was dependent on his writing for extralegislative income.

Beveridge's view of Russia, when he began to send back his observations to the Post, coincided neatly with Lorimer's. As a Hamiltonian, he was impressed by the strong central government of the Tsar, and the voice of the people reached his ears not at all. Claude G. Bowers, his biographer, has pointed out that Beveridge was oblivious of approaching events in Russia, as Gouverneur Morris had been in the France of the Bourbons. He saw only power and authority. "I have never been impressed," he wrote from Moscow, "with the idea . . . that the Russian Government was destined to crumble and finally disappear, perhaps, as some writers have suggested, in a second 'terror' surpassing the awful

days of the French Revolution. Such talk appears to me to be
wild, absurd, ill informed. . . ."

Beveridge planned his articles on Russia and Manchuria while he
was on the voyage home, and they began running in the Post in
November 1901, continuing until late in the spring of 1902. It
was the first time that millions of Americans had ever been faced
with a consideration of what lay across the Pacific, and the articles
were widely discussed, thereby adding prestige both to the senator
and to the Post.

By this time Lorimer had become convinced of Beveridge's
value as a writer, and the friendship between them had ripened.
Sam Blythe was still sarcastic and unrelenting in his *World* observations of Beveridge's conduct, but he was compelled to admit
that his victim was "a good sport." The only part of Beveridge's
conduct that alarmed Lorimer was a characteristic he himself
shared: a tendency to revise copy right down to the last galley.
Often these revisions were done at Wyncote, because Beveridge
always planned to spend a night there whenever he was within
reach of Philadelphia. No one could make him feel so relaxed as
Lorimer. The Boss had a sparkle and wit that the usually serious
Beveridge could appreciate but not achieve. Their correspondence
shows clearly the nature of the relationship between them. Beveridge's letters are full of his plans and ideas and hopes and fears.
Lorimer's are encouraging, prodding, and always witty.

Most of Beveridge's Post contributions were inspired by Lorimer, and the senator always listened to his proposals. He had a
profound respect for the editor's ability to sense the public
temper. A typical Beveridge letter answering a Lorimer suggestion is this one from Indianapolis, dated May 19, 1904:

"Just got back from your stamping ground in Chicago. I will
give you an answer on the Roosevelt matter next week. I think I
shall do it. What do you think about that idea of a joint discussion of issues? Would it not be well, whether I write the article
on Roosevelt or someone else writes it, to have the two articles
appear one immediately after the other? This by way of suggestion. I met your old friend Valentine, of Armour's, President
Earling of the North Western road—or I don't know what road—

and several other fellows in Chicago, all of whom were loud in their praise of Lorimer. You can imagine the pleasure that gave me. I asked Earling whether he had read your book. He said, 'Well, haven't I! I pick it up and read something from it nearly every night.' Isn't that fine? . . ."

At that time both Beveridge and Lorimer were still a reasonable distance from Roosevelt's philosophy. Railroad presidents were their friends and trust busting was not an enthusiasm with them. Then the Hearst papers started the tidal wave of muckraking. S. S. McClure introduced the technique to magazines with Ida Tarbell's articles on Standard Oil and exposés of Wall Street manipulation. Phillips joined the march, writing on something that was close to his friend Beveridge's heart, "The Treason of the Senate." In this article he pointed out a fact that was becoming painfully clear to the senator from Indiana, namely, that there were powerful and influential men in the Senate who were not motivated by high principle, nor by any principle at all except that of vested privilege. Lorimer, the romanticist and dramatist of business life, building a magazine on the nation's interest in business, was not blind to this increasing domination of the nation's legislators by ruthless trusts, and he was wise enough to know that a government dominated by business would ultimately be corrosive to both sides.

Of the two men, Beveridge was at first the more reluctant Progressive. In 1906, beset by ideas which seemed radical to him, he wrote an article titled, "The Rich Man in Politics" and sent it to Lorimer with a note saying it was not for publication. Lorimer was eager to publish it, however, and Beveridge began to weaken in his decision as he witnessed successive outrages of honest government on the Hill. "I am not so dead sure that I don't feel like letting you print that article," he wrote. "It surely needs to be done by somebody, and on the other hand, a defense of the Senate as an institution is needed to be printed by somebody, although, God knows, there could be no defense of some of the men of that body."

The article was published at last in June 1906. It shocked friends of the author, the editor and the magazine. What it said now seems elementary, although the issues it raised are still far from settled.

"We must always remember," Beveridge wrote, "that this is a government of the people; but if public office is occupied by possessors of great wealth, the mass of the people, among whom, after all, throughout all history, the ablest governing ability has always been found, will be excluded from practical participation in the management of public affairs. . . .

"Yes, and a man who is rich and personally agreeable can secure the nomination for, and election to, an office over a man who is far better equipped for public duty. . . .

"Capital is all right in its place. It has a mission, and a mighty and beneficent mission it is. I do not object to capital. I defend it —only let it attend to its own business. And public life and special legislation for its own benefit are not its business.

"But the vote of the rich man in public life, cast in the interest of his own investments, is only the beginning of his practical mischief. Universally, such men are great entertainers. They give sumptuous and delightful dinners. They are friendly men, too; and in addition to that tremendous ability which won their immense wealth, they frequently have a singular charm of manner. Thus they make personal friends among their associates—and blood is thicker than water in public just as it is anywhere else."

This article was the beginning of Beveridge's split with Senator Aldrich, powerful ruler of the Senate, and the clique which supported him. Aldrich and his friends represented the big-business interests which had seized Congress. They were incensed by the article, and it also embarrassed some rich congressmen who were up for re-election. Most important, it served notice on the rulers of the Republican party that Beveridge was not undeviating in his allegiance to them. By 1908 his enemies in the party—and they were also, in the main, the enemies of President Roosevelt—were able to maneuver him out of his deserved selection as keynoter of the convention that year. He had been so certain of the choice that he had already written the address. In this skirmish Lorimer was faithfully at his side. He wrote: "Are you willing and can you write that keynote speech which you are not going to deliver at the Convention, for the Saturday Evening Post?" But Beveridge's disappointment was too keen; he preferred to pass over the slight, for the moment.

After Taft was nominated Beveridge talked with him at Hot Springs and came away convinced that the bulky candidate did not intend to forsake the principles and reforms of the progressive Republicans. On the strength of that visit he wrote a pre-election piece for the Post on "The Issue," in which he further offended his conservative enemies, including some of Taft's advisers. His article asserted: "For the last year there has been a determined effort, not only to check, but also to turn back, this mighty movement for common honesty in trade and righteousness in business upon which the American people have entered. Great forces— the greatest financial forces in history—are determined that it shall be turned back. Master minds—by far the most resourceful in the Republic or in the world—have been planning, and are planning now, to turn it back. Unlimited wealth is at their disposal, the craftiest minds in politics at work. . . . Our whole financial system, which is now a sort of chaos, must be set in order, and put upon a solid, enduring basis. The time has come when we must abandon the logrolling, hop-skip-and-jump method of tariff building and make our customs laws upon exact information, according to modern methods of commerce."

That statement was the prelude to Beveridge's crucial fight in the Senate, in which he and other liberal senators came to an honorable defeat in the battle against the iniquitous Payne-Aldrich tariff bill. His work was commemorated in a New York *World* cartoon titled "Roll of Honor," showing a bronze plaque on a wall and, examining it, a poor mother and her little child, with a "market basket," so labeled, on her arm. The plaque's wording read: "In honor of the ten Republican senators who voted for the people against privilege, plutocracy and the betrayal of party faith." Then came the roll call: Beveridge, Burkett, Bristow, Crawford, Clapp, Cummins, Dolliver, Brown, La Follette and Nelson.

Lorimer clipped the cartoon from the paper and sent it to Beveridge, inscribing it in the lower left-hand corner: "Good for you!" Beveridge replied despondently. After the adjournment he joined his wife at a summer home they had at the time in Dublin, New Hampshire. There he tried to forget his defeat, and invited Lorimer to come up and help him.

"My dear Beveridge," Lorimer replied, "You know perfectly well that no one except a United States Senator can afford to be lolling around during August. I am not a United States Senator, but a humble member of the G.O.P., when I do not vote the Democratic ticket; ergo, I am working. Seriously, we are right up against the biggest numbers in the history of the Post. The only doubt about our putting them out is our inability to print them. What have you up your sleeve about the tariff? We want some hot stuff for our autumn numbers."

This letter was the starting point of another Post article, in which Beveridge returned to the tariff fight in October 1909. He set forth the Progressive point of view: "The insurgents sought to keep faith with the people. They felt that the promissory note of their party should be redeemed at a hundred cents on the dollar. They felt, too, that these promises were based on justice. So that, from the very beginning, the revision of the tariff presented itself to them as a moral question. And the deeper they went into it, the plainer it became. . . . They considered the business side of it as well—the common sense and practicability of it. And so the insurgents fought for moderation. . . . All of them feel that protection has become the settled policy of the Nation. But because they wanted protection beyond attack, the insurgents did fight for many reductions and against any such increases as seemed to them unnecessary and wrongful. . . ."

It was obvious that his tariff fight had cost Beveridge the support of some of his oldest and most potent political friends. In his home state of Indiana the Republican schism over the tariff issue was already dangerous to his political future, and he was urged not to argue his views at the state convention of 1910. Lorimer again came to his aid in this crisis, and oddly enough it was Beveridge's erstwhile severest critic, Sam Blythe, who wrote for the Post one of his most caustic articles about the Indiana split, in which he made it plain that Beveridge was right and the standpatters were wrong.

Encouraged by such support and more determined than ever in his convictions, Beveridge plunged ahead. The Republican party and the President had virtually repudiated him after 1908, but in 1910, when the vacillating Taft advocated the passage of a tariff reciprocity treaty with Canada, the Indianan exhibited his magnanimity by coming to the support of the man who had cast him out. He wrote a Post article arguing the President's case, an act of statesmanship for which he was widely commended. Then he suffered the further injury of watching Taft's own party kill the treaty. His defeat and retirement from the Senate in November were inevitable after that event.

Lorimer helped his old friend plot a new career that would keep him in the public eye and save him from the eclipse that usually overtakes defeated candidates. In 1911 he commissioned from Beveridge six articles designed to enlighten the American public about Canada. The articles were to deal with currency management, the trusts, the railroads, immigration and industrial wars.

The Canadians welcomed Beveridge. Statesmen talked freely with him, as did labor leaders. He attended the sessions of the Board of Railway Commissioners, and he prepared the groundwork for his articles with the utmost care. They began running in the Post in June 1911 and continued until late September. Meanwhile, safely in the public eye again, Beveridge slipped away to Switzerland for a rest. He begged Lorimer to come with him, but the Boss wrote:

"Be calm, my young friend, be absolutely calm. You know perfectly well that between my going to Europe and to heaven, the chances are all in favor of the Golden Streets. We have had to pull the first number of the *Country Gentleman* out of the air, and that is where the second, and the third, and the fourth numbers are now all reposing. I am keeping at it till midnight every night and making a very rotten little country weekly at that. . . . Be good, and if you can't be good, come home where I can treat you by thought waves. I am afraid that my virtue, though Scotch and rugged, is not granitic enough to support you as well as myself at this distance."

From Lucerne, Beveridge renewed his plea for Lorimer to come abroad and the Boss wrote him: "Dear Bev, I see that you are still crazy. I know that you had incipient paresis when you started abroad for a four months' rest, but I had no idea that it would develop so rapidly. If you will promise to stay over there until about the first of October, I think I will then be crazy enough myself to run over for a few weeks. The *Country Gentleman* is taking hold very nicely, thank you, and we are going to put it across hard in the next year. Blythe writes from Yellowstone that he is having a bully time in a temperature of sixty to sixty-five, with an occasional snowstorm in the early morning. We are having a bully time in Wyncote, with an occasional touch of hell between four and five in the afternoon. . . ."

When Beveridge returned, Lorimer did his best to help the ex-senator adjust to a political climate in which the Boss foresaw the storm of approaching disaster that was to overtake the Progressive movement. In this private campaign Lorimer tried to get Beveridge up to Wyncote as often as possible. One invitation in January 1912 made this promise:

"If you come up here to the dinner, as I hope you will, I am going to hold it up when it is about half over, and ask the leader of the orchestra to play some of that low, trembly music, the kind that takes Eliza safely across the ice and that helps the heroine to pour out the story of her life. Then after the spotlight has been turned on you, I shall tell you the story of the Thousand and Second Night, the one which Scheherazade skipped. It will give you an insight into many things which you in Indiana do not know, namely, why the turkey trot is so popular with our best people and why Woodrow Wilson and Colonel Harvey fell out. Till then I beg you to remain perfectly calm."

As the election of 1912 drew near, Lorimer threw the Post solidly behind the Progressives. To those who know the magazine primarily from its career after the first World War, it would be a revelation to examine the issues of 1912. The publication that was to become the voice of conservative Republicanism a decade later was then the enemy of the status quo, and the earnest chastiser of the Republican party in terms as fervent as it used against the Democrats from 1933 onward. Lorimer retained a few Progressive principles until he died. There were many others, however, which he abandoned not long after the movement came to an end.

It was small consolation in November 1912 to observe that the Progressives had polled more votes than the Republicans. Woodrow Wilson and the Democrats were in Washington, which was no surprise to Lorimer. Like some other Republicans-by-nature in the insurgent camp, he had been discomfited by the embarrassing coincidence of party declarations by Democrats and Progressives. That fact had been a potent campaign weapon for the Democrats. Lorimer was still relatively fluid as far as party allegiance was concerned, but he knew where he stood and it was not with the Democrats.

Consequently he did not oppose the return of the Progressives to the Republican fold as ardently as did Beveridge. To the ex-senator this proposal meant a retreat from principles, a defeat as final as the one he had endured in the Senate. To Lorimer, it was more in the nature of practical politics. Nevertheless, the Boss opened the Post's pages to Beveridge's attack on the proposition. His friend raised some pertinent questions in the first article. He wanted to know what the Republicans would do with the millions of Democrats who had presumably voted with the Progressives. He inquired whether the insurgents would be able to come back in the spirit of true compromise, or whether the Republican leaders would make the terms and accept the revolters as returning penitents. Even more important, he pointed out, was the wide divergence between Republican and Progressive viewpoints on such fundamental issues as the regulation of trusts, the initiative, referendum and recall, and on labor, including child labor. "How," he inquired, "can the Progressive party, which has this concept of nationalism as one of its basic principles, be merged with another party that denies that principle? Will the Republican party put a child-labor plank in its platform? Let the merger promoters try it."

But the practical politicians won, and Beveridge was a completely disillusioned man. There was the notorious "Hinman deal," in which Roosevelt returned to the Republican regulars by using election support of a New York congressman as a bridge, and the Progressive party fell apart for lack of a leader. Beveridge was forced to announce his own return to the party in 1916 or face political exile, but he neither forgave nor forgot. To get the bad taste out of his mouth, he wrote an article, "The Rise and Wrecking of the Progressive Party," which he sent to Lorimer to read, warning him at the same time that it was not for publication. His letter added, "I think that history has not one single example of a party or a movement which was used so cold-bloodedly and wrecked so cynically and selfishly as the Progressive party has been used and wrecked."

In another gloomy letter, later in 1916, he told Lorimer: "The whole situation is a cave of the winds for the Republicans and Progressives. Together they may defeat Wilson, but I'll be hanged if I can see how they are going to do it—corn at seventy-five cents a bushel, wheat out of sight, farmers prosperous, workingmen all employed at high wages and striking for higher, currency law passed, and perhaps my tariff commission bill will be passed before Congress adjourns." As he predicted, the bill was passed.

Beveridge's political career was over, for all practical purposes, but he went on working for the Republican party and writing for the Post. In the autumn of 1923 he prepared several articles for the magazine which he hoped would shape the Republican platform in 1924. The series dealt with foreign policy, the five-to-four Supreme Court decisions, railroads, taxation and bureaucracy. They began running in the late fall and continued into the spring. The most important of the pieces proposed that the Supreme Court establish a rule by which no act of Congress could be declared unconstitutional unless the vote were at least six to three.

The Republican platform was little influenced by Beveridge's article, but President Coolidge wrote that for a month he kept the issue of the Post containing the Supreme Court article on the stand at the head of his bed. "It is so plain," Coolidge said, "so simple and strong, that I am sure it will do a vast amount of good."

Lorimer had little faith in his friend's political activity during these later years. He encouraged Beveridge to work on the Lincoln biography, and the correspondence between them on this matter was voluminous. They visited each other often, and Beveridge frequently sent him speeches to read, as he had in the old days. One of the last letters Lorimer wrote him was this one, dated August 28, 1924:

"Dear Bev: I did not leave my spectacles at Beverly Farms but Alma did. She started out with three pair. Somewhere in Canada she sat on one pair and put it out of business. A second pair she left at Beverly Farms and the third reached Wyncote through some miracle.

"There must be something wrong with my system. Here I am living in a humble little shack in Wyncote while you are living in a granite palace at Beverly Farms and Ed Lefevre in a marble one with hanging gardens at Dorset. Incidentally, it was at Beverly Farms I solved a question which has been puzzling me, because you know some of us have been expecting to go to Washington at any time during the last twelve years and make obeisance to you, crying out, 'Oh, King, live forever.' But every man is entitled to just so much good fortune in this world and I can't see why you should expect both to be the President of the United States and the husband of Mrs. Beveridge too.

"My regards to your redheaded boy and don't shelter him too much. Redheaded boys should be allowed to run a little as the color of their hair keeps them on the defensive and they develop into first-class fighting men."

By the time he wrote this letter Lorimer had come a long way from the principles for which he and Beveridge had fought in the Progressive party. After the election of 1912 it had seemed to President Wilson that he might even have a friend in the Post, because it had supported many important Democratic ideas during the campaign, notwithstanding the fact that this championship had occurred under the flag of another party.

For a few years there was, indeed, a strange alliance between the Republican-Progressive Post and the Democratic Wilson. It was the Post's influential support which prompted Wilson to give Sam Blythe the 1914 interview in Mexico, in which he explained

American policy south of the border. The President gave interviews only on rare occasions. He was more acutely aware than less sensitive public figures that a man in high position would not be likely to recognize most word pictures of himself, after they had been screened through the preconceived ideas of a writer and an editor. Early in 1918 he lamented to David Lawrence, who wanted to prepare an article on him for the Post: "I am hopelessly useless for publicity purposes. I have never read an article about myself in which I recognized myself, and I have come to have the impression that I must be some kind of a fraud because I think a great many of these articles are written in absolutely good faith."

The Post supported Wilson in 1916 because "he kept us out of war." To Lorimer's isolationist mind, this was a high ideal of statesmanship, and when Wilson abandoned that policy in 1917, Lorimer abandoned Wilson. He never got over the reversal. It turned him against the Democratic party permanently, and he was thereafter solidly Republican, even when he thought the Republicans might be wrong.

Wilson did not know he had been abandoned until the war was over, for Lorimer's nationalism was of the same stamp as Decatur's "My country, right or wrong." He did not believe in the war, but he put the Post solidly behind the war effort, to such an extent that Wilson felt compelled to write him on April 9, 1918:

"My dear Mr. Lorimer: Public affairs press upon me so constantly that I seldom get a chance to look about me and see what is being said and done, and consequently it is only just now that my attention has been drawn to the admirable way in which you have been filling the Saturday Evening Post with matter which interprets and emphasizes the objects and meaning of the great struggle we are engaged in. The method you have adopted is all the more admirable because it is not carried in headlines but runs like an essence through the whole contents of the weekly. Will you not accept my sincere expression of admiration?"

Lorimer's postwar disillusionment was complete with the birth of the League. He was so utterly opposed to Wilson's internationalism that he welcomed Harding, whom he quickly came to

despise as a man. Nevertheless he committed himself wholeheart-
edly to Harding's party, as against Wilson and the party he represented, and he was more articulate than ever in his nationalism,
which now became extreme. Money, success and the necessary
restrictions of his life at a desk in Philadelphia all contributed to
this increasingly narrowed attitude toward the world.

That attitude was apparent in Post articles, but it was insistent
on the Post editorial page. In November 1919, in an editorial
captioned "Joyriding and Jaywalking," he attacked any idea of
government ownership (in which he had once conceded merit in
some cases) with these words: "The simple and amply proven
fact is that government ownership does not make men, and rarely
makes money. It makes weaklings, dependents, grafters, bureau-
crats, autocrats and deficits. It is the first lesson in Socialism, and
Socialism is the first lesson in Bolshevism, and Bolshevism is the
last lesson in government. The class graduates from that into
Anarchy."

He was most eloquent, however, on the subject of immigration.
In "Self-Preservation," written in February 1920, he argued: "So
further immigration must not only be rigidly limited in volume
but we must analyze the possibilities and desirability of different
races in a way that we have never done before. The matter of
race, as well as the qualifications of individuals, must be given
more attention. Arguments for unrestricted immigration always
go back to some petty selfish reason—never to the greatest good
of the country."

Again, in May 1921, he was even more blunt: "Americanization
talk is futile unless we are willing to face the facts and apply the
remedy, instead of playing with palliatives. That remedy is the
stoppage of all immigration until we can get the immediate problem in hand; and then its rigid limitation to selected individuals
from those races that are fitted biologically for assimilation. . . .
The trouble with our Americanization program is that a large part
of our recent immigrants can never become Americans. They will
always be Americanski—near-Americans with un-American ideas
and ideals."

He opposed further taxation in these words of March 1923:

"Right now, when we are in the grip of a wild spending mania, with its accompanying orgy of taxation, our city, state and national governments, if they were doing their real duty to the people, would be striving in every way possible to reduce our tax burdens. . . . There cannot be too close a scrutiny of present taxes, or too strong objection raised to any increase in them. Taxation is the great world question. It is the opponent of stability, the real breeder of revolutions, the instrument with which communism stealthily works towards confiscation where it is not strong enough to take by force."

Week after week, year after year, until he left his editor's chair, he pounded away on the subject of the war debts, fighting those who would cancel any part of Europe's obligations, opposing bitterly those who sought to restore any part of the economic balance of power. For him it was America first, America alone; she did not need Europe, and Europe only played her for a sucker. The world was shrinking every year as time hurried it on to greater catastrophes, but to Lorimer, America's position in it was much the same as it had been in 1900 when he and Beveridge preached the new imperialism of a dominant America and the devil take those who opposed her.

In 1922, Lorimer wrote: "Europe wants to know what America is going to do for her and America wants to know what Europe is going to do for herself. With the best will in the world America can do little except ruin herself by extending large credits under present conditions." A year later he was even more vehement: "At present every nation hopes that if America goes into European affairs she will prove to be an ally who will back up that nation in her demands; and an uncle who will write off the old debts with one hand and make new loans with the other. That America should cancel the war debts is the one subject on which practically all Europeans, even while discussing repayment, are in agreement. That these debts must be paid is a subject on which all clear-thinking Americans are in agreement. . . ."

By 1926 he was bitter: "When the war ended, America felt that she had made a fairly substantial contribution in men and money to the cause of the Allies, especially for one who primarily

GEORGE HORACE LORIMERGEORGE HORACE LORIMERGEORGE HORACE LORIMERGEORGE HORACE LORIMERGEORGE HORACE LORIMERE LORIMERGEORGE HORACE LORIMERGEORGE HORACE LORIMERGEORGE HORACE LORIMER

was an innocent bystander. But we are being undeceived. As the propaganda grows more intense, we are gradually coming to learn that it was our war; that the Allies fought for us while we basely devoted ourselves to getting rich out of it; and that when we finally came in we did not amount to anything anyway."

Meanwhile, the Post was doing its best to sell two Republican Presidents to the country. Feeling as he did about Harding privately, Lorimer nevertheless believed in the President's speaking tour on behalf of the World Court, and, seeking to help him, assigned Sam Blythe to write his "A Calm View of a Calm Man." It was this article, whose appearance was scheduled to coincide with the President's arrival in California, that Mrs. Harding was reading to her husband when he turned his face to the wall and died, saying, "That's good. Go on."

When the news of Harding's death reached the Post there was a frantic search for references to the dead man in forthcoming issues already made up. Adelaide Neall found a particularly damaging one, a kidding paragraph on the humor page. Lorimer was on vacation, and Miss Neall had to fight a stern battle with the business and mechanical departments before she could get the page replated. Her insistence cost the Post thirty thousand dollars, but saved it from a major embarrassment.

Kenneth Roberts was assigned to help George Christian, Harding's secretary, write the inside story of the dead President's administration. Lorimer had an eight-installment series, at least, in mind, but when Roberts finally sat down with Christian in Washington he discovered that the secretary, after examining all the documents, letters and annotations of the Harding period and working on them for three months, had come up with a narrative exactly thirty-five hundred words long!

Lorimer had a much warmer feeling toward Coolidge. When the silent little man from Vermont entered the White House, Garet Garrett wired to the Boss: "Here's a President nobody knows anything about; let's find out." Lorimer replied that George Pattullo had already been sent to examine him and had reported, "There's nothing in this man." Garrett then met Coolidge and spent an hour with him, after which he urged Lorimer: "Let's have another look at this man." The two men met and, perhaps unexpectedly for both of them, liked each other. They were violently unlike, but there was an instant rapport. They frequently exchanged ideas and Lorimer spent long hours on the presidential yacht.

Coolidge puzzled even so astute a political writer as Garrett. The Post's correspondent wrote to Lorimer in December 1923 that he had seen the President and discussed the Post's campaign to sell the American merchant marine to the people. There was, however, nothing to sell. There was only a Shipping Board torn apart by the struggle between factions equally anxious to get the government into and out of the shipping business, and full of other, even more serious, confusions. When Garrett had finished outlining the situation, Coolidge said he thought the Post would be doing a public service to print the naked truth.

Garrett's letter describing this incident was typed, but he added a postscript in his own hand: "I can't make Coolidge out. He makes very keen sounds and no wrong ones. I could easily believe he has more strength than has been revealed. I overran my time and stopped. He said, 'Go on.' And that was all he said, except to ask me suddenly when I was born, until the end, which I have indicated. No. He said one other thing. He interrupted me to ask how I knew a certain thing to be so. I told him. He nodded and said again, 'Go on.' "

Lorimer often laughed about Coolidge's peculiarities, and sometimes refused to take him seriously. But he was a Republican first and a pragmatist afterward, and he continued to believe that Coolidge, when he spoke, enunciated sound Republicanism. In August 1931 he paid Coolidge ten thousand dollars for his article on "Party Loyalty and the Presidency." The ex-President submitted his manuscript to the Post with a characteristic approach. He preceded it with a letter, which arrived three days before the manuscript, saying he had written a paper that the Post might wish to use. That backward introduction threw the magazine into a turmoil. Working in secret and at top speed in order to anticipate the newspapers, Lorimer ripped open an issue that was on the presses and replaced the first installment of a new serial with Coolidge's message. Three million copies were printed and circulated before the news services got to the story.

After this article was published the response from Post readers was so enthusiastic that Lorimer went up to New York to consult with Coolidge about a second piece. They had dinner together in the ex-President's suite at the Waldorf. When the waiter brought in the menus, Lorimer ordered one of his favorite dishes, roast beef. The plates arrived and the Boss was shocked to see that his portion of meat, like his host's, was meager. He was about to say something to the waiter when he remembered that Coolidge never ate large portions. He had been served a Coolidge portion. Lorimer acceded silently to this nice courtesy on the part of the management and ate his dinner in short order.

"I never eat any dessert, do you?" Coolidge remarked in a tone which implied that he would be appalled if his guest yielded to such a vice. Lorimer replied politely that he didn't, feeling his stomach cry out for apple pie and cheese. The coffee arrived and the two men had an hour or so of conversation over it, after which Lorimer said good night and hurried downstairs to one of the hotel's restaurants, where he put away a large supper.

Coolidge proved to be a popular writer for the magazines after he left the White House. Besides his Post articles, his autobiography ran serially in *Cosmopolitan* before it appeared in book form, and he turned out three articles on peace for the *Ladies' Home Journal*.

During the Roosevelt-Hoover campaign Costain suggested to Lorimer that the Post run articles on the issues by Al Smith and Coolidge. Lorimer agreed and Costain wired Coolidge in Vermont, asking permission to come up and see him and talk about such a piece. Coolidge replied with one word, "Yes," but he filled out a long telegram with explicit directions on how to reach his farm. The wire came collect.

Even when Coolidge was in the White House, Republicanism was in the ascendant, and the market was soaring every day to dizzier heights, Lorimer was privately gloomy. The Post re-

flected the general optimism and prosperity of the country, but
Lorimer was in a state of mind comparable to that of the anti-
New Dealers at a later date. His hatred of the New Deal is better
understood when one sees how perturbed he was by the events of
a comparatively calm world in the twenties. He worried about the
war debts, taxation, immigration, and foreign policy most of all.

"Never in my experience," he wrote to Corra Harris in March
1927, "has there been so much scrambled and uninformed opinion
about everything. Led by the pinks, the preachers and the professors, we seem to be in danger of mob rule. I can't see that the
preachers and the professors are doing their own job well enough
to warrant us in believing that they can successfully run the
country and dictate our foreign policies. They have swallowed
the Mexican, the Nicaraguan, the Chinese, the French and English
propaganda at one big gulp and when the real facts are presented
to them they brush them aside rather impatiently. There is something almost ludicrous in the attitude of the church towards our
army and navy. On the one hand they are preaching total disarmament and on the other they are using the navy and the
marines to protect and save the lives of their missionaries in China.
What happens to our other advance guards of civilization, the
businessmen, seems to be a matter of small consequence to them.
The elements who attack the presence of our marines in Nicaragua
are the same as those that demanded warships from Secretary
Hughes to protect their schools and colleges in Turkey when they
were threatened."

He wrote in much the same vein to George Pattullo, who had
sent him an article about the Chinese situation in March 1927: "I
was delighted to get that Chinese article. It clarified the situation
for me and it will do as much for most of our readers, who are
really in the dark as to what it is all about. We have been propa-
gandized to death over Mexico, the Marcosson series being the
first one that I have seen that gives the real facts in the case. The
same thing is now starting in the case of China. Our emotionalists
and radicals are comparing the present mess to our Revolution and
all that sort of thing. You know the pink patter. I really don't
know what is going to happen to us over here. . . ."

What happened immediately was the administration of Lorimer's friend, Herbert Hoover, whom he had pointed for the
White House since the first World War. Lorimer and the Post
were important factors in elevating Hoover to the presidency of
the United States. It was the one positive political act in the
Boss's life that he never regretted, even though he came to be
disillusioned with this President, too, as he had been with all the
others before him. At first he was unequivocally in favor of the
man who shared his views on so many subjects, but after Hoover
was in the White House they quarreled on the subject of internationalism, and Lorimer was constantly impatient with his man's
political ineptitude. Ever conscious of the President's limitations,
Lorimer remained his friend and, when necessary, his ally as well.
He did not believe in too much mixing of politicians and editors,
but he went frequently to the White House during the Hoover
administration, largely at the insistence of Alma, who had become
a figure in Pennsylvania Republican politics. These visits were not
without their compensations. As Lorimer often said: "One thing
about the White House, it's the best place in the United States to
get a good night's sleep."

The first indication of Lorimer's intention to make a President
of Hoover, or at least help in the process, was contained in an
exchange of letters in 1919 with C. A. Brant, proprietor of El
Tovar, the Fred Harvey hotel at the Grand Canyon where the
Boss always stopped. Lorimer and his friends referred to Brant as
"Baron," because they said he should have been one. Unsuspecting
trippers, hearing this title used, also raised their host to the
peerage.

Brant reported that October that his guests during the month
had included the King and Queen of Belgium, "about two hundred of the Native Sons and Daughters of Arizona," and Sam
Blythe, who had taken the occasion of his visit to discourse to
Brant on the frailty of human nature and the vicissitudes of
politics.

"Mr. Blythe disabused me of one idea I had," Brant told Lorimer, "to wit: that we ought to have a businessman as President.
Mr. Blythe seems to have convinced me that it would never do

in the world because a first-class businessman was nothing more
nor less than a specialist in his particular business and knew but
Damn Little of anything else. . . . Mr. Blythe seems to think that
Mr. Hoover is, possibly, as capable a man as could be selected for
President, but Mr. Blythe stated that he did not know to what
political party Mr. Hoover belonged and, for that matter, coming
to think of it, I have always thought of you as a Republican, because you have been giving particular hell to the Democratic
party for the last year or two, but I think that even a good Democrat would have done so under the existing conditions."

Lorimer replied: ". . . The trouble with Sam is that he labors
under the common delusion that there are no businessmen in the
country excepting the eight or ten that have been thoroughly
advertised, Gary, Schwab, Vanderlip. Incidentally, business is or
should be the specialty of government. One reason why we are in
such a mess is that it never has been. We have been run by professors, lawyers and other professional men. Sam, himself, is thoroughly inconsistent because when I saw him last week he turned
to me and said, 'Why wouldn't Hoover make a good President?'
Now as a matter of fact, Hoover is and always has been a businessman. So far as I know, he had never held a government position in his life up to the day that the war broke out, but his
specialty, business, proved broad enough to cover satisfactorily
and efficiently a situation that was as big and important as national
government itself."

Lorimer admired such Hoover feats in World War I as his solution of the condensed milk can problem. These tin containers
were being made into hand grenades by the Germans, after
Belgian mothers had thrown them away, and the Allies threatened
to cut off the supply. As food administrator, the solution was up
to Hoover, who simply insisted that every Belgian woman turn in
an empty can whenever she got a full one. The empties were
crushed flat by a stamping machine and thus made unusable as
grenade casings.

In the early twenties Lorimer drew closer to Hoover. They
found themselves in agreement on a good many points. What the
Boss did not learn about the man from their long talks he found

out from his writers. Eleanor Egan wrote to Lorimer in 1922 from her Park Avenue apartment: "Mr. Hoover came to see me last Tuesday evening just after his defeat at the hands of the Railway Presidents, and we had a long bitter talk. He is normally doleful, but on this occasion his pessimism was extreme. He seemed to think that the Reds had the country thoroughly undermined and that the capitalists were finally applying the torch that would bring about the inevitable explosion, but he went away laughing at his own views, so he was all right. I am going fishing with him this week end in Chesapeake Bay, and will then discuss with him the further developments of the Russian situation. . . ."

To this Lorimer replied: "Mr. Hoover is not running so wild at that. Personally I am no Pollyanna about these strikes and the general business situation. Let me know what you catch besides fish. . . ."

In May of the following year Lorimer wrote to Garrett that Hoover had spent the night at Wyncote and they had discussed the state of the nation, particularly the railroad and merchant marine situation. The Boss had been impressed by Hoover's views on transportation, and suggested to Garrett that he should approach their man with the idea of doing two or three Post articles on the subject. "Incidentally," he added, "we could present in these articles an outline of what the Administration has in mind for the railroads."

By 1925 the Post was so closely allied with Hoover's career that Lorimer discussed Post political articles with him, and in at least one case promised to go through a particular manuscript "very carefully and eliminate anything that seems ill advised in view of the present situation."

Lorimer had his scouts out a year before the convention of 1928, listening for whispers in the wind. What they heard at first was not reassuring. Sam Blythe wrote him from the Waldorf in January 1927: "It is an extraordinary thing that most of the big folks financially downtown think, firmly believe, that Coolidge will be nominated, that he expects to be and that he will accept. I get this in the highest places and, especially, in Morgan quarters which is supposed to be the main listening post on Coolidge stuff."

As for the Democrats, Sam added: "I saw Al Smith. He says he has the nomination in a bag and that he intends to take it but only on the condition that the Democrats will make the fight on clean-cut Democratic principles. He says the Democrats have elected only two Presidents since the Civil War and that both of those elections were flukes. He says that if the party will put up a clear and definitive set of Democratic issues, he will take the nomination, which nobody can stop him from getting as he sees it and also his friends, but if they go fumbling around with a lot of extraneous stuff and trimming and straddling he won't have it. . . . That's the situation here, with all leading Republican hands trying like hell here and in New England to get uninstructed delegations."

For his part, Hoover appeared to be in no great hurry to rally support for his nomination. In public, at least, he seemed to be disinterested. Lorimer got the first accurate report on his actual intentions in a letter from Isaac Marcosson, written in September 1927: "Hoover is very anxious that you know his position with regard to the presidency. He therefore talked to me on Saturday with great frankness. Hoover said that he would make no effort to get the nomination. He declared that, in his opinion, the scramble for delegates is 'a degradation of the office.' He further stated that most of the party leaders had been to see him, asking him to announce himself and enter the race. This he has so far declined to do. He maintained, however, that if the nomination were offered him he would accept it. Hoover made one interesting point which makes me believe that he is very keen for the nomination. He said that, with the exception of Dawes, every man mentioned would be past seventy years of age if he served a second term. He is the youngest of the lot. I therefore pass this on to you for what it is worth."

When Hoover's friends persuaded him to enter the race they discovered that their troubles were only beginning. The candidate's naïveté astounded and dismayed such practical politicians as Blythe, Garrett and Lorimer. In March 1928 the Boss asked Garrett, who was a good friend of the candidate, to take a day or two off for the specific purpose of advising Hoover. He had already asked Blythe to see if he could find an experienced man who would serve as a buffer between Hoover and the daily press, and he had advised the presidential tyro not to let anyone take a defensive or an apologetic attitude in his behalf toward such questions as farm relief, but to insist that all publicity be affirmative. "I am shooting an editorial and a couple of articles that ought to help," he added in a letter to Garrett. "Perhaps you have something in mind that we could do."

Will Rogers added his bit. On a lecture tour he polled the audience every night on the strength of the potential candidates and he told Lorimer, "It is all Hoover."

From Hugh Wiley there came in April a plea for the Post to do still more for Mr. Hoover. "Dear Boss," Hugh wrote, "this country needs an inspiring bulletin about Herbert Hoover. All the writers seem to pull their punches. You could write a piece *for this country* that might *make* the hardshells nominate him. I think you are the only man who *could* write it." Lorimer was reassuring: "We did our best for Hoover on this week's editorial page and we are following it up with some articles by Henry Ford, Samuel G. Blythe and other well-known artists."

Hoover went to the West Coast in the summer of 1928, and Blythe followed him there to discuss what kind of article could best be run in the Post. The result of their conversation was contained in a letter from Blythe to Lorimer, written from the Palace Hotel, San Francisco, on July 26:

"My dear George, After talking with our peerless but somewhat gun-shy candidate, with sundry of his close advisers, hearing from the East extensively and summing up things as I find and know them, I think the first and best thing to be done, in case you want to do anything, is to write a calm and detached article contrasting Hoover and Smith in the light of the necessities of the country; the theme being that the U.S. is the motor of all the world, that our greatest necessities and advantages are economic—business—that the two platforms, being almost identical, are political and hokum, and the thing the voter must decide is whether Smith or Hoover, judged dispassionately from the angles of experience, education, abilities and adaptabilities for this particular job of President at this particular time, and in this particular situation is best fitted for the office. Of course the showing will be all in Hoover's favor and it would be valuable in my opinion. . . ."

The official notification occurred in August, and Wiley reported from Los Altos that "Sam came up for an overnight stay and we attended in full regalia. The only danger I see at this time is the universal chorus of prominent visiting firemen whose 'all over' song may lull him to sleep at the wrong moment. It is all over on the slide rule but the precincts have yet to be counted and this election will be won or lost in the precincts and not in the parlor. There will be the usual absence of miracles in the Solid South. The Wildcats will vote copiously but kin dey git 'em into de totals is still de main trouble. I am not even sure of California. It is all well enough to say that the eleventh-hour thinker will elect to retain his high wages, but who ever proved that this 'thinker' ever thunk? Mr. Hoover and I did not agree on this, which led me to deplore this happy, not to say prattling, local group of bringers-of-glad-tidings. . . ."

As the campaign swung into its final weeks Hoover followed his own publicity inclinations, with results that did not please Lorimer, as he indicated in a letter to Garrett on August 17: "I also had a letter from Herbert Hoover, saying that he would like to have Governor Allen meet me, and I answered that I should be glad to see the Governor whenever he was in these parts, though up to this point I can't hand him a great deal as a publicity man. I think you might very well say to Mr. Hoover that we would both be glad to meet Governor Allen, but personally you are at work on your contribution to the campaign and that our political features are pretty well planned to the first of November."

From his editor's chair Lorimer had directed the Post's active participation in the campaign to elect Hoover, and his writers had been in the field along with those from other magazines and the daily press. Yet Lorimer liked to feel that he had been entirely independent of the whole procedure; he resented even the implication that the Post had been hand in glove with Hoover.

In a strict sense it had not. Lorimer would never have tolerated any suggestions from Hoover or his advisers, intended toward shaping the direction of Post policy. On the other hand, he believed that undeviating support was legitimate as long as the ideas originated with him. Granted that viewpoint, the Post could and did become virtually a Hoover propaganda organ, and there was no inconsistency between that fact and the assurance Lorimer gave Mabel Walker Willebrandt in October: "I have backed Mr. Hoover because I believe that from every point of view he is the better man. I have not been in communication with Mr. Hoover or any of his lieutenants since long before the convention, and whatever I have done in the Saturday Evening Post has been done on my own initiative without suggestion of any sort from his managers."

This was literally true, but neither Hoover nor his managers could have done as well if they had owned the Post and written the campaign articles themselves.

Lorimer was temporarily exhausted by the rigors of the campaign. He could not even respond as usual to a typical letter from Will Rogers, a few weeks after the election. This was the kind of letter Rogers wrote when he had something to sell:

"Finally got broke and had to go to writing. Now I think I hit on an idea that will give us a pretty good 'Clothesline' to hang a lot of Political Gags on, and that is this idea of taking over the Management of the Democratic Party, For that will be the main topic from now on, I think we can get a lot of Comedy out of managing it. It gives us the best plan too to point out the mistakes of the R—— and get in enough truths about both of them along with the Gags so we can make it interesting, They don't have to be continuous, I have the next one about laid out already, will have it in next three or four days, then can lay off two or three weeks, and then maby write the next one to somebody else, They are going to hold a meeting pretty soon and will do something Komical there, Then you see we got Congress working for us every day so there should be lots of funny things between now and March, Anyhow I hope the idea hits you, Good luck to you and all the Gang. Where is old Wildcat?"

Lorimer accepted the article Will enclosed, but he begged off any more political pieces because, as he said, "we now have the inevitable reaction that comes when people have talked and thought intensively about one subject for a period of weeks." He added a postscript on the activities of Wildcat, who he said had "just bought himself a ranch and is doing a little intensive hustling for the money with which to pay for it. The last piece of land he bought with the idea of raising kumquats or cuckoos or something like that proved to have no water within fifty or sixty miles of it. Sam Blythe tells me that there is a little moisture on this latest one."

Deeply as he might involve himself in political battles and public issues, Lorimer always saw them in relation to his magazine. He was not interested in politics for any personal reason. When Hoover entered the White House he asked Lorimer verbally if he would be interested in any federal post, possibly that of ambassador to some European country. Lorimer replied that he did not think he could leave his responsibilities at the Post. Later, when Charles G. Dawes asked to be relieved of his ambassadorial duties in London, Hoover asked Lorimer if he would be interested in that specific position. The Boss wrote bluntly that he did not want to leave the Post.

Lorimer appeared again as a possible political candidate in 1934, when the Pennsylvania Republican organization was attempting to check a state-wide swing to the Democrats. The party bosses decided to draft a prominent Republican from the Philadelphia district and run him for governor against George Earle. Herbert J. Tily, president of the Strawbridge and Clothier department store, and Judge Harry S. McDevitt were named with Lorimer as the possible choices, but Lorimer wired hastily from Palm Springs: "I am not and will not under any circumstances be a candidate for any office."

It was fortunate that Lorimer did not accept a post in the Hoover administration, because his disaffection began almost at once. The stock-market crash and the dark days following cast a profound gloom on all Republicans who believed that the businessman in the White House would be able to lead them quickly out of the wilderness. By 1931 it was obvious that no such leadership would be forthcoming. A revealing sidelight on the internal state of the Hoover administration was disclosed to Lorimer by his friend Julian Street, in November 1931. Street said he had sent a wire to William Allen White, who was at Rapidan Camp, the day before Hoover went to Detroit to address the American Legion Convention. The wire read: "Beg him to strike out tomorrow with fire and passion, frankly citing lesson of G.A.R. Beg him to voice the feelings of silent, disgusted millions. Beg him to burn the grafters up, not only because they deserve it but because the nation craves spiritual lift of forthright and aggressive leadership we know he has courage and ability to give."

White replied by letter to Street: "I left Rapidan Camp in the middle of the afternoon. Your telegram was delivered there after I left and relayed from there to Washington. The President was still at the Camp when it came and I'll bet a horse he saw it. Anyway, I hope he did. . . . We talked over the speech. He has no dramatic sense and could not do the thing as you and I would like to have seen it done and as the occasion cried for it. He is a grand administrator but has no sense of public relations. He can press a button and call a man in and hire him or fire him wisely, but he can't hold a joint debate with him, and that is the trouble. He is all right. I am very fond of him. But he is not for this hour. . . . The sad and almost hopeless part of the situation is that the man thought he was just raising hell—talking short, ugly words with the bristling barbs! That was his idea of a sizzler. Which shows beautifully how little a man who works with *things* knows about the power of *words*."

That estimation would not have been news to Lorimer. He had spent many a week end with Hoover during which the President would outline what seemed to the Boss a strong and sensible stand on current issues. Lorimer would come home happy and confident, but in a few days or weeks Hoover would compromise and contradict the stand he had intended to make, undoubtedly because of conflicting advice.

The divergence of views on internationalism between Lorimer and Hoover was further widened by Hoover's sponsorship of the moratorium on war debts, an idea completely repugnant to the Boss. Albert Atwood acted somewhat accidentally as a mediator between the men on this issue. In December 1931 he reported to Lorimer a conversation he had just concluded with the President. He had found Hoover "very blue" about matters in general, and particularly about the possibility that the debt moratorium idea might spread throughout Europe. Hoover told Atwood that he believed Lorimer overlooked the psychological impact of this European trouble on America's public confidence. Hoarding and bank failures, he said, were already resulting from apprehension about world affairs, and he had agreed to the moratorium of the preceding June "not to cancel debts, but to save them." Hoover declared his two principal worries were the railroads and the foreign situation. He had faith in the railroads but he was fearful that affairs abroad would become much worse. "He kept repeating," said Atwood, "that you did not allow for the impact of Europe on this country." Hoover may have seemed more pessimistic than he actually was, Atwood noted, because he was equally preoccupied with reading a lecture on Lorimer's policies and "being sore at Congress for not passing the moratorium quicker."

Atwood's letter concluded: "One thing interesting which Hoover said, and seemed to me to be good sense, was that he was trying to make France take the primary responsibility for keeping Germany afloat and that was why he sent for Laval. But France, he says, is trying to squirm out. When he finally stopped talking about European matters and got on domestic, he was his same old keen, analytical, well-informed self.

"I don't know whether you care to have me pass this sort of thing on to you, but I thought I better, for it is the first time I ever heard Hoover so pessimistic. A well-informed newspaperman tells me Hoover's idea is to appoint Baruch the head of the new Reconstruction Corporation which Congress is to authorize after the recess, to try to get both parties behind the business of helping things."

Atwood added this amused footnote: "Hoover said: 'I am as much a nationalist as Lorimer, and that is going some.' "

Lorimer replied: ". . . I should be sorry to have the President feel that there was any unfriendliness on my part towards him personally. I have been extra careful to keep personal criticism of him out of the Saturday Evening Post, but I cannot modify our policies or change our beliefs. They are what they have been ever since Woodrow Wilson wrote his first letter on the debts to Lloyd George. What is happening now is the culmination of a campaign that has been going on with very little intermission since the Armistice. It has never obtained its objectives, but that is not from lack of trying. Whenever the moment has seemed favorable that campaign has increased in intensity. Right now it looks to our debtors as if the time was absolutely ripe and they are engaged in a now-or-never final push. I have no desire to advocate a demand for the last dollar while Europe is in financial trouble, but I can see no good reason for cancellation or for basing a reduction of the debts on present capacity to pay when tomorrow there may be full capacity to pay and probably will be. A moratorium is one thing, and repudiation with our consent quite another. I do not believe that we should co-operate with Europe, as some of our people apparently want to, in plans for repudiation. Let me repeat that I have nothing but the friendliest feeling for the President and a real appreciation of those troubles that are not of his making with which he is confronted."

Within a few days after Hoover's debt moratorium announcement, Garrett and Lorimer were on their way to Europe, where they compiled material for a Post series on the German and general European debt situation. Hundreds of thousands of copies of these articles were printed and distributed at private expense.

The Post once more fought hard for Hoover in the election of 1932. Lorimer suspended his disagreements on principles in the interest of keeping the Democrats out of Washington. His first act after the November defeat was this note to Hoover: "When, as and if you decide to do any writing, either before or after March 4th, I hope that you will consider the Saturday Evening Post in connection with it. Both Mrs. Lorimer and I thought that you made a magnificent campaign, and I need hardly add that we are both greatly disappointed at the outcome."

Hoover accepted the invitation to write, and he contributed his first work after he left office to the Post. They were two chapters from a book he was writing, "The Challenge to Liberty."

Oddly enough, he did not approach Lorimer directly with his contributions, nor did he tell him that he was writing a book. Bruce Barton did the marketing. He telephoned Lorimer as the Boss was sailing for Europe and offered him the articles. The details of the purchase had to be left to others.

The first article was a front-page story in every major newspaper from coast to coast, even in the pro-Roosevelt organs, where it was a direct slap in the face. International News Service called Lorimer to ask him what the Post had paid for the article, and how the price had compared with the price paid to Coolidge for his last two articles. Lorimer refused to give any details, but there was a leak elsewhere and he was startled a day or two later to read in Hearst's Washington *Herald* an INS story asserting, correctly, that Hoover had been given ten thousand dollars for the first article. There had been a higher bidder, the story went on, but he had been refused because Hoover believed the magazine in question (probably *Liberty*) had New Deal tendencies and that his piece would do more good if it were printed in a sympathetic medium.

This incident embarrassed Lorimer. He wrote a long letter to Hoover, telling him what had happened and assuring him that he had given out no information about the marketing of the article or the price paid for it. Then he chided Hoover for not coming to him directly. Getting down to details, he told Hoover that he did not want him to feel that the Post had treated him unfairly in the matter of price. Barton had told him, he said, that the competing magazine had offered twenty thousand dollars for three articles. To compensate for any discrepancy that might exist, Lorimer said, he was instructing the treasurer to send Hoover a check on Tuesday for an additional five thousand dollars, "not because I feel that, everything considered, our first offer was out of line at the time, but because the first article has received a much wider and stronger acceptance than we felt that it would have."

The Hoover articles were part of the Post's campaign against the New Deal and all its works. Of Mr. Roosevelt's numerous enemies, however, it is doubtful if there were any who fought more fairly than Lorimer. He was, in a sense, almost the leader of the opposition in the early years, speaking as he did for three million readers, or more, nearly all of whom, judging by the mail, not only shared his views but were more violent in their own. Yet Lorimer never attacked Roosevelt in a personal way, as did so many newspaper editors. When Steve Early wrote an article for the Post in June 1939 he described the worst of such attacks on the President, and he disclosed that they had been filed at the White House in a fat manila envelope labeled "Below the Belt." Nothing Lorimer wrote appeared in that file. His blows were hard but fair.

This was only one more example of Lorimer's essential largeness of character. In all his years as editor he did not once abuse, or even use, the unfair advantage that small-bore editors love to employ against people with whom they disagree. He would fight harder and better than anyone else against an idea he thought was wrong, but he made no personal attacks upon the men who sponsored the ideas and practices he detested. He once told Bruce Gould that he believed the editor's privilege of the last word laid upon him a very solemn obligation to use it honestly and fairly.

Unlike most conservatives and other anti-New Dealers, Lorimer was not a frightened man. He believed simply that a man should rule his own destiny. The kind of social controls proposed by Roosevelt aroused the same violent antipathy in him that Wilson had stirred in the final year of his administration. In a way there was a curious resemblance between Lorimer and Roosevelt. Both loved the outdoors. Both were in love with the United States, although in such different ways that probably each would have denied that the other understood America at all. Both enjoyed humor, their own and other people's, and they loved the good things in life. Finally, both were strong-minded individualists, not much inclined to listen to advice or to spare anyone else in the hard drive toward his own ideals. It was no accident that both men were called "the Boss."

Roosevelt had barely arrived in the White House before Lorimer was in open revolt against him. Every one of the emergency measures advanced by the President went against the Boss's grain. He could talk about nothing that year except what the New Deal was doing. Up to that time the Post had been primarily an organ of entertainment and enlightenment, notwithstanding its political campaigns. Now Lorimer frankly abandoned that concept of it in favor of an open and continued attack on the enemy. He told Mary Roberts Rinehart at a Palm Springs party in the winter of 1933, "I'll fight this New Deal if it's the last thing I ever do."

The men around Lorimer, most particularly the company's management, were apprehensive of the Post's position. Blythe warned the Boss that Roosevelt would call him Public Enemy Number One if he didn't curtail his opposition to the Administration, and in such an event, that would be the end of the magazine. Lorimer told everyone concerned that he would say what he thought he should say or resign.

According to one editor, the Administration actually had the power to cripple the Post by cutting away its advertising, and an attempt was made to do it by threatening the automotive advertising in particular. As a major stockholder, Lorimer suggested breaking precedent and calling a meeting of the directors to discuss this crisis, but he was persuaded not to do so. No overt action occurred, as less fearful men could have predicted, and the Post went on attacking the New Deal with undiminished vigor. No attempt was made to close it, as its jittery friends feared.

Nevertheless Lorimer was advised constantly by his associates not to defy Roosevelt, and he replied that if matters came to a showdown he had his editorial written. It would say: "We cannot bandy words with the President of the United States."

As Lorimer often pointed out to those who challenged his views, he believed in some New Deal objectives but he objected to Mr. Roosevelt's methods of attaining them. In fact, even in the hectic year of 1933 he had not yet concluded that everything about the New Deal was wrong. That summer he was one of several guests at Ben Ames Williams' summer place on Lake Winnepesaukee, in New Hampshire, when Roosevelt made his radio address outlining the National Industrial Recovery Act. All the guests listened to the speech, and Lorimer remarked, "I think it is a good thing and a needed thing, if it will work." Later that night another guest said he had worked out a code for quahaugs and he outlined it, to the particular amusement of Lorimer, who guffawed over the joke.

During the week end at the Williams place Lorimer told his host that he had lost something of his former interest in fiction because his energy was so concentrated on the fight against the New Deal.

As always, the core of his crusade was on the editorial page, where its course could be followed without difficulty. In the first editorial he wrote after Roosevelt's election, Lorimer was inclined to give the new President every benefit of the doubt. "For weeks before the election," he wrote, "we heard about what was wrong with America, and, according to the campaign orators, just about everything was wrong. Now the time has come to think about what is right with America, and to correct those things that are really wrong. . . . We overstressed the material issues during the campaign. We have had our period of living by bread alone, and we need much more than that—less sectionalism, more neighborliness; less greed, more friendly co-operation; less intolerance and more understanding."

Backing up such editorials as these were the familiar editorial-page cartoons by Herbert Johnson, a perennial favorite with Post readers whose popularity now increased in the heat of battle. A typical Johnson cartoon was captioned "A Fine Old American Family." It depicted an aged, eminently respectable couple labeled Democratic Government and Private Capitalism sitting on a sofa, surrounded by six sons labeled Individual Initiative, Right of Private Property, Right to Wages, Right to Profits, Economic Liberty and Political Liberty. New Dealers were always labeled in Johnson cartoons as crackpot theorists, professors, Reds, radicals, fake liberals, demagogues, academic dreamers and politicians, while the righteous folk who opposed them consistently emerged as the Honest Businessman, the Harassed Rich Man, the Poor Taxpayer, Investor, Farmer and that splendid abstraction, the American People.

As late as July 1933, Lorimer was not ready to say that there was no virtue in anything Mr. Roosevelt had done as some newspaper editors were insisting. He wrote: "There is and probably will be much to applaud and much to criticize in the present Administration. To the extremists among his followers any criticism is lèse-majesté, but that, of course, is pure Hitlerism or Stalinism. No man, however, can fairly withhold from the President both praise and admiration for the boldness with which he grasped the nettle depression as soon as he took office."

But the honeymoon was over by December of that year. "From Roosevelt to Roosevelt" was the title of Lorimer's editorial for December 30, and in it he asserted: "Two Presidents of the United States, both Roosevelts, were given a great opportunity, and both failed to grasp it. We must credit each of these Presidents with high ideals, a sincere purpose to improve conditions in their countries, and with accomplishments of no mean order. But we must debit each of them with a failure. . . ."

The real declaration of war came on April 7, 1934, when the lead editorial became a long declaration of Post policy, under the title, "The Great Illusion." It ran, in part: "The Saturday Evening Post is neither a Republican nor a Democratic organ. It does not condone the abuses of power and trust of the Republican party while it was in office, and it cannot indorse those policies and experiments of the New Deal that look to the left. In our opinion, this is a time when the press and the public must examine thoroughly and feel free to criticize every proposal advanced by the Administration. . . . It is better to be careful now than sorry later. It is safer to put over one sound plan than a dozen doubtful experiments. Recovery is important, but the fundamental issue today is the preservation of Democracy and our traditional American liberties along with recovery. . . . It is impossible to escape the conclusion that today we are having government by amateurs —college boys, irrespective of their age—who, having drunk deep, perhaps, of the Pierian spring, have recently taken some healthy swigs of Russian vodka. We cannot solve our problems with a discredited European ideology and a Marxian philosophy. The great illusion of the moment is that we can gain any worthwhile happiness or prosperity by the sacrifice of our hardly won liberties."

At this point Lorimer fell into the error which beset some of

the editors of influential newspapers who fought the New Deal.
He examined his mail, he listened to his friends, and he concluded
that the majority of people in the nation felt as he did. Thus he
became another of those who professed, some sincerely, others not,
to know what the voters were thinking. He had good reason to
believe that he was accurate, because there had been few people
in America for the past thirty years who had been better able to
diagnose the temper of the nation. Thus he wrote in September
1934:

"When this Administration came into power, the country had
a depression to liquidate. It begins to look now as if it has both a
depression and a New Deal to liquidate. . . . Signs are multiply-
ing that the country will not continue to take the New Deal lying
down or to tolerate in office those left-wing New Dealers who are
suspected of dealing from the bottom of the pack to circumvent
the Constitution and to impose on America a new social order that
is repugnant to our ideal of liberty. . . ."

On the other hand, Lorimer held no brief for the Republicans.
In November 1934 he declared editorially, "Under its present
leadership, the Republican party is not even an intelligent opposition party. It could have been made and should be made, under
enlightened leadership, a fighting liberal-constitutional party."
And in the following year, when the Republicans began to gather
their forces in the search for someone who could unseat Roosevelt, Lorimer advised both them and the Democrats that new
men were needed. He believed it would be a mistake to nominate
Roosevelt and Hoover, to refight the 1932 battle. "Both men inherited the depression," he said. "The first has failed to cure it;
the second was not given a full and fair chance to cope with it.
. . . Justly or unjustly, we do not believe that the sober second
thought of the country wants to continue the present Administration in power or to return to the old one."

When Landon was nominated, Lorimer was not one of those
who thought that any honest Republican would dispose of a man
whom everyone was alleged to hate. He was sincerely convinced
that most of the voters opposed Roosevelt, but at the same time

he could not believe in Landon as a candidate. Lorimer looked upon the dismal campaign of 1936 with dismay. He viewed the spectacle of Henry L. Mencken riding the campaign train with an enormous sunflower in his buttonhole, looking and sounding like a character in one of his own essays. He listened to the hearty voices of his friends, who assured him that "everything you hear around the club is Landon." He surveyed the field from the perspective of thirty-five active political years, and he concluded in August that Landon would be defeated.

"That will be the second successive election we've lost," he told a friend. "It's time for me to get out."

Only two, possibly three, people knew at that moment that he intended to resign from the Post at the end of the year.

Convinced of Landon's defeat, Lorimer steered the Post onto a broad plane, away from personalities. He had declared in May: "There is one issue and only one issue before the country today— the New Deal and all its works, public and private, and its threat to the fundamentals of American government and society. The coming contest at the polls is one of principles and not of men; of ideas and not of spoils; of patriotism and not of partisanship; of the American system against European systems. During the past generation we have admitted many undesirable and unassimilable aliens to our country, but none so undesirable as those alien and un-American ideas that the New Deal party has assimilated to itself."

His final election editorial was even more explicit: "As far as the Saturday Evening Post is concerned, the personalities of the candidates are unimportant, except as they have direct bearing on the ideas for which they stand. . . . Whether Landon or Roosevelt is elected, we shall continue to be non-partisan in the real sense of the word, and criticize the policies of either as President whenever we feel that they are unsound or unwise."

The election was a crushing repudiation of all that Lorimer had fought for, an even worse defeat than he had anticipated. In the last political editorial he ever wrote for the Post he returned to the theme of 1932: "Even though the Saturday Evening Post has been a severe critic of many of the policies and tendencies of the New Deal, we shall return to the position that we took when the President first came into power and suspend comment on the new Administration until its policies and purposes have been made clear by him and the Congress. We sincerely hope that during his coming term in office the President will prove to be a wise counselor, friend and leader of the whole people."

But the battle had stricken Lorimer, underscoring mentally the fatal physical illness which was at work in him. After Election Day his family was shocked to see how suddenly old and bewildered he looked. He seemed to be casting about in his mind for a reasonable answer that would tell him why he had been so wrong in interpreting America, after three decades of near infallibility.

It was true, of course, that no President, regardless of party, had pleased him since the days of McKinley. He had never quite trusted the first Roosevelt—trust busting was essentially distasteful to him—and there had been the disillusionment of T.R.'s final defection—his refusal to run a second time on the Bull Moose ticket when Beveridge, Lorimer and others thought he had a chance to win, and then the subsequent disillusionment of the Hinman deal. He had despised Taft because of what he considered the fat man's vacillating character, and because he had thrown down Beveridge. Lorimer had been betrayed by Wilson with war and internationalism, and he had welcomed Harding only because the Ohioan was the opposite of Wilson; the welcome had dwindled to a weary contempt. Coolidge he had liked for somewhat obscure reasons, but it was not a political affection he felt for Silent Cal; he knew that the little man from Vermont was not a big man for a big job. Hoover had been the greatest disappointment, because he had appeared to have all the qualifications Lorimer demanded of a President, and then, after years of anticipation, he had proved to be the wrong man for the times. And finally Roosevelt—the apotheosis of everything that Lorimer hated in public life, yet maddeningly on the side of those reforms which had stirred the Boss in his Progressive party days.

Lorimer was conscious of three things in November 1936. He

knew that the Post had lost its political influence. He was aware that the feel of America had somehow escaped him, that he lived in an alien land bound on an alien journey. Worst of all, he realized that he was an old man and the fine, golden days were gone.

CHAPTER SEVEN

Lorimer as Editor

The façade of the Curtis Publishing Company on Independence Square said Big Business. It said that Curtis was big business and the men who operated it were big businessmen. Every morning Lorimer climbed the flowing marble steps which would have done credit to a state capitol, strode beneath the severe columns of the portico and into the vast lobby that could have been a bank—except for the lack of cages and for the presence of a broad pool and fountain running the length of the back wall beneath an enormous Maxfield Parrish mural representing a garden, executed in colored glass by Tiffany.

Answering the elevator man's respectful salute, the Boss rode to the sixth floor, strode by the time clock, in which his forever unpunched Time Card No. 1 was regularly renewed, and walked briskly down the corridor to his office. It was an office with a big desk; the room was finished in mahogany with white woodwork, and the sun made it always seem a place full of light and air.

He did not take off his coat before he sat down to work. Lorimer wore his coat in the office on the hottest day; he never unbuttoned himself physically or spiritually. His desk was neat and relatively empty at the start of a day's work. The only picture on it was one of his father.

The Boss's first act of the day was to take out of his bulging pigskin brief case, dark with usage, the manuscripts he had read the night before and start them on their way, either to the composing room or back to the author. Then he ran through the pile of new manuscripts, sending them along to be read.

Turning next to one of the day's most important functions, he attacked the mail. There were three formidable piles of it. The right-hand file was personal mail, the usual potpourri of requests for everything from speeches to articles to money, and a batch of fan letters. These he read first and set aside to dictate the answers after lunch. The middle pile was addressed to the Post and he read those with care, because they helped him to keep his finger on the public pulse. All varieties of communication were in this section. Once a member of an exploring expedition sent out by Tulane University wrote to say that he had discovered a page of advertising from the Post attached to a primitive altar in an Indian hut in Central America. "This proves," he wrote, "that not only do the advertisers in the Saturday Evening Post get the advantage of a circulation far and away beyond that which they pay for, but also that the natives of Central America are just as pagan as the natives of North America, in as far as they both make an idol out of the Saturday Evening Post."

Lorimer designated who was to answer each of the letters in this second pile. When he answered them himself he covered his identity and signed most of them "The Editors." He never answered a critical letter hastily; often he would hold one for rereading next day. "Sometimes," he once remarked, "it helps to know what not to say."

The third pile of letters were those written to staff members which they thought might interest him. He also glanced through the forwarding mail to discover which authors were getting letters from readers. In the last few years of his editorship Adelaide Neall went through the mail addressed to the Post and to the editors, sorting out those she knew the Boss would want to see, just as she had always opened the mail addressed to him during his absences and distributed the letters, or held them, as the case might require. Miss Neall also took over in the last two years the

Boss's chore of reading final page proof, with the exception of certain pages.

With the mail disposed of, Lorimer turned to the issue then being made ready. He would, for example, go over the galleys of several stories with the art director, to determine the proper illustrator.

"Here's an outdoor story. Who've we got?" he would say. The art director would name someone, but Lorimer might object: "No. There's a girl in this one." At last he would okay an artist who could do both outdoors and pretty girls. It was typical of Lorimer's thoroughness as an editor that he not only supervised the art but initialed all make-up and every illustration in the book.

At this point the order of the day varied with the passage of the years. In the younger, more carefree days of the Post, Lorimer listened to a report from Adelaide Neall on general office matters. Those were the days when the Post staff consisted of the Boss, Churchill Williams as contact man, Bigelow on office detail, Helen Walker and Miss Neall as readers, the latter assisting in reading pages and editing copy; and Harry Thompson as art editor.

When the size of the Post got up to 240 and 260 pages, the staff did not increase in proportion. It was still amazingly small, but there was a weekly make-up meeting which all editors attended, and at which plans would be made for the Post that would go to press three weeks later and be on the stands in six weeks. Charts, with a box indicating each page, were kept for three issues at once. They were filled out from the copy list of material on hand, subdivided into articles, short stories and serials.

Lorimer's technique was to place all the serials first in a given issue; then he would look for his best opening feature, after which he would go on to plan the balance of the book. His aim was variety. As he went along in the planning process he would comment, "We're getting too much foreign stuff in this number," or "What we need is love," or a question: "What's the best humorous feature we have? This book is heavy so far." An issue was almost never made up completely at the first session; Lorimer left space for timely features.

By late morning his callers would be waiting for him—authors, artists, politicians, diplomats, all anxious to occupy what he called "the poet's chair" beside his desk. He handled visitors expeditiously. Lorimer could listen to an idea from an author and discuss it with him, meanwhile answering a question of policy from an associate editor and looking over an artist's dozen or so preliminary sketches for covers.

"This one is good," he would say to the artist, while the author shifted restlessly in his chair, "but not for us. Perhaps for a woman's magazine. We might use this one." This one would be, perhaps, a rough sketch of three children, two boys and a girl, looking at a cat in a pet-shop window holding several puppies at bay. "Take out the cat," he might say. "No pet shop would mix cats and dogs. Make them all puppies. Can you draw a dog? And take out one of the figures—so many will confuse your composition. Two's enough."

All this would be done in four minutes, the artist would go on his way, and the author would have the stage again.

At lunchtime Lorimer usually entertained authors, either at the Post or at the Bellevue-Stratford. He planned for the Post while he ate. Other men did most of the talking at the luncheon table; one of the Boss's chief attributes was his ability to sit and listen. "I should say," he told a friend, "that the prime qualification of being an editor is being an ordinary man." Lorimer felt that one reason he knew what the ordinary man believed was because he had the remarkable patience to listen to so many of them talk over the years. Nor was it condescension on his part. He was willing and eager to understand, to learn all he could about men and their affairs.

Back at the office again, he picked up the routine of the morning: callers to be seen, a feature to be read at once and rushed into type, a conference with the head of the mechanical department on some point of make-up or printing, another with the advertising chief or with one of his best customers who wanted to shake the Lorimer hand. About two o'clock—and usually twice during the day—he made a tour of the editorial floor, asking readers what they thought of new pieces, chatting with editors, occasionally not stopping at all but just walking around to let the staff know he was there.

Often he looked in on the secretaries' room, to joke with the girls. He always noticed a pretty new dress or a new hairdo. When the Curtis Company moved to its ornate new home on Independence Square, Bok and Lorimer were each furnished with a set of buzzers connecting them with the offices in their departments of the company. On the seventh floor it was considered a great honor to be on the list "buzzed for" by Mr. Bok. Lorimer was never known to buzz for anyone except the office girl and his secretary. If he wanted to talk to a staff member, or one of the girls, he would send the office girl to ask the needed one to drop in when he had time, or, if he wasn't busy, he would simply go to the other's office himself.

Often, when the bulk of his day's work was done, he would sit down in Miss Neall's or some other editor's office and talk shop. There were few women on the Post staff, and Miss Neall was one of two who were close to the Boss; she remained his editorial right hand for twenty-seven years. The other was Bessie Riddell, who was art editor for a time. Lorimer called her "Bess," and she could make him laugh as no one else could. There was a Post rule, sometimes evaded, that no married woman could work at the magazine, on the Lorimer theory that no woman could do two jobs well. Man or woman, he expected people to work at the Post for less than they might earn elsewhere because it was a privilege; most employees agreed with him that it was.

Before quitting time Lorimer cleaned up odds and ends of work. Usually occupied reading manuscripts at that hour, he would lay one down to take his pencil and, for example, cut and rewrite an advertising layout. He would glance at a page layout and remark, "Have them cut out 'Murder' from that head. The point of the story is not the murder but the mystery."

As five o'clock approached he called in all the manuscripts that had passed the readers during the day, added some of his own, stuffed them all in his brief case (which was always a flap with spring catches; no zipper, no handle) and started for Wyncote. Sometimes, in later years, he left at four to make a quick check of the farm, but he arrived at Wyncote in time for a nap on the couch before dinner. At the table Alma always had something interesting and amusing to tell him, and after dinner he walked with her and whoever of the children was home. Then to work with his batch of manuscripts.

That was his routine for years. When the affairs of the company began to press him he learned to delegate some of his mail to others, and distributed a few chores, but he never relinquished his authority to make final decisions, nor did he cut down his reading, although he always said that no man was indispensable. In the great, golden days of the Post, Lorimer worked every minute of every day; at the end he often had leisure in the afternoon to walk around and visit with the editors, just to kill time.

There was always a touch of his particular brand of humor in his dealings with the office staff. No matter how routine his memos might be, they had sly touches. One to Miss Neall read: "Please look over my cuts on ——— and unless you find they bleed anywhere [meaning whether the transition between cuts was smooth] you can put these pages through." And he added: "If they bleed, stanch the flow."

Lorimer was nervous about going away and leaving the Post in other hands. He respected his editors, but he believed sincerely that without his hand at the helm the whole editorial structure might fall to pieces. If he was not kept fully informed at short intervals while he was away, he would prompt his lagging letter writers with such cables as this, from London: "Have any of my houses burned up is anybody dead have we discontinued publication nothing from you since leaving home except Hoover cables." Miss Neall was instructed to write to him daily, no matter who else wrote.

His trips abroad, usually to England, were taken not only for resting purposes but to give him a perspective on his job. A change in the Post usually resulted from one of these trips. The changes were almost imperceptible. To the casual reader the magazine looked the same year after year, but a close study of it over any two-year period would show how Lorimer fashioned his product and kept it fluid. It was a combination of instinct and genius, this constant refitting of the Post to its market. Lorimer himself didn't know how he did it. He told Garrett: "I could get any number of men who could write a better ten-year prospectus for the Post, but they'd lose the circulation I've gotten."

In the office he paid meticulous attention to detail, particularly in the matter of spending company funds carelessly. One of his last memos to the employees was characteristic: "Please make it a rule never to use the long-distance telephone when a telegram will answer; never to use a straight telegram when a night message or a night or day letter will answer, and always look over telegrams to make sure that there are no unnecessary words in them; and finally never to telegraph at all if a letter will answer."

It was such memos as these that made his friendship with Coolidge more understandable.

The general atmosphere of the Post office was one of benevolent despotism, as far as the rank and file were concerned. On the day before Christmas, Lorimer took his associate editors to lunch and bought them champagne. Every year he gave a party for the whole office force. He ordered the menu himself, specifying such items as terrapin, which he thought they might not be able to buy for themselves. He danced with the girls, joked amiably with them, and at one time gave each a twenty-dollar gold piece— token directors' fees which he usually jingled in his pocket. Momentarily he seemed familiar and human to them, but next morning he was all business again and possessed of his customary office formality.

There was one exception to this rule: the Boss always called the office girl by her first name. If she worked up in the organization, he still used the more familiar term, but there were no other exceptions.

He watched not only his own staff but those of the other Curtis publications. As president of the Curtis Company, he was responsible for them all as time went on. It was Lorimer who rescued the *Journal* from the steady decline it suffered after Bok's departure. The magazine had failed to recover under three successive editorships. Not long before he retired, Lorimer discussed with Bruce Gould, then a Post associate editor, the idea of taking over the *Journal's* editorship. The two men were often in disagreement and Gould's independence once prompted Lorimer to say of him, "Bruce Gould just isn't an associate editor—he's an *editor*."

Gould had already refused an offer to become managing editor of the *Journal* under Loring Schuler, and he showed no immediate inclination to accept Lorimer's new invitation until a dinner party changed the course of events. At this affair Lorimer sat next to Gould's charming wife, Beatrice Blackmar Gould. She made an exceptionally pleasing impression on the Boss, and that night he conceived the solution to the *Journal's* problem. Why not a joint editorship by the Goulds? This idea, when he proposed it, was exactly the kind of proposition Gould wanted, but his wife was reluctant. Her logical argument was that if she stopped being a housekeeper, wife and mother her value to the *Journal* would diminish. But she accepted finally, when Lorimer agreed to the stipulation that her working week should never be longer than three days—the first woman executive to be employed by the company on a part-time basis.

The partnership proposed by Lorimer was one of the best things he ever did for the Curtis Publishing Company, as the *Journal's* current pre-eminence proves.

Lorimer looked out for the welfare of the *Journal* and the *Country Gentleman* when they came under his wing, but he wanted the best for the Post. Thus he wrote to Hugh Kahler about a story originally intended for the farm magazine: " 'Once in a Hundred Years' is much too good a story for the *Country Gentleman* or any other periodical except the Saturday Evening Post."

Away from the office, Lorimer's mind constantly generated Post ideas. Lazing by the sea in Atlantic City with Garrett, he might be silent for hours in the sun, then he would break out abruptly in a flow of talk, outlining in detail the idea for an article or an editorial. This process worked both ways. Garrett was sitting with him one day at the resort, reading the paper, and began to express emphatic views about an item he saw in the news. Lorimer interrupted him: "Wait a minute. That's an article. Sit down right now and work it out."

He read prodigiously on vacation trips, in the search for ideas, but he exhausted ordinary books in no time. Garrett saw him stumped only once. On this trip he had used up his supply of volumes during a stop in Havana, and on shipboard again, headed through the Panama Canal, he found himself without anything to read. Garrett observed him chewing his cigar and pacing up and down, so he gave him Stendhal's "The Red and the Black." Stendhal lasted two days. "I take my time with something really good," Lorimer explained.

All his life Lorimer read and re-read the masterpieces of other centuries as well as the relatively trivial stuff of his own time. Those who did not know him were often surprised by his thorough acquaintance with the Bible and the works of the philosophers. He knew the Bible as well as any preacher, because of his father, but he had read the other great books of the world on his own initiative. As he said, "You have to acquire your intellectual furniture young." Huxley and Schopenhauer he particularly admired. "They would have made ideal writers of special articles for the Post," he asserted. "They wrote as clearly as they thought."

The Boss never denied that he published pieces which were tripe, but he knew they were tripe. Fortunately his likings covered such a tremendously wide range that they inevitably encompassed the likings of the majority of readers.

In his role as editor Lorimer permitted himself certain peccadilloes. For instance he liked women writers if they were good-looking. He liked them to be a little flip and impudent with him, as Nina Wilcox Putnam was. When she came to lunch they usually ate alone in the board room and now and then Lorimer's ringing laugh could be heard down the corridor. Nina, according to the Boss, was the only woman he knew who could make mourning spectacular. Part of the technique was a wide white brow band on her veils.

Lorimer was a deliberate showman with his writers; he could not help dramatizing his relations with them. Whether they were women or men, he wanted them to be writers first and specialists in one field or another afterward. He argued that when people became experts they became bores, and consequently they would bore readers. Rather than send a specialist on a story, he preferred to send a top-notch reporter.

Taken all in all, the Boss as editor was a tough-minded man. He was resistant to high prices for stories and high salaries for his staff, and to some writers he appeared almost sadistic. "Not a hard man but a strong man," was the way Mary Roberts Rinehart put it. It was one of the little paradoxes of his character that he talked like a pacifist because of his strong revulsion against the war, but he was far from being a pacifist by nature. When he arrived at a firm judgment he listened to no one. If an editor liked a piece well enough to hold out for it, however, he would change his mind even though he might not have liked it before—that is, if he had not come to a definite decision on his own account.

Some Post editors had the idea that Lorimer did not like people to disagree with him, and they tried to anticipate his opinion on manuscripts. Early in her Post career Adelaide Neall argued heatedly with the Boss about a story at the weekly make-up meeting. The rest of the staff had voted for the story, he had referred it to her, and she had voted no. Lorimer tried to make her change her decision, but she held her ground. After the meeting Churchill Williams offered Miss Neall some friendly advice. "Don't argue like that with Lorimer," he said. "He doesn't like it."

The story was returned and Miss Neall asked the Boss: "Why did you send it back? You seemed so enthusiastic about it."

"I wasn't enthusiastic about it," he replied, "I just wanted to see if you'd stick to your guns."

If a story came to Lorimer for a final decision bearing four noes on the manuscript's envelope—indicating rejection unless the Boss chose to save it—and it proved to be something he liked, Lorimer would walk around the office, showing the piece to any editors who had not seen it. The word went out ahead of him: "The Boss is shopping for a yes." A listener could invariably tell when he was reading something he liked by the appreciative chuckles which emanated from him.

As he edited copy Lorimer worked with a soft black pencil to make cuts. "Try to cut it down" was his most frequent command to editors and writers. When a story was completely off base he knew it instantly and his instructions were blunt: "Rewrite it." He much preferred to have authors cut their own work, whenever they were willing and able.

"I always have to fix up Socker Coe's women," he complained. Charles Francis "Socker" Coe was the writer whose tough, masculine stories of gangland characters and prize fighters were decorated but scarcely ornamented by females until the Lorimer pencil went to work.

Even Mark Twain was not above his editorial criticism. "If he'd only stopped Tom Sawyer after that scene in the cave," he maintained, "it would have been a better book."

In spite of his professional zeal to cut down copy, he was enamored of "Gone with the Wind" to the last page and wished it were five hundred pages longer.

He used his black pencil ruthlessly on the copy of some writers; others he scarcely touched at all, except for purposes of censorship. Of the 207 articles Kenneth Roberts wrote for him, only one was censored and then the change was in two words: "Polish Jews." Lorimer made it "Poles." The change led to an incident which nearly cost Roberts his friendship with the Boss. A man he had known in Siberia wrote to him from the editorial desk of a large Jewish magazine, protesting against his use of the word "Poles." Roberts replied that he was aware of the difference between Poles and Polish Jews; the alteration had taken place in the Post's office. The editor then attacked Roberts, Lorimer and the Post in print. A terse note came to Roberts from Lorimer, asking whether he had said what the editor had quoted him as saying. Roberts replied by letter that the quotation was correct. A long calm ensued, followed by a telephone call from Alma, tipping off Roberts that the Boss was much distressed because he had written instead of coming down to see him. Roberts caught the next train to Philadelphia. He sat for three hours beside the call desk in the lobby of the Curtis Building before he got into Lorimer's office, where the Boss apologized and said he had not been told that his friend was waiting.

"I don't give a damn how long I've been kept waiting," Roberts said. "I'd have sat there a week, if necessary, to get at you."

Roberts made his peace with Lorimer, and the Boss settled the dispute with the irate editor. Alma had prevented a perhaps irrevocable breach between the men.

Eventually a writer learned the editor's likes and dislikes, but if the Boss suspected that anyone was writing according to "policy" he was infuriated. Once he called in Costain and said, "Max Foster has written the last chapter of this serial the way he thinks we want it. He's given it a happy ending, and that's not in character. Send it back to Max and tell him he's free to sell it anywhere he likes; any other magazine will jump at it just as it is. But if he wants to fix it up and make it logical, we'll take it."

Although he never said so, Lorimer admired the hard, meticulous kind of composition more than the easy, facile style. He often spoke approvingly of Samuel Merwin and Henry Kitchell Webster, who composed their best-selling "Calumet K" by sitting on opposite sides of a table and beating out every sentence word by word. This business romance about a grain elevator, which Lorimer serialized in 1901, was probably the first American novel in which a labor union organizer played a prominent part.

Unlike the editors of other magazines, Lorimer was not finished with his task when he had put together an issue of the Post. He was deeply involved in the business affairs of the Curtis Company, and these responsibilities grew year by year. Paradoxically he was also concerned with the advertising department, although there was no publication where a stricter separation of the advertising and editorial sides existed. Lorimer's relations with that division of the business arose from Cyrus Curtis' conviction that a magazine had something to sell and that the editor, knowing the merchandise better than anyone else, was the logical man to tell the story. Consequently Lorimer came to write a great many of the Post's newspaper advertisements in the magazine's earlier period, and he put his okay on them all.

He had an unusual talent for that job, too; it was one of the several occupations in which the Boss could have been outstandingly successful. The owner of a major New York advertising agency once summoned his first lieutenant and sent him to Philadelphia with instructions to hire the copy writer who was turning out a certain series of Post advertisements.

"Did you get that copy writer?" the chief wanted to know when the lieutenant returned.

"I'm afraid not," said the emissary.

"And why not?"

"I didn't think you'd want to meet Mr. Lorimer's salary."

The Boss's ad copy was cast in the same mold as his editorials. Here is a typical full-page ad, which ran on March 8, 1927, when the top line on the page blazoned the news that Post circulation was 3,020,000:

This is honest circulation, clean circulation, built on the merit of the magazine, without clubbing, cut-rate or catch-penny methods.

The Saturday Evening Post goes to the most intelligent and progressive audience in America—the backbone of the country's buying power.

It has been built up slowly and steadily by appealing to and reflecting the best and most vital things in American life. Its readers are those who support the nation's industries rather than its night clubs.

Its growth has not been based on sensationalism.

It has not been based on an appeal to the morbid and prurient-minded.

It has not been based on thinly veiled indecency.

It has been edited on the theory that the tastes and standards of the American public are steadily growing better.

Its editorial policy is based on the belief that America is fundamentally sound and decent and that it is interested in something more than sex and cheap pleasure. Its circulation is the answer of the public to this policy.

It is first, last and all the time an American periodical, convinced of the essential integrity of American principles and intentions.

In the dark days immediately after the crash Lorimer found something to say in full-page Post ads when other copy writers were paralyzed. This one ran on November 5, 1929:

LEADERSHIP

Wall Street may sell stocks but Main Street is still buying goods. The ticker may slow down but production is going right ahead. There may be less money but there will be more earned money. Fewer people watching the ticker means more people watching their jobs, and sound standards mean a sound prosperity.

AMERICA'S BAROMETER OF BUSINESS
IS THE SATURDAY EVENING POST

The largest number in its history is just going to press. It carries the greatest amount of advertising ever placed in a single issue of the weekly. It reflects continuing prosperity in almost every line of business. It is concrete proof of the confidence of American business in both the present and the future.

Lorimer had realized that the market of the twenties was an artificial one. At a time when everyone with an extra dime was playing stocks as though they were horses, there were few people on the Post floor who were speculating. When editors, writers or friends came to Lorimer for financial advice he sometimes told them: "Put it in United States Steel. You'll lose your shirt in anything else." For himself, he liked the smaller companies better. Often a writer yielded to the gambling fever and invested in something highly speculative. "They always come back for a five-hundred-dollar advance," the Boss would say sardonically.

There was no financial advertising in the Post. It was on the banned list along with real estate, liquor and cigarettes. Lorimer refused these categories even when the Post needed additional revenue. There were several reasons for such prohibitions. Lorimer did not open the door to financial and real estate ads because he wanted Post article writers to feel free to write critically in those fields, and because he didn't want to assume responsibility for them. He could have insisted on that freedom even if such ads had been accepted, but he preferred to avoid the controversy entirely. "Anyway," he told a friend, "I know only one piece of financial advice, in or out of advertising, that means anything: buy stocks when the others are buying bonds, and vice versa."

For a long period cigarette advertising was banned. Curtis felt that it should not be carried as long as young boys were selling the Post.

Of liquor advertising Lorimer declared: "I won't encourage people to drink more." This attitude was derived largely from his father. Lorimer was not a religious man in the orthodox sense, but he had acquired certain high moralistic standards from George Claude Lorimer, and he adhered to them in a broad sense. No teetotaler himself, he was likely to write serious letters to his friends about the evils of drinking. He even helped set straight their wandering feet, as in the case of James Whitcomb Riley, when the Hoosier became the concern of his friends because of his heavy drinking. Riley was visiting at Wyncote and it had been decided to serve no alcoholic beverages during his stay. When the poet asked for a drink he was told there was nothing in the house. Riley appeared horrified. He questioned Lorimer closely, pointing out the risk of being unprepared for such sudden contingencies as illness or snakebite.

"Well," he concluded, "you'll never find the Hoosier poet in such danger." He went to his room and came back proudly bearing a bottle retrieved from his suitcase.

Resistance to liquor, cigarette and financial advertising was indicative of the Post's progressiveness, in one sense. Before Lorimer's day no magazine was free of business office influence. Cyrus Curtis changed that by making the Post and *Journal* one-man publications, and the one man could then maintain an absolute or a limited integrity of the editorial department, as he chose. Lorimer's was absolute. He paid his own way and never took a free ride from an advertiser. Sometimes a company, if it advertised in the Post, would attempt to write off his bill, but the Boss was inclined to be unpleasant about it, if necessary, until he was allowed to pay what he owed. It amused and irritated him to see how often he had to engage in a verbal fight to avoid being given something, but he followed the policy meticulously and insisted that his editors do the same. Nor would he permit his name, with one or two exceptions, to be used to support a cause, no matter how worthy.

The only concession he made to the advertising department in his editing of the Post was to take out, on rare occasions, some such remark in a story as "I hate canned peas." But such editing was done only if the line was non-essential to the story.

Knowing his policy, the advertising department occasionally engaged in a game of hide-and-seek with Lorimer, trying to find out far enough in advance what the editorial pages were going to carry so that tie-in advertising could be worked out. Once someone in the department got wind of a scheduled football article and quietly sold some ads to sporting-goods firms to be keyed in with it. Almost at the deadline, Lorimer smelled out the plot and removed the story. He did not hesitate to switch a story, even in the final proofs, if he suspected an advertising tie-up. "You're buying only Post circulation," he told advertisers.

Naturally there were clients who could not understand such integrity. "Lorimer's tough," they would say, "but I'll bet I could sell him on something if I could sit down and talk to him." These boasters were astonished to discover that Lorimer refused to talk to them. An exception occurred when one of the Post's most prominent customers insisted on seeing the Boss, who yielded only under pressure. Once inside the inner sanctum, the customer said he would like to see some Post editorials advocating the building of homes instead of apartments. "After all," he added sentimentally, "an apartment is no place to bring up a child." As it happened, he said, he was in the home building material business himself, and he remarked in passing that his large Post advertising contract was up for renewal.

"I agree with all you've said," Lorimer replied, "but I'm sorry you said it. We've had quite a bit to say in the Post about homes and pets and gardens as a background for raising children, but now it will be impossible for us to mention that subject again for at least a year. If you or any other advertiser should come to think you could influence what goes in the editorial columns of the Post, that space would have lost its value to you."

The advertiser was stunned. He swallowed, excused himself, and retreated from the office, down the hall to the elevator.

"Whew!" he finally got out as he and his escort from the advertising department reached the elevators. "What a man!" he added.

Next day he wrote a new contract double the size of the old one. In spite of his tug-of-war with the business side, Lorimer was as much its sparkplug as he was its nemesis. He was one of the first to see the possibilities in national advertising. He okayed all Post advertising and his role in that department was one of adviser. In fact the Boss often delivered pep talks to the salesmen in the best tradition of the up-and-coming sales manager, interpreting the Post to them. The men took this inspiration seriously; they were ready to admit that Lorimer was an advertising genius.

He was a business genius, too, as he proved in his management of Curtis properties. His rise in the organization measured his increasing value to Cyrus Curtis: elected a director on October 21, 1903; elected vice-president and chairman of the executive committee on September 19, 1927; elected first vice-president, November 25, 1927; elected president, October 28, 1932; elected chairman of the board on December 1, 1934.

It was not an easy rise. There were strong men in every department, and a continuing struggle for power was waged among them. One of the strongest was William Boyd, head of the advertising department, who cracked a whip over the customers. He was succeeded by Fred Healy, who died in 1947. The head of the manufacturing department, John B. Williams, was another of the giants. These strong men yelled and cursed at each other down the years, but Lorimer was tougher than any of them, singly or in combination, and his will prevailed. Moreover, he made the others like it and kept them welded into a smoothly functioning organization.

Aside from his internal battles on the Post, Lorimer had to contend with Bok in the larger framework of the Curtis Company. The Post climbed and climbed and eventually eclipsed the *Journal* in every way, but particularly in circulation and prestige. Under Bok the *Journal* had become the nation's leading women's magazine, and a success by any standard, but that was not enough. The extraordinary Bok ability that had once enabled him to raise a million-dollar subscription fund singlehandedly from the

Academy of Music stage, to save the Philadelphia Orchestra, could not make the *Journal* a bigger magazine than the Post. In any event, he had other affairs to absorb him and resigned in 1919. While the intense rivalry between Bok and Lorimer went on, Curtis and Bok maintained a well-mannered truce. The saving grace in the situation continued to be the mutual respect which existed between Lorimer and Curtis. It was a respect founded on certain similarities between the two men. They were both self-effacing, although for somewhat different reasons, and they shared an extreme distaste for ostentation. "The only real luxury in life is privacy," was a favorite Lorimer aphorism. Curtis admired Lorimer's editorial and business ability. He watched the jockeying for position in his organization with a wise and understanding eye.

Curtis was highly successful with his magazines, but he was a dismal failure in the newspaper field. There he had no Lorimer or Bok to run his properties, and the record was one of disaster and mismanagement. He tried to make a national newspaper out of the Philadelphia *Public Ledger*, and spent a fortune creating a great foreign staff for it, but eventually he had to abandon the whole operation because his initial premise had been wrong. The nation was not interested in a newspaper edited in Philadelphia. The *Inquirer*, which he also owned, reverted to its original owners when payments could not be met. He followed this attempt with the *Sun*, which proved to be an insufferably dull digest for businessmen; it was a tabloid completely devoid of tabloid qualities. Later Curtis operated the New York *Post* for a time, and that, too, had to be sold. All these failures were not the fault of Curtis, but of others involved in the operation of the properties.

Lorimer had nothing to do with these ventures. In fact when Curtis' fliers in newspapers began, he held out for complete separation of the company and the newspaper business. Curtis turned over a block of his Curtis stock so that he could help support his new ventures, but there was no real connection. Ultimately Lorimer's wisdom in the matter was proved.

Similarly, the Boss was opposed to the inauguration of so-called "yellow dog" contracts, whereby employees bought stock through the company and paid for it by deductions from salary. Many of the top executives took on huge blocks of stock, the company underwriting them. Lorimer asserted that the employees wanted to share with the company in good times, but he wanted to know what would happen if the times turned bad. He got his answer after the depression began. The unpaid-for stock holdings proved to be a continuing headache, which still exists, both for the company and for the executives caught with large holdings.

The Boss's financial sagacity was proved not only in such specific instances, but in his management of the Curtis magazines, particularly during the twenties, when the Curtis Company declared a dividend on its common stock every month—fifty cents or a dollar a share. In 1929, just before the crash, it declared nearly twenty million dollars in dividends. At that time, on April 11, 1929, Lorimer wrote to Curtis:

". . . The circulation on all three publications is above last year's figures, and the advertising looks good. We have just put to press a number of the Post that will show the highest net profit in the history of the company." Lorimer added to this letter a paragraph which went about as far as he ever ventured to overcome the extreme reserve between the two men: "I want to take this opportunity to thank you for the letter that you wrote for my anniversary book. No one more keenly appreciates than I do how much of my success as editor of the Post has been due to your help over the rough places, and your standing behind me from the time when I first took editorial charge of the publication."

The correspondence between them consisted almost entirely of minor suggestions from Curtis and frequent reports on the state of the business from Lorimer. In these reports the Boss demonstrated his grasp of every detail in the organization. A typical 1929 report, for example, noted that the *Journal's* covers were poor and that its pages lacked enough definite feminine appeal. It reported, too, on the Post's recent acquisition of an airplane and how one of the advertising executives had flown in it to Lancaster to see a customer with a grouch. The advertiser was so flattered by the compliment that he forgot the grouch and the account was saved. Lorimer added that the same executive intended to fly out to Battle Creek, Michigan, and attempt to woo back W. K. Kellogg into the advertising fold—"an exceedingly difficult nut to crack." Kellogg had expressed a desire to see the plane and ride in it from Battle Creek to Detroit.

As a businessman Lorimer weathered the worst financial storms. In 1933, when the bank holiday had caused near collapse for other organizations, he wrote to Curtis: "The past few days have been pretty hectic ones, but we are coming through in good shape. . . . We had sufficient cash on hand both to meet our pay roll this week and to provide the postage on our magazines for several weeks to come. We still have some cash over and above our bank balances, with which we can care for unexpected contingencies. However, it looks as if things would begin to straighten out before the end of the week, so that we can tell better what is ahead of us, and that we will either have sufficient cash or clearinghouse certificates to cover our day-by-day needs. . . . We had practically no cancellations over the week end, and put an 88-page Post to press. . . . Everything considered, we are in a good position, and I can see no reason for any uneasiness even with present conditions what they are."

Among his responsibilities as president of the company was the answering of indignant letters from stockholders. One complained because the company had passed a preferred dividend in a lean year; he termed it the "style" among some corporations to pass dividends "on the slightest provocation." Lorimer replied tartly that the largest stockholders were members of the board of directors, and it could be presumed that they had not passed a dividend because of any desire to be in style. "You urge," he added, "a continuance of dividend payments based on a 'faith in the future.' Unfortunately that quality is not convertible into cash, and it is cash which is necessary for the payment of bills and to meet current expenses."

Most stockholders and members of the company were eminently satisfied with Lorimer's conduct of affairs. When it was announced in 1934 that Lorimer would step down as president and become chairman of the board and head of the executive committee—a realignment to relieve him of business detail—several of his friends in the company wrote to him in alarm, wondering whether he intended to relinquish the reins altogether. To one of these inquirers Lorimer replied:

". . . I don't know whether you appreciate just what being editor of the Saturday Evening Post, which has always been my real job, means. I formulate its policies and practically everything in connection with the weekly begins and ends at my desk. I have a very large correspondence which I must answer personally, and in addition to that, after the readers have weeded out the manuscripts, there is still five hundred thousand words a week which I must read personally and from which I must select the stories and articles that appear in the magazine, and that in itself is a full-sized job and it takes five evenings of every week, leaving me two in which to play if I feel inclined to play."

If that statement sounded like a complaint, it was not the Boss's intention. The job absorbed his time but he loved every minute of it. He resented the time he had been forced to give to the purely business affairs of the company. To him the editor's occupation was to edit, and his concern was to please the readers. These readers he had constantly in mind. He visualized them in terms which sounded like a Chamber of Commerce brochure, but the conception was accurate, on the whole. They were, he thought, "the men and women from seventeen to seventy who are growing." He saw them in business as "the gray-haired President with young brains, the never-say-die salesman, the up-and-coming clerks, the get-ahead cubs." In law, medicine, journalism and public life they were "the men who win cases and save lives, who fight for clean politics, and a better America." Rural readers were "the farmer who goes to town in his automobile and the young man who goes to the State College of Agriculture." In college it was "the boy who has more than the batting averages in his head, and the professor who can interest his classes in a dry-as-dust subject." Women readers were those "clear-eyed, upstanding ones who think in terms of something besides cup custards and sex stories."

In brief, good old-fashioned middle-class Americans, notwithstanding the fact that Lorimer hated the term "middle class."

People outside the magazine, all the way from obscure subscribers to acquaintances of the Boss prominent in other fields, respected the editor in Philadelphia from whom the word flowed abundantly every week. Even those who knew him only as a name on the masthead were eager to know more about him. A Salt Lake City man wrote in 1933: "It seems to me, Mr. Lorimer, that you love the Saturday Evening Post as you do your own life. You have truly done a great job and so I tell you what great pleasure and real happiness you have brought to our home. . . . I feast on good biographies and only once or twice have I been able to read anything concerning you and your life. I only wish I could know more about your very interesting and useful life."

Lorimer returned the answer he made to all such requests: "I have always felt that the Saturday Evening Post is a good deal bigger and more important than any of the men who edit it, and its biography is written week by week."

The admiration of the publishing world was his from the beginning. John O'Hara Cosgrave invited him to speak at a 1914 banquet of the Authors' League in these words: "You are the boss editor of the bunch. Yours is the most successful, most widely read publication in the country. You can tell the gathering things about their work they'd be glad to hear. . . . You would be listened to with attention because you have real authority."

But the Boss declined to join William Jennings Bryan, Herbert Putnam and Rex Beach on the speakers' dais. His refusal expressed his reluctance to take advantage of his position. "I think far too highly of the Authors' League to make a speech at its banquet. I have myself suffered so much at the hands of untrained speakers that I must absolutely refuse to be a party to the crime which you contemplate. I occasionally give a little, informal talk to a little, informal crowd on some topic related to editing and publishing, but that has been, and is going to be, my limit. I appreciate more than I can tell you the authors wanting to have me, but the first duty of an editor is to keep the bad stuff out." He added this characteristic postscript: "Also, I could change this, if the first reason were not such a good one—but old Irvin Cobb and I are planning to be somewhere in the lower levels of the Grand Canyon about the time that your dinner is pulled off."

Similarly he refused to be drawn into controversies. One of those literary teapot tempests occurred in 1921, when Upton Sinclair published a full-page advertisement in the *New Republic* and the *Nation*, quoting a letter from H. G. Wells to him in which Wells made a somewhat ambiguous reference to the fact that he had referred to Sinclair in a Post series on "The Salvaging of Civilization." Sinclair asserted in his ad that he had not been able to discover the reference, and he inquired whether the capitalistic Post had suppressed it.

At that time the New York *Globe* was publishing a series of articles in the form of a debate between Sinclair and James Melvin Lee, professor of journalism at New York University, on the subject, "Is Journalism Honest in America?" The debate was based on Sinclair's "The Brass Check." Bruce Bliven, then managing editor of the *Globe*, wrote to Lorimer and asked him if Sinclair's name *had* been edited from Wells's Post series. Lorimer replied: "I have had one of my associates go through Mr. Wells's copy very carefully, and he assures me that the name of Upton Sinclair does not occur in it. This letter, however, is not for publication as I do not care to contribute any advertising of any sort or description to this notoriety seeker."

Bliven in those days apparently shared Lorimer's opinion of the eminent literary crusader, for he answered that he was disappointed that Lorimer would not co-operate. He added that he was well aware of Sinclair's "itch for publicity" and repeated that this "really good case" against him should be printed.

This incident was typical of Lorimer's lifelong avoidance of the public prints, even if they did him injustice. In 1932, when he became president of the Curtis Publishing Company, *Time Magazine* published a story about the promotion which, in little more than two columns of omniscient prose, contrived to amass a total of at least fourteen major errors. The Boss wrote *Time* a forceful letter, setting Mr. Luce straight and reminding him that a telephone call to Philadelphia would have corrected the record in advance. But he requested that the letter be held for future reference; he was not interested in seeing it printed.

Lorimer took recognition of his pre-eminent editorial position lightly, particularly when it came from a foreign source. In 1927 he was given one of the highest honors possible for the Italian government to confer upon a foreigner, but except for his formal thanks to the Italian ambassador, the only notice he took of the honor came in one paragraph of a letter to Kenneth Roberts, sandwiched between a paragraph about the values of Jersey blue glass and his plans for the summer. "I received a letter from the Italian Ambassador last week," he wrote, "saying that on his recommendation I had been made a Commander of the Crown of Italy, and shortly thereafter, the Italian Consul came in and pinned the order to my bosom, remarking that on *his* recommendation I had been made a Commander of the Crown of Italy. As I believe that I am indebted to you for the honor, I am sending herewith my regards and final thanks for it."

All manner of people honored the Post's editor and wished him well. Billy Sunday wrote from Waterloo, Iowa, in 1932 that he "knew your dear Dad when he was a preacher in Chicago and never missed a chance to hear him. I have watched you climb the ladder of success until today you sit on the throne."

Even his writing friends among the Post's contributors were occasionally compelled to express their admiration for something the Boss had done in his magazine. Ben Ames Williams wrote in 1927 to compliment him on the appearance of a short-lived department in the Post titled "Americana," which Lorimer had compiled in an effort to "expose" the machinations of men like Mencken and Nathan, who in their new *American Mercury* had joined those editors and novelists who, in Lorimer's opinion, were attempting "to prove everybody and everything in America rotten." Williams agreed with him. "I know no easier way to attract attention," he wrote, "than by abusing the universe at large, and Mencken, Nathan, et al have made a living at it for years."

While there were some who believed that Lorimer the editor could do no wrong, it was plain to other, less idolatrous observers, that the Post had reached a low point immediately after the first World War. Though the men who had worked with Lorimer to make the Post great were still in the saddle, it was a cruel fact that they had begun to outlive their usefulness, and Lorimer had an understandable reluctance to replace them. A more obvious weakness in the organization was the Boss's apparent lack of concern for the Post's physical appearance. Other magazines were spending lavishly to dress up; Lorimer would not spend a dime. The art editor continued to bring in ideas for his approval, and he picked out what pleased him—but the same things pleased him that he had liked ten years before.

The arrival of Tom Costain in 1920 was the first move in the Boss's campaign to rejuvenate his staff. It was slow going for the new man at first. He was aware of the Post's old-fashioned appearance, and he felt certain that the Post needed photography, among other things. Lorimer had been singularly unappreciative of this art and its practitioners, but he assented readily enough when Costain arranged a luncheon with Margaret Bourke-White, then at the beginning of her career. It was a pleasant meal but nothing came of it. Costain did not dare to press the point. It angered Lorimer if someone reiterated an idea that had found no responsive enthusiasm in him.

As a contact man, however, Costain had more success and soon proved his value to the Boss. He would come back from a New York trip with thirty or forty acquisitions to be decided upon, and Lorimer would dispose of them in an incredibly short time, making his quick, irrevocable decisions. Gradually these trips of Costain's became the source of a steady flow of ideas, and Lorimer accepted more and more of them.

Other new blood was soon injected with the arrival of Arthur McKeough and Wesley Stout. McKeough was an ex-Lost Battalion soldier and New York *Sun* reporter. In the next decade still other editors joined the staff, one by one—Pete Martin, Merritt Hulburd and the Boss's son Graeme. These men helped to accelerate the process of change on the Post; they were the answer to Lorimer's feeling that the magazine needed people who would accept new ideas. For his own part, he worked harder than ever, often staying late at the office to read and okay rush pages. One of the new men, hoping to impress him, began to stay at his desk after hours, endeavoring to outlast the Boss. Lorimer was not impressed. He said nothing the first two nights, but on the third night he put his head in the new editor's office on his way out and remarked, with a twinkle in his eye that the victim did not see, "If you can't get your work done on time, we'd better get someone else."

It took a little time for new staff members to understand Lorimer and his magazine. When he invited several of them to dinner at Wyncote, they remembered the Post's policy on liquor advertising and, mistaking it for the editor's, polished off a pint or two before they presented themselves. They were confounded when Lorimer, with his accustomed hospitality, produced a quantity of alcoholic refreshment and urged it upon them. He seemed astonished by their restraint.

Of the new editors, Wesley Stout was the one most like Lorimer. Coming to the Post in 1922, he looked over his new territory with the kind of meticulous attention the Boss would have given it. The Post seemed a stuffy sort of place to him. He felt that Lorimer could have dismissed the whole staff and put out the magazine himself. Analyzing the Boss's position, he concluded that Lorimer was a man preparing himself deliberately and with considerable enthusiasm for his work as president of the company—perhaps fulfilling at last his early dreams of business success. To Stout, he appeared somewhat self-satisfied, so satiated with his editorial eminence that he had lost some of his interest in the Post. He pointed to the Post's enormous size as the visible proof of his success, but Stout and others thought the magazine was too big, filled with column after column of solid type. Lorimer would not accede to any change in make-up, however, nor to any plan of modernization.

Some of the magazine's best writers had been lost to Hollywood and the influx of new material was still only a trickle compared with the flow it would become. All in all, Stout thought, the Post resembled a great feudal castle, dreaming of its past glories while the world rushed by outside and the stout walls shut out the sounds of change. It was a benevolent feudalism, where the serfs were given delightful Christmas parties at which attendance was compulsory.

The reason for this situation was obvious. Overwhelming success in the Post's golden era before the war had made Lorimer more or less complacent about the magazine. It could run itself while he diverted more of his energies to the affairs of the corporation. In this matter he had little choice. Curtis was growing old and he would ultimately have to retire into the chairmanship of the board, making Lorimer the inevitable choice to succeed him as president. The Boss was not reluctant to assume the mantle. He believed that the position of the Post was so secure that he could be businessman and editor simultaneously without strain. The magazine's nearest rival was the *Literary Digest*, whose revenue and influence were insignificant by comparison. Still around the corner was the publication which would make the first successful assault on the Post's supremacy—that fountainhead of the journalism of omniscience, *Time Magazine*.

When Luce's child was born in 1923, Lorimer did not take it seriously because it was not at first a direct competitor. But its spontaneous reception soon began to be felt in the place where it hurt the Post most of all, in the advertising department. Until that time Boyd had never been compelled to solicit advertising. He had been in the enviable position of being able to tell the advertiser what he could have and what was denied him.

As the Post thus moved into the twenties it became the task of Costain, Stout, Hulburd, Martin, Graeme Lorimer and other newcomers to revive the magazine and give it new life. With Lorimer's genius at the helm to guide them, they succeeded. The Post entered a second and even more profitable golden age before Lorimer's death marked its transition to a different era in its history.

All the new editors were able men, but it was Costain who appeared to have the inside track. At a board meeting Lorimer referred to him, perhaps jokingly, as the crown prince, and it was no secret that he expected to succeed the Boss as editor. The ambitious Costain was more aware of this trend than anyone else. As one observer remarked, "The Boss is captain of this ship, but Costain keeps nudging him and saying, 'Let me take the wheel.'"

Lorimer frequently entrusted the Post to Costain when he was away, but he left the most detailed instructions, covering every possible contingency. He would begin one of these instruction sheets, "As usual, you will be in full charge of everything and everybody on the Post floor during my absence. Use your best judgment and I will, of course, back you up in whatever you may do." Then Lorimer would add, "I should, however, like to add before leaving a word about editorial matters," to wit over several pages:

"In addition to the Ben Ames Williams serial, which I have returned, I have turned down the Darrow article, because it is thoroughly one-sided and gives a false picture of the criminal classes as a whole. We could agree with what he says about one class of criminals, but he took the position that practically all crime was entirely due to early environment and poverty. Incidentally, I thought that what he was planning to write was an article without prejudice and bias on the administration of criminal justice in England.

"I also turned down the first of the Al Jennings articles and told [George] Bye that I did not believe that there was any hope for a series. This first article was thoroughly false and sentimental in tone, and, though Al tried hard to set a backfire, the net result of it was a glorification of the criminal. I think that in 'Beating Back' he really told everything of any importance that he had to tell, and in that series he had the advantage of a wise collaborator in the person of Will Irwin. Stout, Pete and Miss Neall were in thorough agreement with me on all these matters.

"George Allen England sent in a fair article on the smuggling of aliens, which we have accepted, and added in his note that he had been commissioned for three articles, two of which we have accepted, and the third on treasure hunting. I wrote and explained our policy in regard to special articles and stated that in my opinion the treasure-hunting article would be a gamble. You would better look up my letter to him. He, like Cooper, is good for an occasional piece, but not for too many.

"I think the summer numbers have run exceedingly well and on the whole we have a good copy list with a number of outstanding features on it, though there are more ✳2s on it than I like to see. While I am away I wish that you would read very closely, accepting nothing but ⚹1 stuff, trying particularly to add some light, one-part special articles to the list. We need, too, a couple of crackerjack serials, as, while we have a number of them, they are none of them really world-beaters. For the present I think we should lay off on buying many series of special articles, either in the form of reminiscences or biography. Of this kind, only a feature of the most exceptional and outstanding merit should be considered. With the Spring-Rice and Harvey letters and various other fairly heavy series we have had about enough of this sort of thing for the present. I particularly do not want to take on any more war reminiscences or series of articles about the war and its various side lines. Good war fiction is okay but even that can be overdone.

"We should also go light on crime fiction. We have had a very large number of serials and series tied up with crime and it is time to soft-pedal a little in that quarter. Particularly I do not want to add any stories of penitentiary life such as Givens and Coe have been doing for us. Switch Givens off onto stuff like 'Pappy Blue Boy,' which he does even better than penitentiary stories.

"Please confine Prohibition stuff, either for or against, to the editorial page, and then only after I have read and okayed it.

"We have several men writing for us in the Earl Chapin May class, who present subjects that look good and that almost always turn out to be ⚹2s. I think it would be wise to get rid of these men and try to add more special writers who can do first-chop articles for us. As a matter of fact there is no reason why we should ever use either ⚹2 stuff or stuff that is on the line in the Post. We get landed with it either through asking people to revise stories and articles that do not get over in the first instance or by letting some of these special writers come to us with ideas which we say are possibilities. Then, when they have done a lot of work on them and the article is fair, we do not quite feel that we can turn them down. It is really better not to start with them at all. I do not include Reinhardt in this list, because I think he is a very valuable man.

"With the increasing competition we have got to make the Post better all the time and to do this we shall have to broaden our list

of ⚹1 writers, cut out the ⚹2s and watch the length of articles
and stories so as to get more titles in the book wherever possible.
I have been living pretty close to the weekly for the past three
weeks and this is about the net of what I have come to feel.

"Incidentally, the public seems to tire of too much stuff by the
same writers and so we must continually be feeding in the new
men. A lot of the old-timers, the Cobbs, the Kynes and so on, are
really living in the past, and the public is ripe for new names. . . .

"P.S. Hoover is seeing Lowry at the White House, giving him
an interview on the reorganization of the governmental departments, but he cannot directly quote the President in this interview. . . ."

Aside from all this, Costain was to feel free to use his judgment,
and Lorimer would back him up!

Much as he trusted Costain, Lorimer could not like him. The
differences between them were too great, and no doubt the Boss
was conscious of ambition breathing down his neck. The two men
were somewhat ill at ease with each other. Lorimer took out his
anti-British feelings on the Canadian-born Costain with ribbing
that had a sting in it. At lunch one day he complained:

"There's nothing but cauliflower in these sour pickles. Those
damned British are always doing that."

"You speak as though that were a sign of the degeneration of
the species," Costain protested mildly.

"It is," Lorimer replied.

The undercurrent of tension between the two men came to the
surface only once before Costain's ultimate departure. There had
been a complaint about a story, suggesting plagiarism, and Costain
had given the complainant a routine answer. Then a second letter
arrived, of a really threatening nature and implying legal action.
Costain decided that he should show the correspondence to Lorimer before he took any further action.

The Boss was angry because Costain had not shown him the
original letter. For the moment he said nothing, but he brought up
the matter at the first editorial meeting and gave Costain what
amounted to a public reprimand. Costain went back to his office
and without a word to anyone began cleaning out his desk. He

stopped only long enough to type out his resignation and send it in by messenger. Later in the day Lorimer summoned him. The resignation lay on his desk.

"Let's forget about this," he said brusquely, indicating the paper. That was the nearest he could bring himself to an apology, and Costain could see that he spoke with an effort. A few more conciliatory words were exchanged, and Costain agreed to stay. The truce lasted until 1934, when Costain resigned on amicable terms and went to Hollywood, where Hulburd had preceded him three years before. It was freely predicted that Tom's blood would be let by the studio hatchet men. It was. That fortunate assassination led Costain to return to New York, become a book editor, and eventually capitalize on his lifetime hobby of reading English and French history by turning out a series of best-selling novels. Hulburd, it may be added, also rejected Hollywood in time and came back to take the place of Graeme Lorimer, who resigned to write.

All these intraoffice maneuverings, however, were only small interruptions to the pattern of teamwork that Lorimer and his new editors built up in the twenties, and which resulted in the Post's remarkable recrudescence. The peak of that resurgence was reached in 1929. During that memorable year twenty-four new fiction writers were discovered in the unsolicited manuscripts. It was the year that the Post published 386 short stories, written by 121 authors and illustrated by 51 artists. Exclusive of departments, it published 399 articles which were contributed by 165 writers, and 29 serials, most of which appeared later as books and movies. One issue—December 7, 1929—took 6,000,000 pounds of paper and 120,000 pounds of ink, and sixty 45-ton presses rolled day and night for three weeks to print it. That issue was the largest Post ever printed. For a time it seemed that the magazine had returned to the splendid days of 1916, when it had refused business and Lorimer had ruled that no advertising could appear in it which did not run once every four weeks, thirteen times annually.

The Post had led its field for thirty years, while most of the magazines that started out with it had fallen by the wayside. A majority of these casualties were the victims of sensationalism. They had tried for quick circulation, got it, and then were unable to stand the pace. There was a limit to sensation, as *McClure's, Everybody's* and the others discovered. One of the few popular contemporaries of the Post to survive was *Redbook*. It did so largely by emulating Lorimer's policies, eventually under the guidance of a Post alumnus, Edwin Balmer.

But as the Post moved into the thirties it was often out of joint with the times, in other ways than politically, and no one felt this more keenly than its editor. He wrote bitterly to Kenneth Roberts in August 1935:

". . . It does seem these days as though the way to get an opportunity to write is to do something spectacular that has nothing to do with training for writing. If you swim the Channel or if your husband figures in a spectacular kidnaping, the newspapers open their arms to you. In other words the advice to the young would be if you want to write do almost anything except train to be a writer. One could carry the idea further and bring out the fact that if you want to be a Secretary of the Treasury, say, be an apple grower entirely uninformed on financial matters, or if you want to get a job selling dresses in a specialty shop or modeling, be sure to be a member of the Junior League. I can only imagine what your feelings must have been when you saw that Mary Pickford was a best seller!"

Through these changing times Lorimer clung to the principles that had made him a great editor, as well as to those which had served their purpose and might better have been dropped. He was, for instance, meticulous about such apparently small matters as insisting that Post readers be careful of manuscripts and not rumple or mar them, because he well knew how important a financial matter typing stories could be to an author.

The Boss never forgot what it was like to be a beginning writer. He would say: "Writing is a very personal thing. Your story is a little bit of yourself. It hurts to get it back. At least we can make people feel that we have read their manuscripts with interest and have handled them carefully."

He insisted, too, on the nickel price for the magazine. During the war there had been considerable pressure on him to raise the price but he had refused. "I consider it a pledge to the American people," he said sincerely. Nor would he retreat a step from the principle that Post writers must have absolute freedom; no one must write anything except what he honestly believed.

As a result of these policies and the hard work of its new editors, the Post recaptured in the twenties several of its former big-name writers and developed promising new ones as well. In a commanding position once more, Lorimer could contemplate without alarm the advent of new magazines. When *Liberty* appeared in 1924, the brain child of Captain Joseph Patterson, the Boss looked it over and wrote to Ed Howe: ". . . Personally I am inclined to think that the new weekly will find an audience and in the end prove commercially successful. It has not, however, touched and will not touch the Saturday Evening Post so long as it is edited along its present lines and continues the appeal that it is obviously trying to make."

Lorimer felt secure in the knowledge that the Post was the biggest nickel's worth in the country. He had demonstrated that fact dramatically in 1919, one of the worst years in the magazine's history, with the publication and private distribution to agents of a book called "One Issue," subtitled "Just One 52nd of a Year. An Object Lesson in Values." It was, indeed, an object lesson. The volume was designed to show how one issue of the Post would look if published in book form, without the advertising. Lorimer estimated that it would cost a dollar and a half at retail.

The 382 pages of "One Issue" carried a fairly impressive list of reading matter, considering the time of its publication. There were stories by George Randolph Chester, May Edginton, Wallace Irwin and Octavus Roy Cohen, among others. Sam Blythe, Will Payne and Henry Watterson were among the article writers.

But the seeds of the magazine's subsequent discontent were beginning to flower in this book. The lead story, "Man Snatchers," by William Hamilton Osborne, was a typical business story of an outmoded kind. It began: "At half past twelve o'clock on the afternoon of Friday, the thirteenth day of December in the year nineteen hundred eighteen, Pemberton Forbes, seated at his desk in his private suite in the Cedar Street offices of the Forbes Powder Works, Inc., scribbled a brief message on a telegraph blank and pressed a button. He read the message and corrected it. This is what it said: 'Pay all hands one full month's extra wages. Shut down plant forthwith. We quit today.' "

The editorials in that 1919 issue indicated the state of the Post's decline and foreshadowed the way in which it would become politically outdated. These editorials denounced the Bolsheviki, pleaded for a national blue-sky law, half seriously backed an Italian statesman's proposal for a world lottery to reduce war debts, asked for a new kind of Europe, and deplored further increases in railroadmen's wages, unless the country wanted to resort to "the Bolshevik device of paying a big industry more than it produces."

Sam Blythe's article, "A Presidential Potpourri," seemed strangely prophetic in this paragraph: "You cannot teach an Old Guard new tricks. Every circumstance, from catastrophe to candor, has taken a hand at it, but to no avail. The Old Guard surrenders, but it never dies. Right at this minute, despite conditions, both political and national, that are so changed they bear no resemblance to conditions whenever precedent, those ancient and archaic Republicans who think they control the destinies of the Republican Party—think they do!—are operating after the manner and style of 1896. The war hasn't made a dent in them. The new aspect of affairs has had no impress. They are proceeding toward 1920 in the same old way. Day after day they are led into the menagerie and shown the ringtailed gyascutus of the new order; and day after day they chew their straws, shake their hoary heads and solemnly aver: 'There ain't no such animile!' The pathos of it is obscured in the purblindness of it. You can't teach an Old Guard new tricks."

Lorimer's editorial tricks, at least some of them, were so good he did not need to learn new ones, even when the Post finally stood at bay, unchanged in a changing world. His were the editorial tricks that made him seem a hard-fisted dictator to one writer and "the original easy boss" to Irvin Cobb; the tricks that somehow, by sheer ability, put together week after week a magazine that was capable of earning enormous profits and entertaining millions of people. *Cosmopolitan*, by comparison, entertained well enough but its profit-making ability was inferior.

Cobb's estimate of the Lorimer character was conditioned by friendship, but he came close to catching the quality in the Boss that made him supreme among editors—one of "the big, outstanding, human nouns of his day and time," as Cobb put it. They were simple virtues, the humorist thought, but important—things like explaining something complicated in two hundred words or less, knowing exactly what he was going to say when he began to speak and stopping when he had said it. "I never knew him to say no when he meant yes," Cobb said. "I never knew him to say yes when he meant no. I never knew him to say, 'Well, possibly so,' under any circumstances." Taking shortcomings and virtues together, Cobb asserted, "Lorimer more nearly approximates the popular conception—and incidentally the proper one—of the typical American than any man I have known. . . ."

With that comprehended, the secret of Lorimer's success as an editor is better understood: he edited the magazine to suit himself as a typical American, and thus he pleased other typical Americans. There were large quantities of that species extant. The Post was bright but not sensational, instructive without being pedantic, effective without resort to preaching, and good-natured without being silly. It leaned to ridicule rather than scolding, and it believed ardently in the romantic ideal of love.

Lorimer impressed his writers with the sheer impact of his personality as much as with the importance of his position. Cobb, who was not a man inclined to be impressed by anyone, described what it was like to call on the Boss. "You walk along a hallway," he said, "and through an open door into an office slightly smaller than the State of Rhode Island. Behind a big, square desk at the far end of the room sits a man of medium size—a compactly built, rather sinewy-looking man with a long, strong, angular jaw, a small, keen, blue eye and a squarish think-box of a head thatched with brown hair which is beginning to turn gray above the lean temples. He has shapely, slender fingers—the fingers of an artist and a creator. He has deep, witty lines around his mouth, and a kindly twinkle in the blue eye. If you have an idea to present, he listens patiently enough but very often before you are done with the job of outlining it, he breaks in with a short, laconic comment and then realization comes to you that the thing you have been mulling over for weeks was merely half an idea, and this man who probably never thought of it until five minutes ago has, in fifty words, supplied you with the remaining half and made it a structure complete and adequate. At taking mental short cuts I have yet to see his equal anywhere. He never thinks around a subject—he thinks through it and comes out on the other side with the sum total in his hand, all neatly wrapped up and ready for delivery."

The Boss's genius was peculiarly for the magazine medium. He understood the character of periodicals, and he thought it was nonsense to apply book standards to them, or to apply magazine standards to newspapers. He blamed professional critics and professors of English for the confusion arising from attempts to interlock these standards. He argued that the most popular Post serial might not make a good book, and that a fine novel might, and in most cases did, lack the qualities of a serial. A few of the Post writers did their best work in book form, but Lorimer did not buy it for that reason; consequently he was accused of printing only the inferior work of his best contributors. The Boss defined the difference in media this way: "A newspaper is life on the run; a periodical life on a walk; and a novel may be life running, walking or sitting."

In fashioning the character of his particular medium, Lorimer had made it a man's magazine by dedicating it to business. Thus it attracted many more male writers than women, which satisfied Lorimer because it was his conviction that women wrote too many introspective stories.

"What do you mean by introspective stories?" Ike Marcosson asked him.

"Stories in which one looks within and finds nothing," Lorimer replied.

Before the Post came into the field most American magazines appealed particularly to women on the accepted theory that men would not buy magazines. Lorimer believed that if a magazine appealed to men a respectable percentage of women would want it too, and on the strength of that argument he succeeded in reversing the emphasis in American periodicals within the first decade of his editorship.

Lorimer correctly analyzed the reason for the decline and fall of the earlier weekly magazines. They failed, he said, because their owners made too much money and lost touch with the people. He never contemplated for a moment that such a thing could happen to him.

On the other hand, he was correct in believing that one-man power on a magazine or a newspaper gave it character and distinction. "Editors and crowned heads," he remarked, "are the only people in the world . . . with the right to say 'we.' Editors should be the only despots. If the editor does not make good, what the public needs is a new editor, not a dozen editors. No human affair is strong enough to stand the mistakes of two men."

As the Post despot, Lorimer was admired by his subjects, the writers, much more than most despots, including those who were sturdy individualists on their own account. Will Irwin was a basically different person than the Boss, and their association foundered on the rock of politics, but nonetheless he could not help falling under Lorimer's spell. He had met the editor by contributing a series of short stories and three serials based on a faking professional medium. These pieces were later dramatized by Bayard Veiller as "The Thirteenth Chair."

Irwin was a good fiction writer, but Lorimer saw that his talent for reporting and writing feature articles was potentially greater, so he endeavored to combine both talents in the Post variety of muckraking article. Irwin thought these excavations rather mild. That was because Lorimer did not really believe in the exposé. He could not avoid admitting that the exposure of evil was a good thing, but he was committed to the idea that business was more in need of understanding than correction. He stood, in general, for the status quo, once his Progressive days were past, while Irwin and other writers cried aloud for reform.

A large part of what little muckraking the Post did was in fictional form, where it was sugar-coated. Lorimer wanted Irwin, for example, to go after the tin-plate trust, whose watered-stock activities had brought it unavoidably to public attention. The technique, however, was to be a serial, because Lorimer believed that this was an idea which could be put across to the average reader more effectively as fiction than as an article. "Take two men," he told Irwin, "a workman in the mills and a clerk in the office. Carry them from the time when the industry was new. Have the clerk get rich through manipulation. Have the workman get poorer and poorer. Tie it all up with watered stock. Make up the rest of the plot yourself as you go along investigating. You'll have to do some digging. The material is in government files and in the mills."

No writer would have questioned such an order from the Boss, or would have dreamed of arguing that the thing might be done more effectively as an article. The Lorimer word was law. Where the magazine was concerned, even the Boss's friends were not given any special consideration.

No writer was bigger than the Post. If one chose to leave, there were always others to succeed him. Nor could he give any less than his best for the Post, because Lorimer would not hesitate to turn down the work of his highest-paid writers if he thought it fell below standard. He read every contribution as though it were the first piece the writer had submitted.

The Boss would not tolerate anything he considered as "using" his magazine. Floyd W. Parsons, a Post writer who contributed more than three hundred short articles on business subjects, had to do much writing for photographs and material in compiling his pieces, and to aid this work he had some stationery printed with his name on it and "The Saturday Evening Post" printed in small type in one corner. He wrote Lorimer a note on this stationery. Visiting him a few days later, he saw his letterhead lying on the desk and a bleak look on the Boss's face. Lorimer's comment, Parsons recalled, "was cryptic, straight to the point, and altogether sufficient."

The Lorimer editorial omniscience was reflected most spectacularly in what came to be known as "Post luck." Of this the

Hartford *Times* marveled editorially in 1935: "Although the Saturday Evening Post makes up its issues weeks in advance of publication, the timeliness of some of its fact and fiction is uncanny. One might ask if it is prescience."

"Post luck" began with Sam Blythe's Harding article, which was on the stands when the President died. Then the submarine S-54 dropped to the bottom while Commander Ellsberg's story of the salvaging of her sister ship, the S-51, was running in the Post. In 1934 the newspapers were black with the *Morro Castle* disaster while the Post was carrying a story of New York newspaper life by Manuel Komroff, centered on the sinking of the *Titanic*. A year later the Post appeared one week with a lead article, the first of three, on the life of Huey Long. A few hours later the "brooding young intellectual" ended Long's reign. In that same year Jim Collins, a test pilot, told Post readers how it felt to power-dive at 400 miles an hour. While they were reading it Collins was killed making his final test before retirement, when he failed to pull out of exactly the kind of dive he had described.

Then there was Jack Dempsey's article, "The Next Champion," with its prophetic sentence: "There could be a new heavyweight champion and a new runner-up when this is printed."

The superstitious were ready to believe that Lorimer had previsions of death and disaster, after this series of remarkable coincidences. What the Boss did have was a superb sense of timing, a feeling for the flow of events. That quality led to other examples of "Post luck" that were more than coincidence. One of the most startling of these was Gordon MacCreagh's article on Ethiopia, forecasting Mussolini's invasion the week it began. Lorimer had picked MacCreagh to do the piece because he considered him the outstanding authority on Ethiopia. Both believed that war was certain, and the rainy season in Ethiopia made it possible to predict the date of invasion almost exactly.

Another outstanding piece of planned "luck" was Lorimer's prevision on the stock-market crash. Warning signals had flown in the Post's columns all through the twenties. Five months before disaster arrived Garrett wrote:

"When a state of excitement long continued passes into a state of delirium, price ceases to have any relation whatever to values. From there on what causes the price line to rise is the power of suggestion acting on the imagination. People are no longer dealing in stocks; they are dealing in quotations. Simply, they are betting on numbers—higher and higher numbers—as at any other game of chance.

"That rise in the price line is what absorbs at last all the credit there is. The higher it goes, the more credit brokers are obliged to borrow in order to buy and carry stocks for their customers, and there is apparently nothing to stop it but a credit crisis. As it was with a price boom in the world of business, so it is still with a bubble of rapture like this in Wall Street. Everybody knows it will sometime burst—only, not yet."

Again, in the spring of 1935, Lorimer sent the New Orleans cotton expert, Colonel James E. Edmonds, to Brazil so that he could report at first hand the Brazilian boom in cotton which had occurred as a result of AAA restrictions on the American cotton industry. Edmonds hardly qualified as an impartial reporter of this situation, and Lorimer himself was not looking for impartiality; he was intent on making a case against the New Deal AAA. It was a remarkably effective piece of work. Edmonds' trip was planned to coincide with the picking of the Brazilian crop, and his articles were scheduled in the Post for issues in August and September, when the size of the United States crop would be known, for purposes of obvious comparison. Thus a revolt among the Southern growers was touched off by the Post, and the newspapers came trailing after the magazine with the news.

This technique was used time and again by the Post, before and after Lorimer's death. It was a technique he originated, and one which Stout carried on successfully. Its fire was concentrated on the New Deal, and the anti-Roosevelt portion of the daily press did not hesitate to take advantage of the Post's editorial prescience. In the thirties it was not unusual to see newspaper stories whose lead somewhere carried the words, "the Saturday Evening Post will say tomorrow." By this simulation of news, anti-Administration editors were able to join the Post's attacks on Roosevelt without any effort on their own part. The stories themselves were simply direct quotations from Post articles and editorials. Such anticipation of public events was one of the bulwarks of Lorimer's publishing philosophy. It was a philosophy he practiced as well as preached. To him, publishing was "the business of buying and selling brains; of having ideas and finding men to carry them out." There was, he thought, a plebiscite on every issue of a periodical, to determine its worthiness, and no business could so quickly succumb to apathy or contentment on the part of its director.

Critics often complained that the Post was as standardized as the life it reflected, but to the Boss this was heresy. "Drugs may be prepared by formula, steel made true by process, and other commodities standardized," he wrote, "but so long as the word counts for more than the type in which it is fixed, so long as the story counts for more than the picture which draws the eye to it, and so long as literature becomes a lifeless thing in the very act of conforming, the periodical will never be standardized and sold indefinitely on the strength of its pretty package and the uniformity of its contents. Publishing is and always will be a contest of ideas —the last stronghold of unrestricted competition free to all comers."

For most of Lorimer's time in the business that statement remained true. It was only with the growth of giant publishing enterprises in the periodical field that the phrase "free to all comers" had to be qualified with the additional phrase, "who have at rock bottom at least a half million dollars."

Lorimer's concept of publishing was not without its romantic aspects. He wrote: "Publishing is a business that in all its essentials is literally materialized out of air and is always tending to resolve into its original element, leaving behind only a memory, some worthless presses and some battered type. In no other business do labor and material add so little to the value of the product. The most faultless typography, the most sumptuous paper fall dead from the presses unless they mirror life. The product of every machine except the printing press is itself a concrete thing of value which the manufacturer sells and the buyer consumes. The printing press fixes an abstraction for a moment and until the buyer has transferred it from the mind of the writer to his own. Then for him the magazine is simply an empty package.

"A publisher then has nothing concrete to sell to his subscribers —only the thoughts of other men. He has nothing concrete to sell to his advertisers—only a glance and a moment's attention from his readers. Where another business may live a lifetime on an idea and wax fat and prosperous selling it over and over again in neat little packages, the publisher must have new ideas for every month and every month's product must be different, yet the same as that of the preceding month. When a number of his magazine is off press his warehouse is empty, his patterns worthless. There is no comfortable stock manufactured to meet a known standard of public taste, to give him a sense of security when he walks through his plant. His whole stock in trade is again under his hat and in the heads of a dozen men around him and a hundred more scattered through the country, and unless they can again and again make a new thing that will reflect ever-changing yet eternally changeless human nature, he is a bankrupt.

"The printing press is greater and stronger than the man who owns it. A senseless mass of steel, it yet has a personality that subordinates the personalities of men to it, and demands whole purpose of those who would use it. Always it tends to purify itself —to slough off those who would degrade it and to force from those who respect it the best expression of themselves. Money may buy a great journal, but, no more than a man, can it be debauched without its vices leaving their imprint on it. Even the dullest begins to understand this and to see that though they may buy publisher and paper and circulation, the one thing that they really want passes from the printing press at the moment of barter. Only to those who serve it honestly are its rewards given in turn, and of those rewards the best cannot be measured in terms of money."

The reward came to Lorimer in two ways: the success of the magazine he edited, and the approval of an amazingly large proportion of the people for whom the Post was written. The balance

sheets assured him of the first; his mail told him of the second.
Only once was recognition of his genius made formally.

He came to his office one morning in March 1929, the day before his thirtieth anniversary as editor of the Post, and found on
his desk a handsome book where his mail should have rested. Prepared by the editors, this book was Post-size and it consisted of
more than two hundred congratulatory letters, each one mounted
on a sheet of parchment, the whole beautifully bound.

The list of notable names on the letters must have impressed
even Lorimer. It began with President Hoover and former Presi-
dents Coolidge and Taft. Then came such diverse people as Otis
Skinner, Major General Harbord, George Eastman, General
Pershing, Charles G. Dawes, Gifford Pinchot, John Philip Sousa,
David Belasco, Commander Richard E. Byrd, Augustus Thomas,
Christian Gauss, Admiral T. P. Magruder, J. J. Davis, George
Broadhurst, Princess Cantacuzene, Eddie Cantor, Josephus Dan-
iels, E. H. Sothern, Dr. W. W. Keen, DeWolf Hopper, Alfred
Noyes, Roy Chapman Andrews, Harold Lloyd and Peggy Wood.

Most of the tributes were couched in conventional terms, but
there were also more heartfelt tributes. One of these was a radio-
gram from Admiral Byrd at his Antarctic base: "In my little shack
down here at Little America I have thirty copies of the Post piled
on my box. One of the red-letter days of my life was when you
accepted an article from my poor pen for publication in the Post."

The Boss was touched by the volume. He tried to take it in his
usual editorial stride, because he hated the display of emotion, but
those around him saw that he was close to tears. For this formal
presentation was public recognition of what he had sensed in the
steady flow of letters from Post readers. As the editor of the Saturday Evening Post, his whole philosophy, in thought and action,
was directed toward the fulfillment of one ambition—that he
should speak to the people, and that they should answer.

As far as he was concerned, the critics could say what they
liked. George Lorimer knew that he had friends, many more than
three million of them, and they were Americans who ranged all
the way from Presidents to the proprietor of an Iowa small-town
grocery.

CHAPTER EIGHT

The Man Lorimer

"Lorimer has no frills and but few fads," said Cobb. "He likes double-breasted sack coats, large brunette cigars, his friends, chocolate bonbons, his family, the Grand Canyon of the Colorado, three cups of coffee for breakfast, and rhododendrons on his front lawn. He collects Oriental rugs and dinner checks. More dinner checks have passed through his hands than through the hands of any living man. He believes in human beings, the Saturday Evening Post, and large tips for waiters. He dislikes poor cooking, posers, and persons who try to slip across clandestine free ads in the guise of literary contributions."

That was as near as anyone ever came to wrapping up George Horace Lorimer's personality in one package. To those who had dealings with him in the big building on Independence Square, his characteristics as editor of the Post were well established, but to those who saw him relaxed, away from the office, he seemed a different person. His family saw one side of him, and that was far from being the Lorimer his friends knew in their convivial bouts with him at Atlantic City, the Grand Canyon and elsewhere. Mere acquaintances saw him as a rather formal, distant personality. There was only one aspect of Lorimer everyone could agree on: it was clear that he stood alone and no one was really close to him. Most people, too, would have agreed with the verdict of an eminent lady agent: "He is one man in whom pure animal magnetism is translated into intellectual force."

To Tom Costain, Lorimer was like the Duke of Wellington in many respects. He had Wellington's laugh and his unwillingness to delegate authority. Even his general physical appearance, particularly his face, was similar. Wellington had a deceptively mild appearance and underneath he was iron, but Lorimer was steel on the outside, while inside he was sensitive and retiring.

Like one of the characters in Maugham's "Cakes and Ale," the Boss had a trick of winking suddenly when he was looking straight at a man. It was something of a twinkle, and completely unexpected. Sometimes during an argument his friend Garet Garrett would think, "I've gone too far." Then the twinkle would come and erase his doubt.

Lorimer's minor vices were smoking and eating candy. He smoked pipes, cigars and at least two packages of cigarettes a day. Both he and Alma loved candy and ate it all day long. The Boss kept a box of Wilbur's Chocolate Buds handy in his desk drawer at the office, and whenever he traveled West by train he would take advantage of the layover in Chicago to stock up with five pounds of Allegrettis for the next leg of the journey. This was indicative of the expansive temperament he displayed in his private life. To see him indulge his appetites, entertain lavishly and spend money freely, no one would have thought he was the same man who kept a tight rein on himself and the Post's purse strings at the office.

The results of indulgence were never visited upon him. Alma lost her fine figure, but her husband ate his chocolates and quantities of good food without a thought of diet until his forties, when a bout of indigestion caused his doctor to recommend a change. He remained trim and erect, and he was seldom ill until his final, fatal sickness, except for occasional heavy colds and frequent light colds—usually on Tuesday night. These were known in the family as "opera colds."

Away from the Post his abiding love was for the outdoors. His zeal for planting trees led him to plant nearly a million of them in his lifetime, in and around Philadelphia. The inspiration of this passion was his constant nostalgia for the world he had left behind, his Chicago childhood, when the prairie was his front yard and America lay verdant and unspoiled all around him.

Lorimer was always minding the national parks. He knew their custodians well and they would not have thought of planning a major project without asking his advice. On his travels, they passed him freely through the chain of Western parks and he accepted their homage as though he owned the system. The only public offices he ever accepted were appointments by Hoover as a member of the Commission on Conservation and Administration of the Public Domain, and by Wilson as chairman of a committee for Chinese relief. His feeling about the parks amounted to the pride of personal ownership. No one ever questioned that attitude, because no citizen did more for these public domains.

His own private piece of the outdoors was his farm, King's Oak. The farm was six miles from Belgraeme, his home, and he contrived to spend an hour or two nearly every day walking its acres. In his walks at Wyncote he was often accompanied by one of the Wyncote dogs. Lorimer was a dog lover who did not hesitate to sit up all night nursing his scrappy mongrel, Brownie, when the animal was fatally poisoned. Brownie was succeeded in the family by Van, a black-and-white collie whom he named after Van Loan. Later came a German shepherd who had flunked the Seeing Eye course.

Lorimer liked to slip away to King's Oak on a Friday or Saturday. His faithful chauffeur, George Smyth, would stow away a substantial lunch in the car and he would be off for a day or two in the sun. Visitors who saw him in the office, and who thought him severe, unable to relax except with difficulty, would have been amazed to see him striding over the fields at King's Oak, looking like a farmer, except that he customarily wore a gray fedora of an unrural character. He often prepared his editorials on those long walks, and sat down in the evening to write them in the fine old farmhouse filled with the antiques he had picked up on his hunting trips.

At first he farmed hard, but after several years he concluded:

"The less farming you do, the less money you lose." From then on he planted nothing but trees, and vegetables for home consumption. In all other respects, however, the Boss gave King's Oak the meticulous attention he devoted to the Post and the national parks. He talked expertly about farm problems. With a businessman's hand he had assembled his farm property from ten other farms until it reached 1100 acres, and with his editor's mind he had named it for a historic tree which stood at the back of the property.

Much as he loved the place, it was only a substitute, a stopgap between trips West. His compulsion to be in the Rocky Mountain country was so strong that he once seriously considered buying a ranch.

It was on the Western trips that he displayed most often the sign which meant he was feeling on top of the world: when he walked the trails, he raised a little on the ball of each foot. At Estes Park, in his thirties, he loved to ride a big rogue horse named Tuesday, which few others could handle. He enjoyed, too, dressing in rough Western style, except that on cold days he wore the enormous coonskin coat which he often sported in Philadelphia as he rode to his office in an open car during the winter. Smyth, in the driver's seat, sometimes wore his own coonskin coat, and the two made an impressive spectacle as they traversed the city's highways. Lorimer was so attached to this coat that he carried it on his arm when he boarded the dirigible *Los Angeles* for a cruise over Philadelphia.

Getting to and from the West in the early days made Lorimer one of the nation's first sincere motorists. He journeyed across the continent repeatedly at a time when there were no paved roads west of the Mississippi. Smyth did the actual driving. An ex-baseball player, of old Pennsylvania stock, Smyth was a big, solid man, the Boss's faithful shadow on his jaunts away from home, near and far. Together they conquered the problems of terrain and early automotive mechanics.

The more problems there were on a trip, the more it pleased Lorimer. It was not uncommon to see the whole family—he always took Alma and the boys along—sitting on the ground in some sequestered portion of the North American continent while Smyth put the car up on blocks so he could examine it from beneath. These Western expeditions occurred nearly every year. If the car broke down entirely, Lorimer sent the family on ahead by train while he remained with Smyth, but before such a major crisis was reached the party had passed through a series of intermediary crises. The mountains invariably produced near disasters. Passers-by, if any, would be aghast to come around a bend in some remote road and find the Lorimer family sitting near the seat of calamity, while Smyth struggled with ropes to keep the car from going over a cliff and Lorimer shouted encouragement at his elbow.

In those days there were few spectators to such scenes. When their Pierce-Arrow broke down the travelers were alone for hours, at least, if not for a day or two. Occasionally the simple Red Man appeared with a horse or two and offered to pull the car out of a quagmire created by a break in an irrigation ditch. The price was arranged in advance, to an obbligato of grunts on both sides. Lorimer suspected, with reason, that these helpful aborigines patched up the ditches when they needed the water and broke them again when they needed ready cash.

Such experiences had a permanent effect on the family's members. When the Boss's son Burford was a grown man, he was riding with Garrett one dark night in the West, and the car had jolted over unfamiliar roads for an hour, until Burford was obviously in a nervous state. Garrett assured him there was nothing to worry about.

"I know there isn't," Burford replied, "but childhood experience tells me I'll have to get out pretty soon and push."

No one enjoyed traveling more than Smyth. His enthusiasm for it, and for the outdoors, matched his employer's. The relationship between the two men was unusual. Smyth argued with his employer as he might have with another man, yet he never overstepped the line. For his part, Lorimer had a real affection for Smyth and enjoyed a congeniality with him; he considered him his right-hand man and "a grand guy" in the bargain. The practical expression of his feeling was a seventy-five-dollar-a-week salary plus Christmas bonus, and gifts of a house and five acres, private-school tuition for Smyth's sons, and ten thousand dollars bequeathed to him in his will.

As a veteran of Lorimer's antiquing jaunts, Smyth came to be something of an authority on the subject too. In one shop the Boss once asked him what he thought of a certain chest of drawers under consideration.

"Them legs ain't right," was Smyth's verdict.

And they weren't.

When his boss died Smyth was lost. A year after the event Garrett was visiting at Wyncote and Smyth came into his room, a pathetic figure, holding a road map in his hands, one of the many he had pored over with Lorimer. He wanted to talk. For the rest of the evening he rambled on, recalling in voluminous detail the many trips he had made.

All the roads Smyth had traveled led eventually to the Grand Canyon country, to Estes Park, Roosevelt-Sequoia Park, Glacier Park and the others. Lorimer's feeling for the Canyon itself was so intense that he judged other people by their response to it. Moran's huge painting of the spectacle hung in his office for years, and no visitor could miss it. "I can tell 'em by that picture," he would say. If a man noticed it and admired it, Lorimer would be disposed to like him. If the visitor ignored it entirely or spoke lightly of it, the Boss was instantly suspicious.

There was something religious in his attitude. One misty night at the Canyon, Lorimer sat looking quietly into the blue haze for an hour, without uttering a word, until it grew cold and he turned away to go into the bar. Only after the first drink had warmed its way down did he turn to Garrett and say, "I understand why those Indians were superstitious."

Yet Lorimer had to be converted to the Canyon. His first Western interest had been Estes Park, at Alma's suggestion, shortly after their marriage. Alma did not like Estes as much as her husband did, upon further acquaintance, but she had to spend her summers there for many years, meanwhile begging Lorimer periodically to stop off at the Canyon. It was some time before the Boss consented to have a look at what he called a "tripper heaven." Once he saw it, however, he never again took a through train to California without stopping off there, and his motor expeditions were many. His love for Estes Park continued, and he liked California, but he had a different feeling for the Canyon country.

In the early days at Estes Park, Lorimer and the family usually stayed at Long's Peak Inn, owned by a Post contributor, the naturalist Enos Mills. The Boss was fond of teasing the somewhat literal Mills. The proprietor had a sorry horse named Pieface, creaky in the joints and chary of exercise, whom he frequently assigned to trippers who were beginning equestrians. When such neophytes were about to mount, Lorimer would saunter up to them, looking concerned, and say, "Are they sending you out on Pieface? I suppose you've ridden a lot in these mountains. Well, I wouldn't want to frighten you, but——" These tactics were so successful that at last Mills did not dare send Pieface out if the Boss was anywhere near.

It was at the inn, in 1908, that Lorimer met Adelaide Neall. She was a year out of Bryn Mawr, fresh from ten months of travel in Europe, with nothing on her mind. She encountered five-year-old Graeme, invited him to play a game of croquet, and he responded with an invitation to a picnic. Thus she met the Lorimer family and soon was included on many of their trips. Lorimer ribbed her constantly and she was flippant in return, the kind of response he enjoyed most.

"Have you read my 'Jack Spurlock'?" he asked her one day.

"Never heard of it," she responded truthfully.

"Or the 'Merchant Letters'?"

"Never." Also true.

"Well, how about the Saturday Evening Post?"

"Never heard of that either," she said, teasing him.

Lorimer's laughter boomed out. In August 1909, Miss Neall went to work for him and their Post association of more than a quarter century began.

El Tovar, the Fred Harvey hotel at the Canyon, became his rendezvous as time went on. Before many an expedition he would send word to the Coast: "Be at Grand Canyon at such and such a time." That was a summons to his West Coast cronies—Van Loan, Blythe, Wylie, Wilson and the others.

Van Loan shared his love for the Canyon. Charlie's special enjoyment was to push boulders over the rim, at a safely remote spot, and yell after them. One day the Boss's son Graeme joined him at this sport, and in a half hour or so they had graduated to bigger things. Van Loan went to the stables and got a crowbar, with which they pried loose enormous boulders as big as pianos, sending them tumbling down the precipitous sides. Lorimer observed these maneuvers in silence. He made no complaint but he felt that the Canyon should not be so rudely disturbed. Not long afterward he had the territory made into a national park, and one of the park rules forbade the practice of throwing boulders into the Canyon.

That prohibition did not dampen Van Loan's enthusiasm. He enjoyed everything there was to be done at the Canyon, particularly eating picnic dinners on the Painted Desert. He and Lorimer were forever moving about from one place to another, as though they were afraid they might miss something of the spectacle.

Van Loan was a practical joker of considerable talent. One year, however, he played so many jokes on the Canyon gang that Cobb was moved to say, "We will have to fix that boy's wagon." Irvin was, in fact, only slightly less guilty. He had persuaded the proprietor of the hotel to print his much-quoted sentiment, "It is the Saturday Evening Post of Canyons," on the bottom of the menus one morning.

But Van Loan's sins were greater and Cobb devised a revenge. He told the manager, "I want you to present that man with a really whopping bill. Put everything on it you can think of, and I'll add some items of my own."

Van Loan was scheduled to leave next morning, a day or so in advance of the others. His companions sat casually but watchfully in the lobby, in a special corner reserved for them, and observed Charlie come down to the desk and ask for his bill. They saw him contemplate it with growing horror and rage as he noted such Cobbian items as "Flowers in room, $50," and "Conversation with the proprietor, $5." He began to pound the desk and scream, until the manager had to turn helplessly to Cobb and the joke was exposed.

Like any confirmed practical joker, Van Loan hated to be on the taking end. Momentarily he was infuriated, but he got over it.

During his summers at Estes Park, Lorimer came to know the trail up Long's Peak so well that he could escort friends to the summit without a guide. It was a difficult climb. The trail narrowed into a broken thread of path among boulders, then it swerved suddenly into an open space where there was placed a single wooden cross. Someone invariably asked why it was there, and Lorimer would reply: "Read the inscription." The crude lettering said:

TO THE MEMORY OF MARY B——
SHE LAID DOWN TO REST
AND DIED ALONE

Lorimer's guests would look at each other somberly, and the party would toil on upward in silence. At 14,000 feet the trail reached a place called the Narrows. This was a ledge along which the climbers had to worm their way to reach the summit. A 2000-foot drop made the passageway look even more precarious than it was, and before the Boss took his party across he would point over the brink to a rounded mound far below on the rocks.

"See that?" he would inquire.

The others shivered assent.

"Well, that's poor old Shorty Bain," Lorimer would say in a reminiscent tone. "Shorty had been over the Narrows so often he got a little careless and lost his hold." Pausing to gauge the effect, which was always satisfactory, the Boss went on, "Of course they couldn't get him out so they just poured cement around him."

Traveling on his own, or with the more adventurous of his cronies, Lorimer established a reputation as an explorer of the Canyon's trails. With Van Loan he broke the tourist record for the Hermit-Tonto-Bright Angel trip. The only casualty was Charlie's mule. It had to be retired to pasture and never recovered.

While he enjoyed himself, Lorimer never forgot that he was editor of the Post. He climbed trails and camped out with Post authors and often used such trips to plan a new story or series for the magazine. Cobb's "Roughing It De Luxe" was an example. One summer Lorimer took his family to the Yellowstone and made several exploratory trips in the territory. He made no mention of his job, but as soon as he got back to the office the Post ran one of its best series on conservation.

Lorimer's jaunts around the country were comprehensive. He crossed the continent by car several times, made shorter trips by Pierce-Arrow and train to the West, the Middle West and the South. He stopped off in small towns, talked to people, and never went in a store without buying something. That was his method of keeping close to the Post audience. When these trips became fewer, and he was compelled to spend more time at his desk, his "feel" for the American people began to diminish.

The Boss's idea of relaxation was to make a twenty-four-hour non-stop sprint on the last six hundred miles of a long motor trip. On one expedition he sent Alma and the boys on ahead by train while he and Smyth made a non-stop thirty-six-hour run across the Great Salt Lake Desert and Nevada. The family was reunited at Reno, where Lorimer astounded the room clerk at a hotel by appearing at the desk in his traveling clothes a day or two after Alma had arrived and asking to be shown up to his wife's room. It hadn't occurred to him that husbands in Reno, at least the legal ones, never made such requests.

There were frequent trips abroad, too, but Lorimer grumbled about them. It was Alma who insisted; she enjoyed the trips to London every other year or so because they included social life and shopping. As for the Boss, he loved London but he disliked the British and nothing that happened to him in England was calculated to change his feelings.

One of the earlier trips was enough to sour him permanently. It was at a time when Lady Astor was the reigning queen of London society and was currently displaying George Bernard Shaw as her great tame lion. When she heard that the editor of the Saturday Evening Post was in town Lady Astor invited Lorimer and Alma to luncheon, along with Garrett, who was with them. She intended, so Garrett thought, to get herself admired by the Americans and exhibit Shaw at the same time. (Later the Lorimers often visited Lady Astor, who had been at the Anne Brown School in New York with Alma.) Lorimer and Garrett viewed the ordeal with apprehension, but they were no more apprehensive than Alma, who feared that her unappreciative escorts might disgrace her.

They arrived at the Astor town house, and while Alma went upstairs the two men strolled on into the drawing room and stood before the warmth of the fireplace. Shaw came in abruptly, saw them there, and remarked in his customary manner, "Well, I see you Americans have all the money to travel with, as usual." Lorimer said nothing. He only looked hard at Shaw, and the three men stood rather uncomfortably before the fireplace until Lady Astor came in, sensed the tension, and hurried everyone to lunch.

The meal was a hostess's dream of hell. Lorimer and Garrett were obviously at swords' points with Shaw, Alma was nervous, and Lady Astor was determinedly cheerful, trying to hold the party together. She got Shaw talking about his coming expedition to Russia, but that topic came to an impasse when Shaw remarked, "One thing we shall not find in Russia is a whore." Lorimer looked bleak. He disapproved of frank language in mixed company.

Lord Astor began talking hurriedly of postwar conditions in England, and immediately plunged the conversation into a new deadlock by observing, "As a result of the war, a lot of people who are not entitled to it are in possession of industry."

"How does an Englishman determine who should have it?" Lorimer inquired sharply.

Lady Astor rushed into the silence with a change of subject that, had she known it, could hardly have been less tactful.

"Mr. Shaw has written a new piece, Mr. Lorimer," she said, "and it's really priceless. I think you should have it for your magazine before any other American periodical gets it. Tell us about it, won't you, Mr. Shaw?"

Mr. Shaw readily told about it, at length. Lady Astor noted

despairingly that Lorimer appeared to sink deeper into his chair during the lecture. When he had finished, Shaw said, "Of course the American magazines are all after it. Hearst has offered me a very fancy price." He went on to describe, with enjoyment, the competitive bidding of American publishers for his work.

"I see you're on the auction block," Lorimer said in a tone so final that it closed the subject at once.

The luncheon went on in an atmosphere of tension; step by step everything Nancy Astor proffered was disadmired, until she was nearly hysterical before it ended. Desperately seeking a safe topic, she began to tell Alma why she was so successful in politics—"because the others are so stupid, you know."

"I'm in politics too," Alma reminded her.

Lady Astor opened her mouth, closed it again, and looked vague.

The hostess turned to Lorimer. "I understand you're interested in rugs," she said in the accents of a Bette Davis mad scene. Lorimer was a qualified expert on the subject. He tried to conceal his irritation while Lady Astor chattered on about rugs; he looked like a Caruso listening to the musical theories of a Sinatra.

Garrett had said nothing through the entire meal, except to make an occasional sour remark. It was to him that Lady Astor directed her final remark as the party broke up at the door in an atmosphere of utter chaos. By this time she had given up being the hostess; she was plain Nancy Astor.

"Good-by, you gloomy Gus," she said to Garrett with sweet venom.

The ride back to the hotel was as strained as the luncheon. Alma was furious.

"You were disgraceful! *Disgraceful!* You'll never be invited again!" she told them. The "you" was characteristic.

"Not at all," Garrett said cheerfully, "we'll hear from Lady Astor, believe me."

They had not been back in the hotel five minutes before the telephone rang. It was Lady Astor, extending another invitation. Garrett had reasoned correctly that the hostess would be determined to retrieve her social reputation.

Lorimer's own report of this incident, in a letter to Graeme, was succinct: "Had luncheon with Lady Astor Saturday and met Bernard Shaw. He talked prices, just like any other author. Said they'd bid him up to $1.25 a word on his coming trip to Russia, paused, and I changed the subject pleasantly by saying he seemed to be on the block. He monopolized the conversation and made a number of humorous remarks that I should call wisecracks if Mayor Jimmie Walker had made them. The British present all snorted with laughter before he opened his mouth. He started to pan America to mother, but he didn't get very far and again the subject was changed. . . ."

There were compensations in the trips abroad, of a kind one would expect the Boss to find. He wrote to Kenneth Roberts after a 1925 voyage: "I am back and darn glad of it, not to use any stronger language. I didn't buy much abroad but what I picked up was first chop and included a little old silver, a little old china, a set of unusually fine ladder-back chairs, a Queen Anne settee, a pair of very fine oblong-shaped Gothic tapestries, which ought to help the tout ensemble of my library, as we say in Paris. . . ."

In sharp contrast with the London trips were the Boss's expeditions closer to home. On those occasions he could be himself, and could precede his arrival with such a note as this one to Kenneth Roberts:

"Under separate cover I am sending you a portrait of a gentleman, by Van Dyke. Also, I am going to follow it in the flesh about Wednesday the 21st, and turn up in Kennebunkport on towards dinnertime of the 22nd. I have asked Dere Mable [Mrs. Atwater Kent] to kill a frying chicken, but if she has left your inhospitable climate by that time I shall depend on you to fry a steak. In any event, I am going to graft at least one square meal from you."

Much as he enjoyed his visits with friends, Lorimer preferred to be at home. After dinner every night he walked, clippers in hand, with Alma on the lawns and woodland paths of Belgraeme. One night he stood with Graeme on a slippery mat of needles and fallen cones beneath a stand of thirty-foot pines. "These were a foot high when I set them out, son," he said. Graeme had never heard him speak of the Post with more pride.

The sapling oaks he had planted touched and interlaced across the drive, and everywhere on the grounds bloomed the prize azaleas and the high banks and masses of rhododendrons he loved so well. In the fall the dead leaves on the place were not burned but were carefully tucked about the roots of the Boss's "rhodies." More leaves were added each year to rot down. In the early summer, after the blossoming was over, Lorimer commandeered friends, family, authors and anyone else in sight to help with the seeding. They picked off the young seed pods so that all the strength of the plant might go to new growth. He spent hours at this work himself. "I find it most conducive to thought," he explained. In the last year of his life he was still planting, planting— dogwood and hemlock, added to all the others.

When darkness sent him indoors, he began his reading, which averaged a hundred thousand words of manuscript a night. He sat cross-legged on an upholstered settee that was the width of two chairs. As he settled himself, he sat with one leg hanging down, a red slipper dangling from his foot. The other leg was tucked beneath him, but as he became absorbed in his reading, he drew it up until he sat tailor-fashion.

One night Lorimer read aloud to the family from a manuscript, an unusual digression for him. The manuscript (ultimately turned down by the Post) was the reminiscences of Texas Guinan and over a particular anecdote in its pages the Boss laughed until he cried. This story concerned a transcontinental jaunt by Texas and two girls. They boarded the Chief at Chicago, bound for a Los Angeles hot spot, and by dinnertime they were bored to tears. Three women playing poker together in a drawing room was no inducement to revelry. Always ready with a good idea, Texas suggested that they patrol the dining car and invite the first three unattached men they saw eating steak to sit in on the game. The foray was successful. Two flashy youngsters and a quiet, elderly man constituted the haul. This sextet played poker all the way to the Coast, and time passed quickly.

The young men were met in Los Angeles by a covey of de-

tectives. They turned out to be bellboys from a Chicago hotel, who had absconded with quantities of the hostelry's cash. The quiet man, who had played close to his vest and won consistently, then disclosed himself as Thomas Riley Marshall, twenty-eighth Vice-President of the United States.

Lorimer finished his manuscripts about midnight, after which he retired to bed with a book—occasionally a novel, but more often something on economics or a biography—and read until one or two in the morning.

At breakfast he employed a trick device to hold the newspaper so he could read the front page and eat. Alma listened to his conversation and made notes of anything he said that had to do with the household, their business affairs or the conduct of her Republican Women's Club. Occasionally Lorimer, after expressing himself violently and cogently on some topic of the day, would peer around his newspaper and see Alma making notes, on which he would remark, "Now damn it, Alma, don't use *that* in your club magazine." Alma usually used it.

No man believed more firmly than the Boss that his home was his castle. He presided as the loving lord of his particular manor, right down to the smallest matters. On the Fourth of July he set off the firecrackers himself because a pinwheel had once broken loose when everyone had taken part in the firing, and he never bought Roman candles because he was afraid they would backfire. At Christmastime there was an enormous tree in the library (a sharp contrast to that first Philadelphia Christmas) and Lorimer worked until long past midnight decorating it.

The Boss's feeling about his home was expressed dramatically on the night after Lindbergh's son was kidnaped. After dinner that evening, Graeme and his wife Sarah drove to Belgraeme and found Lorimer sitting with a revolver on the table beside him. He looked exceedingly grim.

"I'm going to see that nobody gets into this house," he said to Graeme. "You'd better get a night watchman."

After the Hauptmann verdict, it was the Post that settled doubts in many minds with its Arthur Koehler article, "Who Made That Ladder?" This article, constructed with all the suspense of the best mystery fiction, told the story of the dogged Wisconsin wood expert who traced the ladder's lumber to its sources.

There was frequent entertaining at the Lorimer home. The Boss did not let it interfere with his work, however. He entertained his guests until ten o'clock, then he excused himself and went upstairs to read manuscripts and write editorials.

The guests were of all varieties. DeWolf Hopper came one evening, accompanied by his sixth bride. After dinner, as the conversation warmed up, Hopper discussed his first five wives, elaborating on their good points and comparing them with his sixth, who appeared to be not at all disconcerted. Warming to the subject, Hopper's thoughts soared onto ever higher planes, aided by alcohol, and his vocabulary kept pace with his lofty thinking.

"When I read about such cases as the Hall-Mills trial," he said, "I marvel to think that people impugn the morals of the stage, chaste and ascetic, even liliaceous, as they are by comparison."

Later in the evening he was off on a new tack, discussing the philosophy of beauty. He recalled a Paris convention of artists and sculptors at which the delegates chose the most beautiful animal.

"Man, of course, ranked first," Hopper said. "Horses were naturally the second choice, and women were picked to show."

Lorimer enjoyed such entertainment. He took every occasion he could to indulge his love for good food, good drink and good friends. These pleasures took the place of sports, which he shunned, and of music and the theater, to both of which he was generally insensitive. He was not a gourmet in the Lucius Beebe sense, but he understood and loved food. When his friend H. Gordon Selfridge sent him some Stilton and Cheddar cheeses as a Christmas present in 1929, accompanying them with a rather apologetic letter, Lorimer replied: "I have met Stilton and Cheddar on their native heath and I am a great admirer of them. My preference is for whichever is milder at the moment. There are many delicious odors in the world besides those that are made by the perfumers of Paris."

As a cheese lover, Lorimer was naturally interested in pie. He had a passionate craving for blueberry pie done in the proper fashion, and he sought it avidly whenever he toured New England. He seldom found a good one, but he never stopped hoping. After he and Roberts had cruised the Northeastern countryside they came home with mouths that stayed purple for a week. The pies, unfortunately, were usually either too runny, not runny enough, mucky-crusted, hard-crusted, or not sufficiently sweetened. The Boss was as right about blueberry pies as he was about Navajo rugs.

Aside from the social aspects of family life, Lorimer was at once a good and bad husband and father. Whatever differences in temperament and ideas separated him from Alma, he took her everywhere and maintained the appearance his intense family pride demanded. She tried him sorely at times, but he held his tongue. With his two boys, the survivors of his four children, he was kind and considerate, but his natural reserve and the fact that they, too, were temperamentally unlike him, created a gulf. He knew it existed but he was never able to build a bridge. Both boys were writers. Graeme followed that occupation successfully, but Burford, who had several diverse talents, like his father, never fulfilled the promise of his early published pieces. Writing seemed too easy for him and after a time he stopped. He turned to other affairs and today owns and operates successfully a sixteen-thousand-acre plantation in Georgia.

Burford was one of the few people who dared to criticize Lorimer, a fact that the boy himself recognized. At the breakfast table one morning Lorimer was holding forth on the right of every man to express his opinions freely. "Take Smyth, for example," he said. "Smyth doesn't hesitate to disagree with me. Do you suppose, for example, I'd question his right to try to make me change my political opinions?"

"Oh no," Burford said. "You'd only fire him."

Lorimer might have fired any other household employee who talked to him as freely as did Smyth, but his relationship with Smyth was the kind that nothing could sever.

Burford and Lorimer engaged in a discussion of Proust one evening when Kenneth Roberts was at Wyncote. Lorimer didn't care much for Proust. Roberts asked for one of the Proust volumes to read in bed, and Burford said he thought volume two of "Remembrance of Things Past" might interest him. Roberts went upstairs with it. At breakfast the next morning Roberts asked Burford how he had liked volume two. Burford's reply was enthusiastic. Roberts said that was odd, since the pages of Burford's copy hadn't been cut. Lorimer's delight was profound.

Perhaps the greatest sorrow of Lorimer's life was the passing of his second child, Belle, who died of spinal meningitis in 1908, four days before Burford was born. It was a severe shock to him. Belle's death made him even more tender and understanding to all children than he otherwise would have been. Coming home from Europe on the maiden voyage of the *Europa*, he sent this cable: "Home Friday. Bringing bear to children." He loved the excitement that awaited him on his arrival, and he knew that the grandchildren were not disappointed when he presented them with a magnificent teddy bear.

When they gave him presents, he devoted his best literary efforts to thanking them. To a five-year-old, who had given him a homemade calendar, decorated with golden stars, he wrote: "Dear Sarah Lee, Your present is at once beautiful and useful. When the real stars, that are the watchmen of the night, go to bed for the day, I shall have your stars to remind me that they are coming back in a little while to their appointed place in the sky. . . ."

The father tried hard to come closer to his sons. When Graeme was recuperating in the hospital from an illness, Lorimer stopped every day to see him, but he was unable to carry on a conversation. His habitual manner was either jovial or critical, and neither attitude fitted the occasion.

His patience with all the members of his family was remarkable, but on at least one occasion he could not contain himself. It was a blistering-hot day in Maine, and the Lorimers were visiting friends at a relatively cool point on the coast. The friends urged that travel contemplated for the occasion be restricted to the coastal road, but Alma wanted to drive inland to Concord, and in spite of the protests of everyone else in the party, she prevailed. Two miles inland the temperature rose so rapidly that Alma was obliged to lay aside her fur cape. Ten miles inland she was gasping and complaining of the heat. Perhaps, she said, they had better turn back.

"No, by God," Lorimer said. "You insisted on going to Concord, and you're going to Concord." They went to Concord, but the suffering was intense.

Lorimer ruled that his wife was not to visit him at the office, and her appearances on the sixth floor were consequently rare. Wesley Stout once encountered her in the corridor as the Boss was escorting Alma from the office to the elevator. As they exchanged greetings and stood waiting for the cage to rise, Stout said courteously, "It's nice to see you, Mrs. Lorimer. Why don't you come around and visit us more often?"

"I'd like to," Alma began seriously in her high, penetrating voice, "but——"

The rest of her sentence was drowned by Lorimer's shouting. "Down, down," he yelled, trying to suppress the revelation that he did not encourage visits.

Occasionally Alma was invited to lunch in the directors' dining room when an author who was to speak at her club was being entertained there. She would be driven to the Curtis Building by her tall, handsome chauffeur, George Justice, who had been appointed a special police officer, complete with gold badge and gold-braided cap, by a mayor grateful for Alma's political feats. Succeeding mayors followed the precedent, which greatly simplified Mrs. Lorimer's parking problems.

After depositing his employer at the Curtis Building, Justice would repair to the company dining room for a meal on the house, sitting resplendent in his police chief's uniform. One day when Alma and Mary Roberts Rinehart had come down to join Lorimer for lunch in the directors' dining room, they passed by the main dining room and observed Justice already busy with his meal.

"Who *is* that distinguished-looking man?" Mary inquired.

"That's my chauffeur," Alma replied demurely.

Lorimer howled with delight when he heard the story, and told it frequently.

Alma controlled the Boss's activities outside the office as rigidly as she could. Once they had gone to San Francisco on a trip, and as soon as they were safely registered in the hotel Lorimer called up Sam Blythe, Wilson and a few other cronies, summoning them to a reunion that night. The gathering was a riotous affair, of the kind Alma particularly disapproved.

They had planned to stay several days, but the next morning Alma declared abruptly that they must leave that day on the next leg of their journey. She complained specifically of a heavy fog that had rolled up during the night.

"I'm so sorry the fog is driving you away, Mrs. Lorimer," Wilson said.

"It isn't the fog, Mr. Wilson," she replied frigidly.

But this lady who loved society and the Republican party with equal fervor could astound everyone, including her husband. The Lorimers and Garrett were in Palm Springs one night, having dinner on the desert at a kind of night club which looked like a gangster's hide-out. Alma had never been in such a place. She surveyed with awe the strong-arm men guarding the entrance, and the heavy iron grillwork on the windows. The club made its living from the gambling rooms, and after dinner the Lorimers played roulette. It was Alma's first experience with the game, and having recovered her balance by that time, she kidded it until even the proprietor was weak with laughter and offered her more chips so she could stay in. It was grand comedy. No one enjoyed it more than Lorimer.

It was the Boss's sense of humor, which he shared with Alma, that lessened the inevitable tensions of their life together and mitigated the family sorrows they shared. Their teasing, of other people and themselves, was merciless. Yet each had a different brand of wit. Lorimer's laughter was hearty, booming, Homeric, so contagious that everyone within earshot had to laugh too. Alma's humor sprang from her vivid, complex personality and it was inclined more in the direction of hell-raising than of simple enjoyment.

They reconciled many of their essential differences by compromises. Lorimer, for example, liked to smoke in an open car.

Alma did not smoke and she liked to ride in a limousine with the windows closed. On the way to the opera or to the theater Lorimer smoked a cigar in the family Pierce-Arrow (a limousine with arches over the doors and so much headroom it seemed as though a stepladder would be needed to dust the upholstery) while the windows remained closed, on Alma's order. The arrival on these occasions was spectacular. When the door was opened a cloud of blue smoke would billow out as though the car were on fire and the occupants would emerge into fresh air with eyes red and streaming.

Sometimes Alma would remark acidly that there was no point in wearing perfume if her hair was going to smell like a tobacco auction room. But it was always the same. Lorimer smoked. Alma wouldn't open the windows.

Alma was a genius in her own right, and she made an indelible mark on Philadelphia's life. Married at seventeen and thus deprived of a college education at Vassar, she nevertheless outstripped most of her formally educated contemporaries. At an early date she was active in the Women's Club of Wyncote and eventually became its president. As early as the first World War she was a moving figure in the Red Cross, acting as chairman of the Independence Square Auxiliary, for which she was awarded the Red Cross Medal with four stripes for distinguished service.

She moved into the political arena in the presidential campaign of 1920, as vice-chairman of the National Ways and Means Committee. Later she organized the Republican Women of Pennsylvania, a chartered state club, became its president, and edited a propaganda organ, called the *Republican Woman*, which was circulated in several states. She was chairman of the state committee for the Philadelphia Sesquicentennial, and in 1932 the local Chamber of Commerce appointed her chairman of the Women's Washington Bicentennial Committee. This committee, under her direction, created the "living memorial" of Japanese cherry trees and pink-and-white dogwood stretching magnificently along River Drive in Fairmount Park. This was perhaps the climax of her work in a dozen or more clubs and organizations.

One of Alma's most remarkable political achievements came in

1936, when Herbert Hoover had offered to speak in Philadelphia for Landon. Local Republicans were cool to this idea, doubting that Hoover would do their hopeful much good, and the Union League refused the sponsorship. Thus a delicate situation was created. Hoover planned to speak in Philadelphia but the stalwarts of his own party did not intend to sponsor him. Alma proposed that her club, the Republican Women of Pennsylvania, be the sponsor. She organized the rally, ran it almost singlehanded, and filled the capacious Academy of Music for the speech. Hoover, who stayed at Belgraeme during his visit, realized that some sleight of hand had taken place, but he never discovered what had happened.

For this and other accomplishments Alma was given the Gimbel Award as the outstanding woman of the year, and later, at a testimonial luncheon in her honor at the Bellevue-Stratford, she outdrew a similar affair given the week before in behalf of Senator George Wharton Pepper. There was no standing room at Alma's luncheon, although it occurred on a weekday and everyone had to pay his own way.

Alma was a woman who could put over a hard job, at home or in local politics. Hers was a mercurial, dominant personality that won her extremely few friends. It was the kind of personality that enabled her to issue an ultimatum to her doctor when she sprained an ankle: "I'll give you just twenty-four hours to heal it." It was also the kind that led her to examine critically the foundation sketch of her portrait, and when the artist, Leopold Seyffert, was safely out of the way, she took the liberty of altering the cast of her mouth and chin, which had not pleased her.

Her life with Lorimer was full of the conflict generated by such close association of two strong people. She alienated some of his friends, often moved him to rebellious irritation, yet he laughed with her, was proud of her considerable accomplishments, and was fascinated by her right up to the end.

They moved together in one of Philadelphia's social circles that included Judge Charles Sinkler and his wife, the Robert Sewells and the Atwater Kents, among others. Lorimer was particularly fond of Mrs. Kent, whom he called "Dere Mable," and she returned his regard, frequently laying herself open to Lorimeresque laughter in so doing, as when she once said adoringly, "Oh, George, you say things so brilliantly! I wish you'd write a book!" The author of the "Letters from a Self-Made Merchant" allowed that he might someday get around to writing one.

To Mrs. Kent he would say things he would not dream of saying to anyone else, man or woman. She arrived one night dressed for the opera, adorned with a little more than the usual jewelry.

"Mabel," Lorimer said, looking her up and down, "all you need is a nose ring."

The Boss's humor was on the sardonic side; it was one of the attributes he had in common with Cyrus Curtis. He was especially amused by the story of the time Curtis invited his grandchildren for a week end to show them his new yacht.

"How do you like it?" the old man inquired.

"We love it, Granddaddy," they chorused.

"I'm so glad," Curtis observed, "because you're paying for it."

The Boss loved to tell the story of Ike Marcosson's first trip on the Curtis yacht. Ike was much pleased to be included in the party, and he was anxious to make a good impression. As the guests were eating luncheon the yacht began to roll in a heavy swell and poor Ike grew greener by the minute. Suddenly he rose in his seat and looked wildly about. He clapped his hand to his mouth, but it was too late. The worst overtook him.

The dignified Churchill Williams, a tall and proper Philadelphian, had risen with Marcosson to help him out. Now he led him from the table, shaking his head solemnly and murmuring, "Too bad, too bad." A horrified silence accompanied this exit, then the Boss's laugh touched off the general hilarity.

Lorimer could laugh at himself, too. At the Paris Exposition of 1920 he rode on the chute the chutes with Burford and Graeme. It was a terrifying experience, a fact that tickled his sense of humor because he had previously disdained the contraption as a foreign imitation of good American rides.

His big, wholehearted guffaw rang out most often in company, but there were at least two family jokes which never failed to amuse him. Soon after the first World War ended he went to

Europe on the *Leviathan* and returned with such celebrities on board as Albert Lasker and Senator Smoot. There was no liquor on board except what the passengers carried with them; consequently there was a pooling of convivial resources. The men gathered in the smoking room at night to trade scotch and stories and argue the questions of the day with ever more fluency as the evening progressed. On the third evening out, Lasker was discoursing with particular eloquence but what he said was more vehement than coherent. A foreigner sitting with the Americans listened intently, but he thought his failure to understand was because of his unfamiliarity with English. At length Lasker paused in his oratory, and the earnest listener seized his opportunity.

"But vot is your point?" he asked earnestly.

Lorimer told that story many times and the question became a family byword. Another byword originated with Graeme, who was an unhappy child given to moody conversation. On one of the family's trips he had been running on in a dark vein when Alma interrupted: "Oh, Graeme, why don't you talk about something pleasant?" The boy looked at her with innocent wonder.

"What is there pleasant to talk about?" he inquired.

A formal setting did not deter the Lorimer mirth. Returning to Colby as an alumnus for some academic ceremony, he sat through a program during which a serious young man arose to recite a poem about the wind. The end of each stanza—and it was a long poem—called for a plaintive wo-o-o-o, in imitation. At the end of the first stanza Lorimer barely suppressed a loud chortle when the youngster craned his neck and emitted a woo-o-o-o that would have done credit to a nor'easter. At the end of the second stanza Lorimer emitted a whoop which startled the declaimer and momentarily unsettled him. After that it was an unequal contest. Lorimer finally gave way to uncontrollable howling and the young man gave up.

No one ever heard the Boss laugh louder or longer than he did one afternoon at the Grand Canyon, when he was entertaining the Peter B. Kynes. The Kynes were simple people, but they sometimes spent money in unexpected ways. On this particular occasion a riding expedition into the Canyon had been planned, and Mrs. Kyne appeared in a new riding habit. It was an eloquent outfit made up of a checked coat and checked jodhpurs, and it shone all the more by comparison with the rough clothes the others wore.

Mrs. Kyne's mule seemed to know that his passenger was dressed for the wrong party. At a particularly muddy spot in the trail he appeared to slip—Lorimer always said it was intentional—and plumped Mrs. Kyne over his head into the mud. For once the Boss forgot his never-failing courtesy. Momentarily he lost his accustomed reserve. He was nearly hysterical, and it was a half hour before he was able to go on.

At the beginning of his career Lorimer's laughter was heard often, and the Post was a gay place to work. The parties with his friends were distinctly convivial. Unlike most of the others present, he could unfailingly recall what had happened at these affairs. He wrote to Robert W. Chambers in March 1910 about one especially wet occasion:

"Far be it from me, knocking or casting up, but the way in which you and Phillips threw down the crowd at the conclusion of the Periodical Publishers' dinner was exceedingly unsportsmanlike. There was a brief session in the Palm Room after you retired, and then a few of us adjourned to Bill Hibbs' rooms where there was a very interesting and illuminating discussion of esoteric Buddhism. The argument was so interesting we were all greatly surprised to find, by looking out the windows, that it was breakfast time, so we adjourned to the Shoreham for a bite. It was there that the celebrated Glow Worm Quartet was formed. Its function was to radiate music and good cheer through the remainder of the daytime, though it was slightly handicapped by the fact that no member of it knew more than two lines of 'Glow, Little Glow Worm, Glimmer.' The way in which our revered leader, Mr. Samuel G. Blythe, rendered these few lines brought tears from the eyes of the most thoughtless. . . ."

These affairs of the Periodical Publishers' Association were inclined to be exceedingly damp. Usually the members rented an entire hotel at Atlantic City and had themselves a week-long brawl, after which they would adjourn somewhere else for a brief business meeting to transact the necessary affairs of the organization.

Lorimer's letters to Chambers and his other friends of the early days were full of poignant reminders of these gatherings, the reminders being mixed with business matters. In a letter to Chambers disclosing the fact that Lorimer was working with his blue pencil on a serial by the author, and had transformed his heroine from "a sort of Amélie Rives-Ella Wheeler Wilcox girl" to one "as cool and collected in the revised version as a plate of Neapolitan ice cream," the Boss added: "Thompson gives a very different version of that luncheon from the one which you sent me. I rather gather from him that he had luncheon in a crèche, and that the liquids which he had partaken of were administered to him in a nursing bottle."

It was not solely the pleasure of imbibing that drew Lorimer to the bottle; he loved the feeling of being relaxed with his friends after long hours of work under tension. The stories of his alcoholic exploits were numerous. One week end he went to Atlantic City with Garrett to work on an editorial, as he frequently did, and stopped at his customary hotel, the Traymore. Looking out the window in the evening, he saw the lights of the Brighton and asked Garrett, "Is that where you get the punch you've been talking about?" Garrett had told the Boss of the Brighton concoction of rum and rye named the Garrett Punch in his honor—a variant of the equally famed Brighton Punch.

"That's the place," Garrett said.

"Then let's have one," Lorimer said, putting on his hat.

They had two. One was considered sufficient for an average customer. Walking back to the Traymore, Garrett could feel the boardwalk swaying gently beneath his feet, but Lorimer remarked, "I hear they've got Canadian ale down at the Inlet. Let's have some."

Garrett went along, but he drank coffee. Lorimer had two quarts of ale.

By this time Garrett had recovered sufficiently from the punch to remember that the Boss had an editorial due in Philadelphia the next morning. He glanced warily at Lorimer.

"How are you feeling?" he asked.

The Boss guessed what was on his mind.

"Don't you worry about that editorial, my son," he said reassuringly. He wrote it before he returned to Philadelphia.

Whenever he stopped at the Traymore, Lorimer asked for the apartment atop the lofty hotel. Usually he got it, but occasionally the manager would apologize and say that another gentleman had preceded him. This jockeying back and forth continued for some time and Lorimer never learned who his anonymous competitor for the suite was until Graeme's wife, Sarah, happened to mention the matter to George Arliss, on a visit to London.

"So *that's* who it was!" Arliss exclaimed. "I was the other man, and for years I've wondered who the chap was who always did me out of my apartment when I wanted it!"

Garrett came to Wyncote for dinner one evening during a period when Lorimer had been on the wagon for several weeks. The host was always hospitable, however, and as soon as they were in the library he asked, "Wouldn't you like a drink?"

Out of courtesy Garrett refused. A moment later Lorimer asked him again, and Garrett said, "No, thank you," politely. The Boss fidgeted for ten minutes, then he said, "Are you *sure* you don't want a drink?"

"Quite sure, thanks," Garrett answered.

"Well, goddamit, I want one," Lorimer said.

They spent a satisfactory evening in the library, and next morning Garrett came down to breakfast feeling that he should have taken the pledge the day before. Lorimer was cheerful and about to plunge into a huge breakfast. He sat back to survey his guest critically.

"You look as though you'd been drinking," he said in gentle reproof.

On the way to Atlantic City for week ends of conviviality and editorial writing Lorimer often stopped in New Jersey to see Garrett, either for a visit or to take him along—and sometimes he got no farther. Smyth would drive him home early in the morning, while everyone else was still recovering.

Once he appeared at Garrett's place and said, "Let's go up to

Atlantic City and see Eddie Lefevre." The two men walked to a little gas station near the farm and Garrett called Lefevre. While he waited for the call to go through Lorimer fell into conversation with the station's Italian proprietor, Tony, and when they left, the Boss gave Tony ten dollars. Six years later he said to Garrett with a faraway, reminiscent look in his eyes, "How's your friend Tony?" He had liked the man and never forgot him.

Some of Lorimer's forays with friends and a bottle lasted three days or longer. On the day he came back he invariably ordered a Spanish omelet for lunch. It settled his stomach, he said.

Among the parties he remembered best were those at Sam Blythe's house, and the details he recalled were not the conventional recollections of what state he had been in when he departed. He never forgot the dinner at Blythe's when Sam, as usual, was showing off his Chinese cook, a wizard at pastry. The climax of the meal was a special cake which arrived on the table decorated with fancy Chinese lettering. Someone who had a smattering of the language deciphered the legend.

"I leave tomorrow," it said. And he did.

Lorimer liked to travel on German boats because they had good beer, though beer was not his favorite drink. He seemed to have no favorites, but on his antiquing expeditions through Lancaster Valley he leaned toward the cognac of the region—applejack. If he had occasion to buy a historic flask from one of his antique-dealer friends in that section he often had the new purchase filled with applejack. The bottle would then be tapped lightly at intervals.

"About time for a touch," Lorimer would say. He would touch the flask, wipe the neck politely, and then his companions would touch it, wiping the neck carefully each time. A half-pint flask would last for six or seven hours.

Always blunt in his opinions when completely sober, Lorimer was painfully frank when he had absorbed a few drinks. At such times he said exactly what he thought and damn the torpedoes. His expressed opinions to the editors who were trying to make a success of Curtis' newspaper properties were, in such circumstances, blistering.

On the subject of overdrinking, he gave succinct advice to everyone: "It'll always catch up to you sometime. Everybody, man or woman, who ever takes a drink will inevitably take too much."

When Lorimer visited his friends in Kennebunkport he stayed frequently at a local hotel which served no liquor. There he and Alma once prefaced a dinner party by serving liquid refreshments in their own suite. When the guests went down to dinner Lorimer, who was currently on the wagon and had sat drinkless through the party, was the last to leave the room—or thought he was. But in a mirror one of the guests saw the Boss scrutinize an unsampled cocktail standing idly on a table. Looking sharply in Alma's direction, the Boss quietly snatched it and downed it as neatly as a flycatcher absorbing a gnat.

It is not unlikely that Lorimer took a critical look at the glass as he held it up. Stiegel glass was one of his favorite antiques; and bottle collecting was one of the aspects of antiquing which held an almost morbid fascination for him. Alma had bought the family first antiques, but he had ignored them for years; then he fell from grace completely. As his interest in drinking was curbed during the twenties and the old appetites of his youth diminished, his enthusiasm for antiques increased. It was an exercise which kept him close to his friends, and it took him into his beloved outdoors during the long months between trips West.

Lorimer soon became a master in the field; he would never have been content to be an ordinary collector. He started from scratch, beginning with old silver. Then he took up Navajo rugs, and in three months he knew as much about every sort of rug as the most experienced rug merchant.

Glass was his particular fancy. There was glass everywhere in his house; every panel in the walls was a covering for glass. It was glass, too, that fascinated most of his antique-hunting comrades and became the subject of sharp but friendly rivalries between them.

Roberts knew an antique dealer in Biddeford, Maine, who one day turned up an unusually beautiful Stoddard three-mold pitcher with a blue rim. Roberts bought it for seventy-five dollars and wired Lorimer: "Have bought you a fifteen-hundred-dollar Stoddard pitcher for seventy-five. I want the seventy-five back and a blue flask as commission."

A week later Roberts brought the pitcher to Wyncote. They discussed the deal after dinner, Lorimer sitting cross-legged, as he always did, before cupboards of Stiegel, Stoddard and historic flasks. He began fingering his collection.

"How do you like this piece?" he asked Roberts, picking up an amethyst Stiegel creamer.

"Fine," Roberts said. "I'll take that one."

"Well I guess *not!*" Lorimer protested. "It's the only one I've got!"

After caressing scores of flasks, not one of which he would consent to give up, he eventually found two blue Washington flasks, apparently just alike. One of them was flawed, and with this one he parted reluctantly. Learning later that Roberts had bought the Stoddard pitcher, McKearin, the glass collector, wrote to him and offered twelve hundred and fifty for it.

At one period Lorimer collected eagles. Driving through Washington, Roberts saw a fine carved eagle with an eight-foot wingspread outside the antique shop of Krupsaw, who had repaired the Capitol furniture for many years. Roberts learned that this handsome eagle had once hung in the Supreme Court of the United States, and he bought it for the unexpectedly low price of thirty dollars.

During the following summer the Boss visited Roberts and for the first time saw the Supreme Court eagle. With true collector's cunning, he offered casually to buy it.

"I don't want to sell, but I'll swap," Roberts offered.

Lorimer's glance was cold. Swap for what? he wanted to know.

"That Chippendale master mason's chair up in Burford's room," Roberts said.

"What?" Lorimer howled. "Why, that master mason's chair cost a thousand, and this damned eagle only cost thirty!"

"Maybe so," Roberts said, "but you can get master mason's chairs in a lot of places; you can't get an eagle like this anywhere in the world."

Much as he wanted the eagle, Lorimer could not bring himself to give up his cherished master mason's chair.

The bargaining went on for six or seven years, but no deal was made. After Lorimer's death the chair fell to Burford in the disposition of his father's collection, and Roberts got it at last by exchanging a full set of his own first editions, autographed, for it.

In spite of the professional competition among these non-professional collectors, who were nonetheless experts, Lorimer was extremely generous about buying things for other people—so generous that Roberts often refused to comment about an article because any exceptional enthusiasm might inspire the Boss to buy it and give it to his friend or his friend's wife. Yet this was the same Lorimer who could write to Roberts: "It causes me much pain to notify you that I have just found and purchased in Princeton, New Jersey, the best Sheraton sofa in America, not excepting that in the Metropolitan Museum."

Alma regarded her husband's antiquing expeditions with alarm, among other reasons because they resulted in further additions to a crowded house. Lorimer would say, "I've bought a little thing for the house," and a few days later a huge crate would arrive, containing a piece of furniture bulky enough to necessitate the building of an annex. He once acquired a lowboy, a handsome museum piece, but he was chary about taking it home.

"I can't let Alma know about this thing," he told Roberts. "She'd keep reminding me that I've already got one. Got to sneak it into the house."

The two motored to the Lancaster Valley shop where the lowboy was in residence, loaded it into Lorimer's automobile and returned to Wyncote half an hour before dinner.

"Alma should be out about now," Lorimer calculated.

Smyth slid the car quietly up the drive and the conspirators peered guiltily into Wyncote's quiet hallway. Alma could not be seen. Lorimer and Roberts picked up the lowboy, carried it up to the Boss's room, and exchanged it for the lowboy already there. Then Smyth spirited away the discarded piece to the third floor, where Lorimer kept enough rejects to equip a museum.

"There," Lorimer chuckled, stepping back to survey his work

with satisfaction, "she'll walk past that a hundred times a day and never notice a thing."

The camaraderie between the antique hunters was of a special kind. Roberts, Hergesheimer, Lefevre, Hugh Kahler and Lorimer were more than friends: they were fellow devotees. Like all hobbyists, they scorned people who collected other things, and stared in wonder at the unfortunates who collected nothing at all. They even disapproved of each other on occasion. Kahler, who refused to take antiquing seriously, insisted on collecting mustache cups. His comrades were aghast.

The correspondence between them sparkled with the peculiar wit that antique hunters reserve for each other. Few of their letters concerned with more serious matters failed to contain some reference to current antiquing activity.

Promising to finish an article on a particular week, Roberts added: ". . . and if you are going to be receiving along about Tuesday, October 8th, I will put the world's largest three-mold pitcher into a hatbox, well surrounded by Scott Tissue, and run over to the great city to have a little pea soup and cheese omelet with you. Take it for granted that you will be there, as I see by the papers that several others won't. I had a telephone from Mabel [Kent] proposing a run from Portland to New York in the good ship *Alondra*, leaving tomorrow. When I complained that I had to work and couldn't go, she assured me that I could work on the boat. Any time I fall so low as to do work while on a private yacht, I will consider myself an outcast from all human society. . . ."

To this message Lorimer replied: "Tuesday the 8th is fine. Hope you can stay over and look at a few additions that Eddie and I have picked up en tour. I have two very fine Martha Washingtons, one the best that I have ever seen, and I paid $175 and $250 respectively for them some five or six years ago. Since you were in Wyncote I have picked up six unusually fine Philadelphia Chippendale chairs, a tall Pennsylvania clock painted with tulips, and several other articles of virtue and some not so virtuous, but all above the average. . . ."

Eddie Lefevre, whose serious articles on Wall Street informed

Post readers about financial problems, entertained Lorimer particularly on the antique-hunting expeditions. Sober in his articles, Eddie was lighthearted and gay away from his desk. His passion for bottles was regarded jokingly by his fellow collectors as a foul disease. Lefevre was the explorer who accompanied the Boss on what must have been the apotheosis of antique hunts—a month-long motor tour through England and Ireland, stopping at every antique shop within human view.

Typical of the letters Lorimer wrote to Lefevre was this one: "Thanks for the check. I told Mrs. Jacobs nothing except that you were an exceedingly rich and erratic collector who had a touch of bottle mania. What more could you expect or want? Hergesheimer writes that he was so alarmed at seeing to what depths of degradation and depravity the collection of flasks could lead one that he has decided to sell all his glass with the exception of a few specimens. These few specimens, of course, will include everything in the collection that is better than Woolworth. I am holding your bottles under the sink as hostages against your return to Wyncote."

When Eddie was occupied for too long with sterner affairs on the Street, Lorimer missed him, and was likely to send such a reminder as this, unbelievably flippant to those outside the collectors' circle:

> *The seasons come, the seasons go*
> *The ground is bare, now white with snow;*
> *But what the hell is Eddie-O*
> *A-doing?*

Eddie's bottle mania was a constant source of fun in the correspondence between his friends. Lorimer wrote to Hergesheimer after one trip in 1927:

"Eddie Lefevre took a little run up to York, Pennsylvania, with me last Saturday and gave an exhibition of exceedingly bad antiquing manners, for which I had to reprove him sternly and to enforce the lesson take possession of the article which was the cause of his brutal and unseemly conduct. In three different shops I had permitted him to absorb all the bottles in sight, though four rather fine ones offered at a low price aroused my cupidity. Finally we stopped by the house of Mrs. Bergstrasser's sister and while Eddie was busy poring over all the bottles in the corner cupboard, the lady invited me in the front room to see an odd piece of glass which she had there. It happened to be a fine green Wistarberg piece shaped very much like your blue Wistarberg with the amber rim and the price was ten dollars. I reached for it with one hand and for the ten dollars with the other just as Eddie, imitating a flying wedge, dived over my shoulder screaming, 'I'll take it, I'll take it.' We were hardly on speaking terms for the first hour after leaving the shop. So does the pursuit of antiques engender envy, malice and hatred in an ordinarily kind human being, just as in another case with which you are familiar it engendered a complete disregard of the conventions."

Many of Lorimer's letters to Hergesheimer combined business with the pleasures of antiquing. Thus a letter might begin with the Boss expressing his opinion that a certain series of stories was fine, except that he thought it a mistake to omit quotation marks from direct conversation. But with these matters out of the way, the second paragraph would begin: "I am in the few class myself right now, but I haven't seen anything that interested me particularly since my return from Europe. . . . The Adams mantel executed by Wedgwood that I bought in London is now in place in the drawing room as well as the two Hepplewhite satin-wood cabinets and also a couple of rather nice Hoppners and a good Rembrandt Peale of Thomas Paine. All the glass and porcelain that I bought came through without a single break, although a dinner service in Chinese armorial that belonged to Chief Justice Chase of Maryland is yet to come and that may spoil the score. We must arrange sometime soon to exchange views on our latest acquisitions. The three things that you mention in your letter sound as if they were exceptionally choice and calculated to give me a sinking spell."

Often the transition from business to pleasure was abrupt. "My dear Hergesheimer," Lorimer wrote in one letter, "A man who knows his business doesn't need to be told when he has done a fine job, so I shall confine my remarks about 'Natchez' and

'Albany' [part of the 'Quiet Cities' series] merely to saying that a check will be returned by the treasurer on Tuesday. Eddie and I had a really delightful run to New Orleans and back. On the whole the roads were very good and the hotels fair. We made about three hundred miles a day, though on account of floods and consequent detours we were obliged to make four hundred and fifty miles on the first leg out of New Orleans. . . ."

Roberts memorialized the antique-hunting trips in his "Antiquamania," a book full of the quiet, special humor that pervades Lorimer's letters on the subject. His chapter titled "The Bottle Collectors" describes a particular expedition that had its Lorimer version in a letter the Boss wrote to Adelaide Neall:

"We got back home Sunday night about midnight, all feeling moderately friendly towards each other. Our young friend Ken Roberts was still droning over the frightful hardships that he had endured when he left for Maine. He was a total loss physically on the trip, sleeping part of the time both ways in the car and pop-eyed with exhaustion at either end of the run. We started out Saturday morning and ran two hundred and eighty-five miles straight to Harrisonburg, sixty-seven miles down the Shenandoah Valley, making stops at all the dealers en route. We repeated the process the next day but by a different route, leaving Hergesheimer tired but happy out at West Chester. Yesterday Lefevre and I started out together, as Ken refused to accompany us, and made a circle through the Pennsylvania Dutch country, encountering a terrific thunderstorm just outside of Allentown, that lasted till we got home. I have never seen a heavier rainstorm in my life, and the lightning and thunder were terrific, as we kept moving along with the storm, and every now and then a bolt seemed to strike within one hundred or two hundred feet of the car.

"We were all soaked to the skin when we got home but the trip was worth it as we picked up some rare three-mold glass and a Liverpool pitcher. Eddie indulged in a bottle debauch that has no equal in all history. He gathered together over fifty bottles on this trip and after spending all his money borrowed two hundred and seventy-five dollars from me. He was out of the car and into a shop while it was still moving and by the time the rest of us caught up with him he had all the bottles off the shelves and was pawing them over. This is absolutely the most unique case of bottle mania that I have ever encountered. I got a lovely piecrust table and a beautiful claw-ball Chippendale wing chair in Hagerstown, not to mention some little knickknacks of Stiegel and a Pennsylvania Dutch tulip table that I picked up in the Shenandoah Valley. . . ."

As far as Lorimer was concerned (and it may have been equally true of the others), friendship was the most important part of antique collecting. Writing to his fellow collectors, he could add such postscripts as this, to Roberts: "One of our bright young women authors was dining in a New York restaurant last week. Joe Hergesheimer was at the next table with a strange lady. Our author, as she took her seat, heard Joe say, 'The world is full of cold contacts.' Did he mean cold feet?"

In the actual buying process, however, the Boss was as much a businessman as he was at the Post. He did not buy simply for the sake of buying, and as he became expert in the field he insisted on the highest standards. He wrote to Hergesheimer: "You will be interested and amused to know that when I stripped down the Chippendale wing chair I decided that it was a fake and sent it in to Bateman for a careful examination. He thinks that it was made in England not more than twelve years ago and that the legs have been turned out with a band saw instead of a hand saw. Instead of being mortised it is doweled together. Back it goes to—— ——, who I don't think had any knowledge of its doubtful history. That is the trouble with nine out of ten dealers nowadays. They really don't know their business and are not grounded in woods and cabinetmaking methods. It is a lesson to me not to take anything on faith even from a man who is obviously sincere in his beliefs and who should apparently know what he is talking about. The next chair I buy will be stripped down on the spot and examined with a glass."

Lorimer's critics claimed that he had no real distinction as a collector, that he indulged a rich man's fancy. That criticism could well have been made of others much richer and much less discriminating—men, for example, like Henry Ford, who appeared as a distinguished collector to the uninitiated thousands who viewed the vast museum of Americana he compiled at Greenfield Village. Yet Lorimer and Ford were separated by a world of knowledge. Ford loved Americana and he had the money to buy every sample of it he could separate from the owners, but his knowledge of what he bought was scanty, to say the least. He had to employ experts to do the judging for him.

Other men who made fortunes in Lorimer's time filled their homes with art objects from the galleries of Europe and America, but in most cases it was done without discrimination or knowledge. Unless an expert was hired to buy and arrange the acquisitions, their homes were inclined to look, as so many in Chicago and New York did, like a museum curator's nightmare.

Lorimer, however, earned the respect of other collectors; his antique-filled home was arranged with perfect taste by his own hand, and after his death the best of his early American glass and colonial furniture, considered one of the finest private collections in the world, was placed in the Philadelphia Museum of Art, where it may be seen today. It would have pleased the Boss to see it there. This museum collection represented his finest pieces, in accordance with his will. There was enough remaining, even after his sons had taken other choice pieces, to bring more than a million dollars gross at a series of public auctions in New York City.

The slurs made about his antique collecting were characteristic of the manner in which Lorimer was misunderstood by people outside the Post. It was a self-inflicted misunderstanding. There was about him that faint austerity which made others feel that he kept a part of himself to himself, that a large portion of his life was lived only for Lorimer.

One of those closest to him explained the Boss this way: "He was really a great guy, practically unknown because of his insistence on playing a lone hand—due to the enormous number of people who wanted to fatten themselves through him. That's one reason why he had so few friends—the few people who didn't need or ask anything from him."

He played golf only with Mr. Curtis, on the publisher's private course, and then not unless he was drafted. After Curtis died he never played the game again. In fact he hated all games— cards, tennis, any form of sport. Even when he rode it was not for the love of riding, but only to get somewhere.

He was a man of extremely simple tastes in most things. In the matter of food he was a champion of ham and eggs. "You can't go wrong on them," he often asserted. Seeking to please him, Roberts once gave him the special Roberts steak, rubbed with garlic. Lorimer tasted it experimentally and his comment was succinct: "Why gild the lily?" The Lorimer taste ran more to rare steak, raw young onions, and potatoes Lyonnaise.

His taste in clothes was plain but good. He wore steel-gray, dark blue and brown business suits, double-breasted, cut in the finest English style by one of Philadelphia's best tailors. He was, in fact, named as one of the ten best-dressed men in the city at a tailors' convention.

His musical tastes were even simpler. Lorimer went to the opera on command, but it was evident that he did not enjoy it. Gilbert and Sullivan was as far as he would go, and that amorphous body of composition known as semi-classical was his ordinary fare. One day he stayed out two hours for lunch, an occurrence so unusual that it was the major topic of conversation in the Post office until a friend came back and reported the Boss's whereabouts. He had been lunching in the Bellevue-Stratford, and toward the end of the meal the hotel orchestra had broken into his favorite song, "Ciribiribin." Lorimer was still sitting at the table, his friend related, and, having tipped the leader, he was listening to "Ciribiribin" played over and over again.

In his rare moments of boredom Lorimer's active mind was seldom at a loss to find something amusing. One summer he paid a visit to his brother-in-law, Hulburd Dunlevy, who lived at Spring Lake, Michigan, and after a few days on the Dunlevy farm life palled on him. On a particularly quiet afternoon he rummaged in the barn and found some bright red paint that had been used on the outbuildings. He let it be known among the young fry on the place that he would give a bounty for all the snapping turtles they could catch. The inspired youngsters shortly rounded up a fine mess of turtles, and Lorimer proceeded to paint their shells with the paint he had found. When the job was done he put the turtles out to dry for an hour or so, then urged the scarlet herd back into the lake. He had worked hard at this task; it took him most of the afternoon. And although he was not there to see it, the result of his labor was gratifying. For years afterward natives and visitors alike were bemused by the red turtles of Spring Lake.

In a sense the simplicity of Lorimer's tastes extended to his financial affairs. He was meticulous in all money matters. Collectors could never find the slightest error in his income-tax returns. If a ten-dollar or a twenty-dollar royalty check came in after the forms had been filled out, he would insist on doing them over again.

When he went to Philadelphia, Lorimer's first stock purchases were five-share units of the ultra-safe and conservative Insurance Company of North America. He had fifteen hundred shares of this stock by the time he died. Most of his remaining wealth came from the Curtis Publishing Company. For a time the company made as much as fifty-two million a year, and a large share of the stock was made available to key executives. Lorimer had substantial holdings of both common and preferred. About 1926 he sold the preferred, an act which astounded some of his business friends, who reminded him that the stock was still going up. "I can only sell while it *is* going up," he pointed out.

His concern for the company governed all his dealings in Curtis stock. During the depression, when Curtis was at 30 and General Motors stood at 20, his son Graeme wanted to trade his Curtis stock for GM, but the Boss refused to let him sell it. "Because it would look bad for the company if my son unloaded his stock," he explained. Lorimer did not sell his own common stock until after he had resigned from the company.

Among the Boss's other investments were bank stocks, motors and basic industries. Sixty to eighty per cent of his total investments were in bonds, government and municipal. He owned a piece of virtually every sewer in Pennsylvania.

The principle Lorimer followed in making a fortune was simple:

"Save at least a third of your income [from investments] and buy a little bit more every year. Never worry about whether you're buying at a high or a low price. Don't try to outthink the market operators."

That principle enabled him to survive the vicissitudes which wiped out or seriously diminished the fortunes of his contemporaries when bad times came. Lorimer happened to be in Philadelphia's Union League Club on the night in 1923 when Edward Stotesbury, Morgan's partner, came in and announced gleefully that he was worth a hundred million dollars as of that date. Lorimer did not envy him. His own fortune was at its apex that year, about ten million dollars. It was still ten million when he died fourteen years later, after the crash and the depression, and by an odd coincidence, ten million was the approximate value of Stotesbury's estate at the time of his death.

Lorimer was generous with his accumulations. He gave a Colonial Room to the Philadelphia Museum of Art, and he deeded a tract of his King's Oak farm along Pennypack Creek to Montgomery County for a park—it should be specially reserved for little girls, he said. Few people knew until his death that he gave both time and money to the Abington Memorial Hospital. Other bequests went to the Franklin Memorial Fund (a hundred and twenty-five thousand); the Franklin Museum, where he created a "museum of electricity"; and the Philadelphia Museum of Art. To Colby College, of which he was a trustee, he gave the magnificent two-hundred-thousand-dollar Lorimer Memorial Chapel, in memory of his father, around which the new Colby campus is built.

These were the generosities which came to light after his death. Unknown except to a few people were the innumerable kindnesses of his lifetime—financing anonymous Thanksgiving and Christmas baskets through a grocery store, supplying small sums to an endless stream of hard-luck pleaders who drifted in and out of his office year after year, letting people live rent-free in his properties. He never could resist a plea for charity involving children. At any time, and particularly at Christmas, he could be touched at that most vulnerable point.

It was part of the Boss's character that he never mentioned his charities or referred to the honors given him. Colby, Colgate, McGill and Yale awarded him honorary degrees, but he thought little of them: he believed that children were better educated at home.

The only clubs he ever joined—in fact, the only parties, societies or movements with which he allowed his name to be associated— were the Yale Club of Philadelphia, the Huntingdon Valley Hunt Club, and the Franklin Inn, a luncheon club. He was almost never seen in any of them.

Lorimer liked the luxuries of the rich but he was not concerned with them. It was far more important to him if the California redwoods were in danger from the lumbermen; then he would defend the trees as though they were constitutional principles.

America and the Post were his twin passions, when all was said and done—crossing and recrossing the continent, studying the sky for signs of rain, inquiring about the crops and talking to hundreds of people; putting out the nation's number one magazine with inexhaustible energy and enthusiasm. These things were his life.

If it had been physically possible, this would have constituted Lorimer's idea of a perfect day: to put an issue of the Post together, read a hundred thousand words of manuscript, ride a trail to the bottom of the Grand Canyon and back, take a four-hundred-mile antiquing trip with his cronies, spend the evening in sociable drinking and conversation with these friends and Sam Blythe, and, as the day ended, walk the acres of King's Oak and admire the rhododendrons at Wyncote.

Such a day, impossible though it might be, would certainly have ended in the same fashion as many an actual Lorimer day. The Boss would rise, stretch his square, solid frame, sniff the air, and remark, "Well, this is going to make a grand little sleeping night." And so to bed.

CHAPTER NINE

The Last Year

In the last year of his life Lorimer tried to give up smoking. He coughed frequently and there was sometimes a huskiness in his voice. There was no suspicion in his mind, apparently, that the annoying "smoker's cough" might be the symptom of illness, but he made an earnest effort to stop the steady flow of cigarettes and cigars because smoking had begun to hurt his throat. The attempt was futile. He was forever borrowing cigarettes.

The Boss seemed more reflective that year. He stopped often after work to have a beer with a new Post editor, Martin Sommers, at the Bellevue-Stratford's rathskeller, and over the foam he lovingly recalled the old days on the Post for this man who had never heard the familiar tales.

Early in the year he took a short vacation and went to the Coast. He made a stop in San Diego, where he had his usual tower room in the El Cortez Hotel, overlooking the bay. His friend Stuart Lake came to visit him there and the two men talked quietly for an hour or more. Lorimer gazed out at the magnificent vista and paid little direct attention to his visitor. He appeared to be thinking of something else.

"I'll tell you something," he said at last, "but you must keep it to yourself. I'm going to resign from the Curtis Publishing Company later this year, to take effect next January 1."

Lake was probably the first person to hear this news. Lorimer looked out the window again and there was a faraway look in his eyes.

"For thirty-five years I've been in a squirrel cage," he said. "I want to get out and climb some trees."

Back in Philadelphia, he showed no indication of a desire to quit. He worked harder than ever, with most of his energy directed to the editorial page, where the Post was fighting the Roosevelt second term. Lorimer answered many of the letters which were critical of the Post's policy; he saved the toughest ones for himself. Sometimes he would take a whole afternoon to answer these letters, so earnest was he in the anti-Roosevelt crusade. It seemed not to matter that his practical political sense told him he was laboring in a lost cause.

In August he told Wesley Stout that he intended to resign; it was the first intimation Stout had that he would fall heir to the editor's desk. The formal resignation came soon after, on August 28. It was a characteristic Lorimer document, only four paragraphs long, reviewing his career on the Post, testifying to the present excellent condition of company affairs, and formally recommending Stout as the man best qualified to succeed him. He concluded: "Need I add that I resign with regret because I have been happy in my work and fortunate in my associates. But I want a little more leisure, a little more time to attend to my personal affairs, and a chance to do some other work, including some long-deferred writing. I am confident that my good friends and associates in the company will maintain and increase its wide margin of leadership, and carry on the fine tradition that Mr. Curtis bequeathed to us."

The Boss's retirement was announced to Post readers, and to the world in general, in the issue of December 26, 1936. This announcement, which took up the entire Post editorial page, was the only signed editorial Lorimer ever wrote. In it he disclosed what was news to some readers: "Up to the hour when this number of the Saturday Evening Post goes to press, I have formulated its policies, planned the numbers, and personally read and selected the material for them. I have had an able and hard-working staff of associates beside me, but as mine have been the final decisions, I accept full responsibility for the policies of the weekly."

After he had paid his compliments to the staff, and particularly to Stout, the Boss went on to restate those policies for which he had been willing to "accept full responsibility." He reaffirmed his belief that economic law ultimately had the last word, in spite of what President and Congress might do, and he professed to see a tendency in President Roosevelt and other New Deal leaders to swing back to the policies which he, Lorimer, had advocated, especially in the field of monetary policy—and here Lorimer took a parting shot at the "aliens" whose foreign money and investments he still believed were a threat to America. Then he made his final pronouncement on politics:

"As we have repeatedly stated on this page, we are in sympathy with some of the New Deal objectives. Our criticism has been for hasty measures that have not been thought through, by which it has sought to remake our country overnight. For many years we have advocated the protection of investors; proper regulation of child labor, particularly in the mills, the factories and in some farming operations; slum clearance; the conservation of natural resources, and other reforms.

"As we have often said, the curse of America has been our haste to develop and to overdevelop everything in sight for the sake of a quick private profit and a continuing public loss; to graze and to overgraze our ranges; to bring in hordes of aliens, regardless of their fitness or unfitness for Americanization, to meet the demand for cheap labor. Even our farm problem was, first of all, a real estate problem in many of its aspects, the outgrowth of promoters' drives to sell land to prospective settlers, regardless of the fitness of either the land or the settler. . . . But we must walk steadily forward, instead of running to meet these problems. We are already out of breath with running, and when in our haste we overtake a problem, we discover that it is not one but a group of closely interrelated problems."

The editorial's peroration was an affirmation of faith in the kind of America that George Horace Lorimer believed in so passionately. "I have passed through one panic and one depression after another," he wrote. "In my own lifetime I have seen such ruthless exploitation of men and resources, but in spite of this America has always forged ahead on the courage and initiative of its private citizens. And steadily, through all that period, I have seen business practices and ethics grow better; I have seen sentiment developing against the waste and exploitation of our national resources, and a public conscience hardening against the old abuses. Could a paternalistic government have done better? I venture to doubt it. Granting all the waste, the ruthlessness and the loose ethics of the past, America has done a pretty good job and no Ism would have done a better one. To exchange one form of ruthlessness that is steadily growing less, for another that is steadily hardening, would not be a sound trade. Every time we enact a panacea into law, we take something fine and sturdy from the American character, for character cannot be imposed from without."

In the following week's issue of the Post, Stout's name occupied the place on the masthead where Lorimer's had been for nearly four decades, and his hand turned out the long editorial. Under the title, "Au Revoir, but Not Good-By," the new editor paid his respects to the old and told his readers: "A younger generation to whose hands he has turned over the command have been trained under him. That is their boast and your assurance." An addenda disclosed that Lorimer had been asked to continue his editorials, and it quoted his answer: "Whatever writing I do, the Post will have first claim on, of course. But I planned no such fixed task as a weekly page and I will make no promises. I want sixty days of rest without a responsibility. When I have had that rest, I'll consider the page."

Stout added: "If you share our conviction that this would be a strange page without Mr. Lorimer, our belief that he would miss the page, our certainty that his bass voice would be missed in an age of tenors, we invite you to join in this petition. It has always been George Horace Lorimer's page. That is what we propose to call it if he accepts. . . ."

The response to Stout's plea and to Lorimer's final editorial was one of the most remarkable outpourings of mail any periodical ever received, and certainly the most heartfelt tribute ever paid to any editor. The hundreds of thousands of letters represented a cross section of Post readership, and if the Boss had entertained any doubts about the kind of people who sat in judgment on his work, they were removed by the letters. A sampling of them would run like this:

From a Texas schoolteacher: "You seem to want to know whether the readers of the Post want a George Horace Lorimer Page or not. By all means yes. This comes from a dyed-in-the-wool Democrat who often disagrees with the Editor of the greatest magazine of the age."

From a man in Oakland, California: "I can never be sure about anything until I know what George thinks and says about it. He certainly can figure things out. This country needs his clear mind, his calm sincerity and plain hoss sense."

From an anonymous reader: "The reason I have always liked the Post is that it was intended for the average citizen like myself. It has given us the problems of American life in a straightforward, unbiased, intelligent way. While I did not always agree with Mr. Lorimer, his fundamental principles were the same as all patriotic Americans', and he was always fair and just in his criticisms of the other side."

From a man in Seattle: "To lose Brisbane was a tragedy. To lose Lorimer would indeed be a catastrophe. For almost thirty years I have relied upon the editorial page of the Saturday Evening Post for a basis upon which to found my opinions."

From a man in Goshen, Indiana: "When the Post came last week with the announcement that George Horace Lorimer would no longer edit the publication I felt like a very good friend had died. P. D. Armour and my grandfather were close friends. Perhaps Mr. Lorimer's father and my grandfather were friends too. At any rate, George Horace has seemed like my friend, these long years, though I have never had the pleasure of even knowing what he looked like until I saw his picture in this issue. His character is stamped in his face. . . . One look at him and it is easier to understand the success of the Post and what it has stood for."

From a Brooklyn doctor: "My recollection is that I first subscribed to the Post on or about 1900 when the Post was a very thin little magazine indeed. There was something about it, however, that attracted me to it. Before studying medicine I had been a world wanderer—sailor, soldier, newspaper kid in South Africa, beachcomber in India, gold hunter in Australia, range rider in Colorado, wrecker and deep-sea diver off California and finally the long drudgery of the study of medicine made doubly hard for me because of lack of systematic training in study (I was scarcely thirteen when I ran away to sea). Perhaps it was this background that made me so fond of the Post as I pursued a wide medical practice in a small Virginia village. I was seeing the world again through the spectacles of George H. Lorimer. . . ."

The cartoonist, Nate Collier, sent in a self-caricature portraying himself as horrified by the news of Lorimer's retirement. This legend ran beside the picture: "Airplanes without Lindbergh, flivvers without Ford, hamburgers without hamburg, eggs without bacon, radios without Roosevelt, literature without Shaw, armies without rifles, and buckwheat cakes without maple syrup —I can imagine all these, but the Saturday Evening Post without George Horace Lorimer? Impossible! Of course continue those inimitable Lorimer editorials!!!!"

From a man in Roseburg, Oregon: ". . . I have taken an active part in every presidential election since and including the one of 1872, and never was so much disturbed about the issues at stake as I was at the ones brought out in this election. To old folks like me, who have supported with arms and taxes a constitutional government such as we had in the United States of America prior to 1933, your defense of that government with your splendid editorials in the Saturday Evening Post, seemingly has done more towards curbing the half-baked young brain-trusters in their mad hoedown macabre on the very vitals of our free institutions than any other thing. . . ."

One letter was typed on a thin, noisy slice of copper from "The

Richest Hill on Earth," in Butte, Montana, with the notation: "I hope you appreciate this rattling good letter."

From a Los Angeles man: "For thirty-five years, or since I was twelve years old, I have read every issue of the Saturday Evening Post, no matter where I was or what I was doing. It formulated my viewpoints through its editorials, entertained, instructed and amused from then until now. Its advertisements have sold me my cars, food, clothing, necessities and luxuries. Its advertisers have never failed me, nor have its views of policies ever disappointed me."

A rural woman in Michigan, who said that her tribute "comes from a very humble home indeed but is nonetheless heartfelt," added: "My first thought upon looking upon him [his picture in the Post] for the first time was 'Isn't he just too absolutely sweet!' And I took the picture and pinned it on the wall over my desk. My husband noticed it there and asked, 'Who is the guy?' And I said 'That's my feller.' (With tears behind the smile.)"

An ex-newspaperman from Brockton, Massachusetts, an outdoors lover, took the occasion to recall Post errors—how Ben Ames Williams had made one of his Maine woodsmen tell a sweet young thing in apple-blossom time that the trout were thin because they had just spawned. "I'm told," said the correspondent, "that Mr. Williams now casts a pretty good fly in Maine trout pools and no doubt he now knows that trout spawn in early winter. . . ."

Many readers told how they first happened to get the Post, and included their life stories in the description. The best of these came from a woman in California who wrote: "The Post first came into our home, as near as I can recall, in 1898 or '99. I was eleven and brother Frank was nine. We had lost our mother, and father, broken in health, had gone into Lane county, Oregon, and taken up a homestead in the Coast Range, where he was eking out an existence eighty miles from the nearest railroad at Eugene, and in the winter it took the mail three days to reach us over the mountain trails.

"Our postoffice was Minerva, where the mail came once a week, on Saturday. Through the long rainy days when two lonely children and a more lonely man coughed his life away with the dread, lingering consumption, we read everything we could get our hands on, and our dream of Heaven was a public library where we could have all the books we wanted to read. Brother Frank was nine and one day he saw an advertisement stating that a new weekly could be had for six weeks for the sum of twenty-five cents, and more wonderful of all, he had that sum that he had earned by raising garden truck and selling it in Florence, a town twelve miles distance, which meant a day's journey from our homestead. But the twenty-five cents was sent out and in due time the first copy of the Post arrived.

"I can recall its arrival in my world as though it was yesterday. Brother Frank had gone the two miles for the mail, and as he came running out of the woods into our clearing and over the big six-foot fir log that formed our dooryard fence, he was shouting at the top of his voice, as he waved it at arm's length, 'It's come, it's come and it's a dandy.' I can see him now, a tousle-headed, thin, dirty-faced, barefooted boy; all he had on was an old ragged shirt and patched, ragged overalls with one leg rolled up over the knee; the other had dropped down unnoticed. From that day on the Saturday Evening Post has been our constant reading companion. I haven't missed reading a single copy that I know of from then to the present date, and no one can know what it has meant to us in forming our life's destiny."

A Chicago businessman wrote: "When I was a mere lad out in the sand hills of Kansas, my older brother always had the Saturday Evening Post and when I could steal it from him, I got down on the floor, spread myself out on my belly and looked at the pictures and tried to figure out the spelling of the words which did not look too formidable; in fact, there is some question as to whether my knowledge of spelling was gleaned more from the Saturday Evening Post or from Guffey's Reader. A good many years have now rolled by and said belly has increased to such proportions that an attempt to read the paper in the former position would probably give me a feeling of illness, such as seasickness or looking down from a great height. However, I am still a faithful reader of the Saturday Evening Post."

From a prisoner in Missouri State Penitentiary, with whom Lorimer had corresponded and to whom he had given a Post subscription: "Just a few lines to say hello, and to again thank you for making it possible for me to get the Saturday Evening Post. I shall never forget your kindness. . . ."

From the proprietor of a small business in Chicago Heights, Illinois: "Your distress signal noted and we lamped you bearer of the fiery cross and what you have and you can put us down as having the boss write some of his editorials and fur him to keep his page. We have read the Sat evening post fur nigh unto thirty years and we have sung your praises high and low, as being fearlessly American at all times and having no strings tied to what you put out, and the other year we papered our wash house, we use the term wash house to be polite, with a bushel or so of rejection slips and there are several of yours there. Now if my letter is not strong enuf and it takes more than this to get the big boss back well bounce this back and I will write again in big red letters. Let the old boy continue to fill his page or at least part of it."

A grateful Iowa man wrote: "One particular instance in which he favored me, which I would like to cite, was the position that he always took in his various articles on foreign government bonds as an investment. Fortunately, I saw the light and sold in time, due to his editorials. . . ."

A Brooklyn man said simply: "Let George do it!"

From a Baptist minister in Fort Worth: "I regard it as a great American institution, retaining its high ideals regardless of the trend of popular opinion. It has been no weather vane, showing which way the wind was blowing at the moment, but more like a magnetic needle pointing toward the pole star. It was one of the last of the great magazines to begin carrying cigarette advertisements, and I believe I am correct that it does not now carry liquor advertisements. I searched the current issue before I bought it. It is my opinion that a periodical's advertising pages should reflect the character of the periodical, and have been forced to deny my favorite monthly entrance to my home because the most fine illustrated pages in it advise my boy and girl to drink liquor in order to be smart and brilliant. I am not a crank, but there is a limit to my tolerance. I may as well be frank, I had read the Post a good many years for its fiction alone, then became interested in its non-fiction articles, and finally became a reader of the editorial page, which has since become the first thing I read. . . ."

From a man in Auburn, California: "Me an' George started together with the Post. In anger I stopped the paper when he started us turning over to page 8 or 10 to finish the story. I got over this but G.H.L. never did. I did not realize that the adver-tisers were paying for my enjoyment. More than anything else that has made success for the Post is the strong, virile editorial policy maintained. I have often wondered who the writers were. It never occurred to me that G.H.L. did that part of the work. . . ."

A man in Ocean Grove, New Jersey, wrote: "I am enclosing page 23 from this week's Post. Won't you please sign your name right over the face of that picture and return it to me? There is nothing in this world that I want more. I am not an autograph collector, but ask this favor because of the boundless respect and admiration I have felt for you since I was a young man in your subscription department twenty-five years ago. . . ."

From a boy in West Springfield, Massachusetts: "Having fol-lowed the Saturday Evening Post and its policies, although I am only sixteen years old, for several years, it is with regret," etc. Then he asked for an autograph.

From a lawyer in Yankton, South Dakota: "Your retirement announcement . . . caused me much sorrow that my lifelong political and economic guide and mentor was no longer to sit with me in my parlor each Monday night—and there help clarify my thought on the recurring problems. . . ."

From a man in Santa Monica, California: "I am just one of one hundred and twenty million people who go to make up our great country. I am unknown except among my small circle of friends and acquaintances. But I wish to make my personal feelings regarding your resignation from the Saturday Evening Post known to you. We read your editorial in the December 26 issue, my wife and I, and to say we felt deep regret would be putting it lightly. You know, Mr. Lorimer, this country has no over-abundance of leaders and when we do lose one either through death or retirement his loss is keenly felt. I am not easily moved, sentimentally, but I don't mind saying that as I read your article aloud to Mrs. O'Leary I had difficulty in carrying on. I had the same feeling about Mr. Rockne and Mr. Rogers—two people we could ill afford to lose. . . ."

A Denver doctor wrote: "As a young man in Boston it was my great joy and inspiration to hear your distinguished father at Tremont Temple on Sundays and his lecture on the French Revolution on weekdays. While you are taking a two months' rest it will give me great pleasure to be your private physician, travel with you and be serviceable to you as interpreter in case you wish to go to Germany and France. The question of money is no object as I have income of my own. . . ."

From an Arizona newspaperman: "I am one of those millions of readers you have had who has derived a real and tangible personal benefit from what you have written and published. Those books of yours . . . coupled with such inspiring articles as those of 'The Bloody Six' by Edward Mott Wooley and 'The Making of a Newspaperman,' by Sam Blythe, I read when as a young man I was blundering about trying to decide whether to be a forest ranger or a farmer. Those books and articles inspired me to the belief that if those people could do things so could I, that there was no patent or copyright on what they had done. Curiously enough, things have turned out much better than I ever dreamed they would, and I am still a fairly young man with many years of opportunity ahead of me. Your retirement will be like the loss of a weekly friend and intimate adviser."

Thus the letters ran, every one a testament to Lorimer's knowledge of his audience, and providing in themselves a composite picture of that audience. Only one did not join in the demand for a Lorimer page; only one was unfriendly.

It took weeks to dig out from under the avalanche of mail. Stout wrote a form reply, which was worked out in several variations: "The heavens opened and the letters descended. The Boss worked all New Year's Eve and New Year's Day trying to acknowledge those addressed to him, before he got away by car Saturday morning. The rest we are acknowledging by form letter

with extra girls typing them, and still they pour in. All will be
sent to California to be read at his leisure. . . ."

As though to summarize the end of an era, Stout wrote a short
history of the Post at about the same time. Published in pamphlet
form, without the author's by-line, it was distributed free to any
reader who asked for it. Copies went also to the Post family of
authors, who were as pleased as the magazine's subscribers. Sinclair Lewis said he had read it "with the devout care of an early
member of the congregation," and Harry Leon Wilson wrote:
"What an exciting tale it is! And, considered as a matter-of-fact
recital (instead of someone's pipe-dream) where else on this exciting planet could it have occurred? And every time I found my
own name in the thing I felt merely like a minor character in a
colorful play. . . ."

On his last day at the Post, Lorimer left the office before his
customary quitting time. His old friend, Mary Roberts Rinehart,
was with him. Driving out to Wyncote together, they stopped at
Adelaide Neall's home for a cup of coffee.

"Well, what will you do now?" Mrs. Rinehart asked the Boss
as they relaxed around the hospitable Neall table.

"I'll be happy," Lorimer insisted. "I've got so many things I've
been wanting to do."

During the few subsequent weeks that he spent in California it
appeared that he would, in fact, achieve the peaceful, leisured
life he seemed to want—although no one could imagine the Boss
leading that kind of existence. He went first to Palm Springs,
where he spent much of his time riding about the desert. As an
office joke, in the old familiar manner, he sent the Post staff a
picture of himself posed on a stuffed bucking bronco, with his hat
in hand, fanning the animal in true Western style, and dressed in
cowboy garb.

The staff wired him that they were delighted with the picture
and had given it to the papers. This brought a hasty wire from
the Boss: "Don't use bucking bronc photo. Look at it through
microscope and you'll see why."

The picture looked all right to them, the staff replied by return
wire. "Use mirrors. I did," the Boss answered. But the picture ran

in a Philadelphia paper, to the general amused astonishment of Philadelphians, and the staff sent a final retort: "We took you for a better ride than your stuffed bronco did."

On his return to Philadelphia, Lorimer prepared to construct his new life. He wrote to Roberts: "I had a lovely loaf for sixty days in Southern California, spending most of the time at Palm Springs and Phoenix, with an occasional day's run up to Victor Hugo's new restaurant in Beverly Hills to get a real luncheon. I intended to run up to San Francisco to see Sam, but the weather was so beastly up there and Sam was so sick that I gave it up in the end. As a possible trustee of Colby, I shall from time to time be making trips to Maine and detouring on occasion to see you and perhaps to look over Rubinstein's assortment of junk. While I am not taking on the editorial page, I am writing a few pages to help out during the emergency. Of course, exactly what we both felt has happened. Now that Roosevelt has a second term, he is planning to crack down harder than ever. What suckers these businessmen who declared that he was going to play ball with them during his second term made of themselves. . . ."

In spite of his continued political bitterness, Lorimer appeared to his friends a mellowed man. Not long after his return he remarked to a friend: "Well, I suppose Stout will make a clean sweep of all the Lorimer people on the Post. By God, that's what I'd do if I were Stout."

But it was plain to those close to him that his heart was not in his new life. Perhaps he had a premonition of death. He had liquidated his Curtis stock, and he had gone through the motions of setting up new quarters, in room 1024 of the Public Ledger Building, next door to the Curtis Building. Visiting him in this office, Garrett noted that the stationery he now used was plain, in sharp contrast to the handsome, two-toned letterheads he had delighted to use at the Post. The Boss's old friend looked at him sharply when he saw that stationery, and he thought, "The Boss knows he won't be here long."

Lorimer was full of plans, however. His files were crammed with material for an autobiography, he remarked that he wanted to write something about Mr. Curtis, and he told Sarah Lorimer that he would like to start a new magazine, completely free of advertising influence; he did not explain how a magazine could be any more free than the Post had been. But none of the projects he contemplated was ever begun. He complained that he was tired, and an occasional Post editorial was the extent of his work. A nagging cold he had contracted in the West made him miserable early in the summer, and he spent much time in the sun at Atlantic City. It was on one of these trips that Alma urged him to stop on the way and consult a specialist about his respiratory troubles.

He had already made two such trips. While he was still editor, he had been plagued by a persistent sore spot on his tongue and had gone to see a famous Philadelphia skin specialist. He had to wait, although he had an appointment, and Lorimer, who had work waiting for him at the office, did not stay to be examined. Next day another doctor cured the symptom but did not diagnose the disease. Still later the Boss consulted a throat specialist, who incredibly missed the diagnosis.

It was only after months of coughing that he responded to Alma's urging and went to Dr. Chevalier Jackson, the noted specialist, on August 13, and learned the truth. In the few weeks of life that remained to him, Lorimer fought the throat cancer that had begun to strangle him. He fought it with science and his own stout heart. Dr. Jackson gave him thirty-one X-ray treatments in an effort to burn out the diseased tissue, but it was too late. It was plain that Lorimer was dying.

His old friends wrote anxious letters. Hergesheimer asked Alma if there was anything he could give the Boss, and she replied that he would like a fresh, clear cologne. The most touching letter came from Booth Tarkington, now nearly blind and himself ill, who wrote in his own hand to Graeme in great, sprawling letters on a sheet of heavy orange paper: "Don't have any anxiety about silence here: nobody could better understand your father's wish [that his friends not be bothered] or that your mother couldn't bear sympathetic letters. I've known all about that since the days when my eyes were going out. . . ."

Four times the Boss pulled back from death, until on an October evening, the twenty-seventh, he gave up the life he had so much enjoyed.

Sarah Lorimer's brother, the Rev. Frank H. Moss, Jr., a Protestant Episcopal missionary to Japan, who had been visiting the family, officiated at the burial. The list of honorary pallbearers was a roll call of distinguished names. There were his familiars— Sam Blythe, Tarkington, Hergesheimer, Garrett, Lefevre and Roberts. There were statesmen: Herbert Hoover, Justice Owen Roberts and former Senator George Wharton Pepper. The Curtis Company was represented by Stout, Walter D. Fuller, its president; and Fred A. Healy, the advertising director. And there were such neighbors and friends as A. Atwater Kent, Robert Sewell, Judge Charles Sinkler, and J. B. Lippincott, together with the renowned Philadelphia names of Dr. Thomas S. Gates, president of the University of Pennsylvania; T. Stogdell Stokes, president of the Pennsylvania Museum of Art; Joseph Wayne, Jr., president of the Philadelphia National Bank; Edward T. Stotesbury, Isaac H. Clothier, Frank H. Moss, Sr., George S. Tyler, Percy C. Madeira, and John Gilbert.

In New York the Boss's friend and contributor, Edwin Balmer, editor of *Redbook*, paid him an unusual tribute by pulling out an illustration from an issue just going to press and inserting a black-bordered note that said what many another magazine editor and writer was thinking: that Lorimer was "more than a mere editor. He was a veritable tower of strength. He was a man whose fairness and honesty established new and higher standards in the profession. For a writer to be 'accepted by Lorimer' meant to arrive. For an editor to know Lorimer meant an inspiration. A gentleman of the old school, an indefatigable worker and clear-headed thinker, he will be long remembered as one of the few truly great personalities produced within our lifetime."

Again the mail descended on the Post and on Lorimer's family. It seemed as though everyone who had written at the time of his retirement now wrote again to pay tribute. A merchant in Polo, Missouri, summed up what the Post readers felt: "There was a lump in my throat the other day when I read of the passing of George Horace Lorimer. . . . Merely as one of the 3,000,000, I am prompted to write this note expressing my appreciation of his influence in helping me to think straight, and of the innumerable hours of pleasure and profit that came to me through his editorial genius. I felt that I knew him well, through his weekly calls via the pages of the Post, and especially through his editorial page."

There were dozens of letters like the one from a New York *Daily News* writer, who had been a spasmodic Post contributor: "It was a most severe shock to me as I watched the machine ticking out the news in the wire room here. I felt a deep personal loss, though I had never met him. . . ."

What Lorimer's influence had meant to his fellow professional workers was expressed by George Foxhall, Sunday editor of the Worcester (Mass.) *Telegram:* ". . . I think people like myself, who began in journalism during the period from 1905 to 1910, must feel, in addition to the sense of loss in the passing of a great man, a personal sadness. For Mr. Lorimer was the beau ideal of our professional youth. He was not only our ideal of success. He was the demonstrated success of our ideals. I, for one, felt in him an integrity of purpose, an intellectual force, and a human quality that touched life as it seemed to me to be true. To me he has been, through all the years of my professional life, the one constant standard of editorial fineness; avoiding stunts, avoiding affectations and claptrap, yet finding that an enormous public could find a common interest in those everyday qualities that make life—both in the practical and the romantic world. . . ."

The authors who had contributed to the Post were almost unbelieving of the fact that Lorimer was no longer in the world. T. S. Stribling wrote to Graeme that he and his wife "had been planning how we could get your father to come to lunch with us as we went North this year. I had a new novel that I wanted him to read, one that was not at all for the Post. I thought it would entertain him and I wanted to know what he would think of it."

It was P. G. Wodehouse who summed up what all the Post family of writers was thinking: "I feel as if a great bit of my life had gone. I think that, outside the family, those who are saddest today are the authors who worked for him."

The Post's own editorial obituary was written, but not signed, by Garet Garrett. It began: "His face was to the weather. He had

a mariner's eye and a mariner's step, with that little rise on the ball
of the foot. As some have a special sense of time and can tell you,
without looking, what o'clock it is, so he had a sense of the wind,
knowing always where it was and when it changed and what was
likely to be riding it. Both sunshine and storm excited him. Life
was a voyage, in a barque of one's own, very lonely in the
moments of peril and decision. The meaning? Who knew the
meaning of it or where the port was? The direction was important, and the faith to keep it simplified every problem of
navigation."

The editorial closed with a promise: "With this issue, the name
of Mr. Lorimer returns to the masthead, there to remain as long
as there is a Post." That promise was kept only during Stout's
regime.

As Garrett noted in his obituary editorial, Lorimer would have
liked the grand eulogies that followed his death. He would have
thought they needed editing. And he might have been amused at
the readiness with which the daily press, which had been so quick
to criticize him and the Post, now leaped to the mourner's bench,
from the great New York dailies to the obscure weeklies of the
hinterlands. The tributes were no less magnificent because they
were belated. The New York *Times* obituary asserted boldly that
the Post had "probably had more influence upon the cultural life
of America than any other," and it paid Lorimer the highest compliment it could think of by terming him the "Henry Ford of
American literature."

As for the *Herald Tribune*, it declared editorially: "It is not too
much to say that George Horace Lorimer . . . was the most
notable magazine editor of our times," and it went on to say that
the Post had "left a definite imprint upon the lives and thinking habits of what, for want of a better term, may be called the
great American middle class. . . . Since the war," the editorial
added, "it has been the custom in certain quarters to speak dis-
paragingly of some of the things in which Mr. Lorimer believed.
It was said that his magazine was fearful of the facts of life; that
it was old-fashioned; that it was an apologist for big business; that
it lacked what is known as an alert social consciousness; and that,

in general, it printed second-rate literature. We suspect that much of this is nonsense. Mr. Lorimer was a businessman; he wanted his magazine to prosper. If it is wrong to be clean and respectable, then Mr. Lorimer was wrong. . . ."

It was Lorimer's monumental integrity to which most of the eulogists ultimately returned in their tributes. Time and again its effect on individuals, those who knew him and those who were strangers, was reaffirmed by grateful people. The publisher of a small Illinois magazine wrote in his editorial columns that he had become a "scholar of Lorimer's" when he was "young, idealistic and emotional" and took his job seriously. Subsequently, he recalled, "I do not know how many times I have written for the unpopular side of many discussions because I knew that far away in a world other than my own there was at least one other man who—could he know—would understand and . . . understanding, confirm my course and cheer me on. Over and over, again and again, when I have had to choose between the loss of revenue and the loss of my self-respect, I have kept . . . my self-respect. . . ."

The comparison with Arthur Brisbane was made repeatedly. Damon Runyon, who had worked for both men, thought that they were probably the greatest editors in their fields that the country had ever produced. Each had frequently expressed admiration for the other, but they had never met. Runyon noted that they were unlike in personality but their methods of editorial operation were similar in several respects. Both were uncannily intuitive about the needs of the people they reached, a fact reflected in the enormous circulations they achieved. Both were masters of human interest. The primary difference between them, said Runyon, was that Brisbane found enjoyment only in his work, while Lorimer took time out to play and was not as deadly serious in his attitude toward life. "He laughed more and louder," Runyon wrote. "He liked to hear jokes that would have gone over Mr. Brisbane's head, if Mr. Brisbane had listened to them at all." And he added: "Steady production was the thing that appealed to both Mr. Lorimer and Mr. Brisbane in a writer. They could even bring themselves to forgiving an occasional sour one from a steady producer."

Earlier writers had often compared Lorimer with Ben Franklin. In an article written in the accepted critical vein of the late twenties, Benjamin Stolberg had said of the Post's two great editors: "Both were poor immigrants to Philadelphia from Boston. . . . Both were enamored of printer's ink, managers rather than writers, though their writings say what they want to say shrewdly and well. Both grew in influence and affluence and the control of their fellows' inferior minds. They both loved the common virtues, if properly salted and spiced. Above all, they both worship at the shrine of plain American horse sense, and the fact that they are polished communicants of this simplest of all creeds merely dignifies the homeliness of their democracy.

"Franklin and Lorimer are both arch-Americans in their profound belief that the meaning of life is not hidden but wrinkled on its surface; that its secrets come out in the astute living of it; and that its supposedly ineffable values merely make for confusion and failure in this responsible world. This defense of the surface they do not hold naïvely, but as an archly integral social philosophy. . . . Franklin was our first pragmatist and behaviorist, the forerunner of Dewey and Watson and our Big Business leaders, who would recondition all reflexes into the best means of living and call it a life. Mr. Lorimer helped to manipulate this philosophy into an American folklore."

Stolberg concluded that Lorimer was "very important in and to his own day, and not at all significant in the making of American history," a verdict to which there could be found little agreement when Lorimer died.

Perhaps the best estimate of the Boss came from a veteran newspaperman, Harper Leech, in his Chicago *Daily News* column: "Somebody said of Bruce Barton in the age of Coolidge that he had the wave length of the American people. Maybe Coolidge said it, and he should have known about that wave length, because he had it himself for several years. But the late George Horace Lorimer had it for the first third of the twentieth century, and then some. And because of that the files of the Saturday Evening Post are a mirror of the American mind from 1900 to date. Lorimer's passing has evoked the usual success story that appears after a man who has done a big creative job moves on. But the way it strikes me is that Lorimer couldn't have helped being a great editor. He knew the folks."

Ten years after Lorimer's death it is much easier to assess the Boss's place in American life and letters. Those who knew him best still see him in several different lights, and the only area of agreement lies in an intense admiration that remains undiminished. It is remarkable that the glow of Lorimer's personality persists so strongly a decade after his death. There is little in the magazine that he created to recall him as editor, and the kind of America he grew and prospered in has been permanently altered by the tide of cosmic events.

It is remarkable, too, this persistence of memory, because Lorimer was bound in by his times. He was born in a republic, not a democracy—an individualist who never changed in his feeling about the nation and the world. Attitudes and principles surrounded him and slowly strangled his original elasticity. As the citizen of a republic, he was not in favor of democracy; he considered his own position as realistic and that of the democracy lovers as Utopian. This fundamental conflict is far from being resolved in America today, and only Lorimer's essential largeness of character saved him from the excesses of bigotry.

Into the defense of his principles the Boss poured his enormous vitality and nervous energy, and as long as he remained the spokesman for his own generation he was highly successful. Then, toward the end of his editorship, the world changed and he found himself unable to change with it. He resisted that change in every possible way. It was not that he was blind to the trend of events. He foresaw the conditions that would arise, and he discredited them in advance as inconsistent with the world as he believed it must be.

It was hard to convince Lorimer of anything in which he did not fundamentally believe. America was changing and the Boss was against it because he was convinced that the change was wrong, and no one could persuade him from his belief. He held the Post to that belief at the possible cost of the magazine's future. And at the end he was lonely. He knew it was time to go.

He gave the same careful attention to his death as he gave to his life. Long before he had any idea of dying he bought a lot on the side of Laurel Hill Cemetery that slopes to the banks of the Schuylkill River, only a mile or so from the stand of memorial cherry trees inspired by Alma. When he bought the lot the cemetery had not spread that far and the nearest graves were some distance away. "It's a fine spot," the Boss said, and that settled it.

It is a fine spot today, even with the cemetery grown around it and the traffic roaring by just below on the River Drive. The friendly trees cluster over it and the river smiles up as it did on the day Lorimer chose it. The family mausoleum where he lies is circled by his beloved rhododendrons, and the sunlight filters into it through the English-designed stained glass which he bought, presumably, at some now forgotten antique store. The glass throws a subdued rainbow of light across the words engraved on his tomb. They are words written by George Horace Lorimer, to be read in 1937 at the breaking of ground for the Lorimer Memorial Chapel. They were intended for the memory of his father, but they speak with equal eloquence of the son:

"Religion is the cornerstone of character—not necessarily religion as expressed through any particular church, but through every church and every creed that is based on the broad precepts of the Golden Rule, of charity, and of justice tempered with mercy."

Bibliography

LETTERS:

Private files of George Horace Lorimer, and office correspondence taken from Saturday Evening Post files at the time of his retirement.
Files of Miss Adelaide Neall.
Files of Mary Roberts Rinehart.
Letters to the author from Wesley Stout, Kenneth Roberts and the Hon. Herbert Hoover.

INTERVIEWS:

Edwin Balmer
Thomas B. Costain
Garet Garrett
Joseph Hergesheimer
Alan Jackson
Graeme and Sarah Lorimer
Adelaide Neall

Mary Roberts Rinehart
Kenneth Roberts
Martin Sommers
Wesley Stout
Sophie Kerr Underwood
Ben Ames Williams

BOOKS:

Barrett, James Wyman. *Joseph Pulitzer and His World*. Vanguard, New York, 1941.

Bowers, Claude G. *Beveridge and the Progressive Era*. Literary Guild, New York, 1932.

Doran, George. *Chronicles of Barabbas*. Harcourt, Brace, New York, 1935.

Irwin, Will. *The Making of a Reporter*. Putnam, New York, 1942.

Marcosson, Isaac F. *Adventures in Interviewing*. John Lane Company, New York, 1919.

One Issue. Curtis Publishing Company, Philadelphia, 1919.

Pollard, James E. *The Presidents and the Press*. Macmillan, New York, 1947.

Roberts, Kenneth. *Antiquamania*. Doubleday and Co., New York, 1928.

White, William Allen. *Autobiography*. Macmillan, New York, 1946.

Who's Who

Who Was Who

PAMPHLETS:

A Brief History of Tremont Temple from 1839 to 1944, Edgar C. Lane, Senior Deacon.

A Short History of the Saturday Evening Post. Curtis Publishing Company, Philadelphia, 1937.

The Saturday Evening Post, The Editors. Curtis Publishing Company, Philadelphia, 1923.

MAGAZINES:

Advertising Age: Obituary, November 1, 1937.

Advertising and Selling: Parsons, Floyd W., "Personal Impressions of George Lorimer," January 14, 1937.

Author and Journalist: "Editors You Want to Know," July 1929.

Bookman, The: Cobb, Irvin S., "George Horace Lorimer, the Original Easy Boss," December 1918.

Collier's: Kennedy, John B., "Nothing Succeeds Like Common Sense," November 27, 1926.

Curtis Folk: Files.

Fox Valley Mirror, The: Fowler, Leonard, "George Horace Lorimer—A Reminiscence," April 1937.

Outlook and Independent: Stolberg, Benjamin, "Merchant in Letters," May 21, 1930.

Printer's Ink: October 28, 1937.

Reader, The: Garrett, Charles Hall, "The Arrival of George Horace Lorimer," October 1903.

Redbook: November, 1937.

Rochester Commerce: The Editors, "Getting Out the Post," September 8, 1930.

Saturday Evening Post: Complete files.

Saturday Review of Literature: De Voto, Bernard, "Writing for Money," October 9, 1937.

NEWSPAPERS:

Boston *Transcript*, September 1904.

New York *Herald Tribune*, October 23, 1937.

New York *Post*, October 23, 1937.

New York *Sun*, October 23, 1937.

New York *Times*, October 23, 1937.

Philadelphia *Inquirer* (30th Anniversary), 1929; February 1934; October 23, 1937.

Pottsville (Pa.) *Journal*, December 1936.

The Villager (Greenwich Village, New York City).

MISCELLANEOUS:

Biographical sketches: Three unsigned manuscripts, edited by George Horace Lorimer, and a fourth uncorrected but probably written by Lorimer.

Brief in the case of *O'Reilly vs. Curtis Publishing Co.*, May 25, 1940.

"Notes on Publishing," manuscript, by George Horace Lorimer.

Scrapbook of clippings about George Claude Lorimer and his children, belonging to George Horace Lorimer's nephew, Lorimer Dunlevy.

Index

Index